LIFE AFTER MURDER

LIFE AFTER MURDER

Five Men in Search of REDEMPTION

NANCY MULLANE

PUBLICAFFAIRS
New York

Published in the United States by PublicAffairs™,
a Member of the Perseus Books Group

Book Design by Brent Wilcox

Library of Congress Cataloging-in-Publication Data
Mullane, Nancy.
Life after murder : five men in search of redemption / Nancy Mullane.
p. cm.
Includes index.
ISBN 978-1-61039-029-3 (hardback) —
ISBN 978-1-61039-030-9 (e-book)
1. Murderers—United States—Biography. 2. Murderers—United States—Biography. I. Title.
HV9304.M85 2012
364.152'3092273—dc23

2012002450

First Edition
10 9 8 7 6 5 4 3 2 1

To Max and Nayeli

Contents

Author's Note

I never thought I would meet a murderer face to face—at least I hoped I wouldn't.

I suppose I lived my life with an unconscious fear it could happen. But just as unconsciously I reasoned that if I was careful not to walk alone down dark streets or hang out with the wrong type of people, I could avoid that most horrible of encounters.

Absent knowing a real murderer, I filled in the gaps with lurid news stories and grainy mug shots as the faces of people to look out for. Each time I was reassured: the vile, terrifying images didn't look like anyone I knew.

It's only natural that not many of us know what murderers really look like. When a person commits murder, if he (or she) is arrested or turns himself over to the authorities, he is immediately locked up in county jail to await prosecution. With a trial pending or negotiations for a plea deal moving forward, he doesn't talk to anyone beside his attorney and immediate family. If he ends up pleading guilty or the jury convicts him, he is sentenced, handcuffed, put on a bus to a prison, and locked away to do his time. Years pass. If he is ever released from prison, he makes every effort to fade back into society, anonymous.

That's why we don't know the people murderers become. We don't know whether the saying "once a murderer, always a murderer" is really true. The murderer in prison isn't allowed to talk to us, and the paroled murderer riding on your subway car is probably afraid to.

In June 2007, my radio editor asked me to do a story about overcrowding and the skyrocketing costs of California's prisons. Instead of producing a quick-turnaround story using statistics and a few talking heads from local universities and government, I decided to try to talk to the people most affected, and that meant getting access to a real prison and the people locked up inside.

That's when I met Don. Then came Eddie, Richie, Phillip, and Jesse. Looking into each of these men's faces, studying their expressions and their body language, I realized that each of them was much different than the monster I had envisioned as the "typical murderer."

Over the next four years, I made dozens of trips to San Quentin. Holding on to my erratic press access with a mix of Irish luck and a reporter's persistence, building trust with both prison officials and the imprisoned, I was rewarded with exclusive, extensive, unheard-of access to men behind the walls.

The men in this book all did the unthinkable—for some, the unforgivable. They killed people, tore families apart, and devastated communities. Sentenced to life in prison with the possibility of parole, they were offered a promise of sorts: that if they complied with society's demands—if they paid the price for their crime and reformed—one day they could earn a second chance at freedom. Each man took that hope to heart and worked for years to turn his life around.

But redemption and hope are not enough to get out of prison if you're a convicted murderer serving a life sentence with the *possibility* of parole. You must first face the scrutiny of parole board commissioners appointed by the governor, and in a few states, such as California, Maryland, and Oklahoma, the governor—the person holding the most politically charged office in the state—has the power to reverse the board's decision.

All five men admit they committed murder, and therefore, their stories invite the judgment of those who read this book. I imagine some readers will feel comfortable making that judgment. Others will be satisfied the parole boards, the governors, and ultimately the courts have made the appropriate ruling and that justice has been served. Some may never again want these men to see the light of day outside the prison walls; others may be more forgiving.

The question is: Who is responsible for making the final call?

Though I have not interviewed victims' families, I do not mean to imply that they are in any way marginal to this story. They have suffered and continue to suffer immeasurably from senseless violence and loss. I am sorry for their grief and hope the telling of this book does not bring them additional sorrow, but answers.

By focusing my story on murderers and the institutions responsible for them, I do not in any way intend to negate the seriousness of their crimes or the suffering they caused. I would like to take you along on the same journey I made: from fear and hatred of our society's most reviled citizens—and an ignorance of the flawed and costly policies by which we carry out their sentences—to an understanding of who these men were when they were young, stupid, and selfish, and who they have become more than twenty years after they committed murder.

Life After Murder is their story.

I wear it for the prisoner who has long paid for his crimes
But is there because he's a victim of the times.

—JOHNNY CASH
"Man in Black"

one

FACE TO FACE

JUNE 2007

A half hour north of San Francisco, just past a string of car dealerships and a shopping mall, a deep-green official highway sign announcing the exit to San Quentin State Prison hangs over the freeway. Even at zoom speed, you can't miss the massive clump of warm, vaguely mustard-colored walls and uncommonly long buildings just beyond the tidal grasses of the bird estuary to the east.

When I moved to the Bay Area, I was surprised by how close the prison was to everyday life. Driving by, I would squint into the distance, trying to catch sight of life in the narrow slits of windows. I wondered if prisoners could see out, or if it was only people on the outside who couldn't see in. It was a reminder that we, the civilized of society, are protected from the truly dangerous people.

With a story assignment burning on deadline, I take the San Quentin exit for the first time. I didn't have to go *inside* to get a story, but if I wanted to get a radio story, it meant getting the sounds of the prison and the voices of the prisoners.

After a few calls, I connected with Claire-Elizabeth DeSophia, a volunteer helping inmates at the prison become drug and alcohol counselors. She let me know right off the bat it wouldn't be easy for a reporter to get inside, but once she was satisfied I was not bent on doing some sensationalist crime story, she said she would try to help. "You'll have to get cleared by the warden's office. I can't bring you in without their approval. You can tell them I invited you. But if the warden doesn't like you . . . "

A week later I received word: I was cleared to go inside the prison, home to more than 5,000 inmates. Lieutenant Eric Messick, the public information officer at San Quentin, gave me clear instructions: "Don't wear blue jeans and don't expect the warden to trade you for a prisoner if you're taken hostage."

As a reporter, nothing is more thrilling than a new story, a new "beat." But now, driving down the freeway, the closer I get to the prison exit, the edgier I feel. My trusty reporter instincts and equally reliable instincts for self-preservation alternate in a stream of questions: Will I be allowed to talk to inmates? Will they be kept at a safe distance in handcuffs? What would it be like to be a hostage? Were they serious about not trading me for a prisoner?

I park in a dirt lot outside San Quentin's east gate and walk up to the imposing rack of black metal.

"Who are you?" the uniformed officer demands in a tone designed to turn away anyone without a legitimate reason to stand between him and the entrance to the prison. He looks at the ten-year-old photograph on my driver's license for a long time before dialing Messick to let him know I'm here. While I wait, he points to a wide white line on the ground about fifty feet back down the road and warns me: no photos beyond that point. "You're on the free side. This is the other side. Okay?"

Minutes later, a balding white man in shirt and tie approaches the gate from the prison side. Collecting my ID from the gate officer, Messick motions for me to step through. "Be sure you have it when you leave," he says, handing my license back to me. "Photo IDs are like currency inside."

We walk at a quick clip down a long exposed sidewalk that leads into the massive fortress looming ahead. Another glowering guard stands just inside the passageway that leads through the thick stone wall. He double-checks my photo ID, pats me down, inspects my microphone and recorder, and marks my bare wrist with a stamp visible only under ultraviolet light.

Clunk. The steel-barred gate pops open. Messick grabs hold of one of the thick round bars and pushes the gate into a large cage. I follow him inside the cage, and he pulls the massive gate shut with another ear-popping *clunk*. Fifteen seconds later a wall-size set of bars on the far side bounces open.

Stepping out over the steel door's high sill, we emerge from the dark stone passageway of the sally port into blinding sunlight. In the courtyard along a gently curved pathway are rosebushes thick with colorful blossoms. In the middle of a big circular pool, a fountain shoots a heavy stream of water into the sky. Behind us, the back side of the steep wall is topped with rows of razor wire looping around and around like an unwound, lethal Slinky. High above the center of the wall is a bell tower.

Following my eyes, Messick explains, "At 1600 hours every day, all of the prisons in the state take a count. Here at San Quentin, when we ring the bells, everyone knows the count has begun."

A two-story white building with barred windows borders the green grass of the courtyard on the left. "That's AC," Messick says, "The Adjustment Center is where prisoners who haven't adjusted to prison live in solitary confinement."

At the AC's farthest corner is a squat, octagonal building.

"That's Four-Post," Messick says as an officer steps out, swinging a long black baton back and forth. Hanging from his wide leather belt are handcuffs, a collection of keys attached to the end of a chain, a short solid-steel extendable club, and a large blue can of pepper spray. "The officers keep track of the movement of all prisoners going through the courtyard to the chapel or the library."

Straight ahead and a little to the right is the prison library. The two-story nineteenth-century brick building with long wood-frame windows and tall, worn doors has an unexpected elegance. A graying, hunched-over prisoner shuffles nearby. Using a long-handled hoe, he digs at the dark brown soil at the base of the rosebushes that flank the path. He stops, peering over at us before looking back down at the dirt.

"That's Bird Man," Messick says. "He's been here for years. He takes care of the rosebushes and the family of wild ducks that return every year."

Picking up his pace, Messick leads me past the prisoners and the fountain and pulls open one of the double glass doors to the Protestant chapel. Fold-out tables pushed up against the wall are piled with Bibles and church pamphlets. Down the hall a set of golden oak double doors leads to the sanctuary.

Midway through my tour, Messick's cell phone buzzes on his belt, startling us both. He murmurs a few words into the phone, then turns to me. "I have to take care of this. You can wait here until I get back."

Opening the door to a small office opposite the sanctuary, he motions me inside. "Don't worry," he says. "You'll be fine." A quick smile and he disappears, closing—and I presume, locking—the door behind him.

The room is small—perhaps seven by ten feet. Stackable plastic chairs line the walls. I sit down and keep an eye on the door. As I take in my surroundings, I begin to feel a sense of claustrophobia: I'm all alone, unprotected, in prison.

A good fifteen minutes later, the door opens. I jerk my head up, expecting to see Messick, but it's someone new, a man wearing a light blue shirt and dark blue jeans. He stands in the frame, staring at me.

All the air seems to leave the room. In a flash I remember Messick's warning not to wear blue jeans. Denim is what "lifers" wear—convicted murderers, or worse. In a matter of moments, the man is sitting down across from me. Three more inmates follow, similarly dressed. Four convicted murderers, alone in a small room with a single, defenseless woman.

Think quickly, I tell myself. *Don't make any sudden movements. They probably have shivs stuffed inside their socks under the cuffs of their jeans, and now they're communicating in signs about who's going to make the first move.*

The men start talking to one another, apparently about some kind of test they've just taken. One asks the others how they answered question fifty-nine.

"That was a hard one. Was it substance-induced delirium or substance-induced psychosis?"

"I think it was delirium."

"That was the hardest test I've ever taken," another prisoner adds, to nervous laughter all around.

My heart pounds louder with every passing second. The door opens again. Finally Messick has come back to save me. But no: two more men in prison blues walk in, glancing at me with confusion. My eyes dart to the ground a second too late. The room falls silent. I have the murderers' full attention. I furtively reach over to my recorder and slide the power button to "on." *If I don't survive, at least it will all be on tape. . . .*

"Who are you?" one of the men finally asks. "What are you doing here?"

My breath rattles in my chest. I lift my eyes to see the men staring at me. They look upset, their brows furrowed, their mouths closed tight. The man who spoke is to my right, his face inches from mine. His skin is pasty, almost translucent, unhealthy. I can't tell how old he is—thirty-five or forty, at least. Around his lips, a close crop of dark stubble seems to stretch up over his head fading to a deep receding hairline. He is wearing wire-rimmed glasses. I think about my husband and my daughter; how strange that the morning started off in the usual way, yet now I am going to die.

In a voice shallower than I want, I manage to tell them I am a radio reporter working on a story and that Messick asked me to wait here. "He's probably just outside the door," I add. "He'll be back any minute." The men look at the door and then back at me.

"We didn't know the press was going to be here today," the man in the wire-rimmed glasses says, his blue eyes growing large.

"It's a story for National Public Radio. Claire-Elizabeth DeSophia is going to speak with me."

Eureka. Smiles break across their faces. They all lean back, relaxed. "Oh," says the nearest man. "If Claire-Elizabeth says you're okay, no problem." He offers his hand for a handshake. "My name is Don Cronk. What's yours?"

The air seems to be moving again, like a window has been thrown open. One by one, the men in the tight circle stretch out their hands and introduce themselves. I try to smile back, relieved.

"You don't look so good," says a slightly built man with intense blue eyes who introduces himself as Bryan Smith. "Do you want a glass of water?"

Before Bryan can make good on his offer, a full-bodied, middle-aged woman with a head of wavy, dark hair appears at the door. I know in an instant who she is.

"Nancy?" asks Claire-Elizabeth, concern filling her face. "Where's Lieutenant Messick?"

"Oh, he left her here," says one of the men.

"All by herself?" asks Claire-Elizabeth, her eyes wide.

"Yeah," one of the men answers. "We came in and here she was."

"I would have come for you if I'd known. Are you all right?" she asks.

"Yes. I'm fine," I say, standing for the first time on shaky legs, adjusting my jacket.

I *am* fine. Really. But this has been one of those before-and-after moments. I survived being in a small room, alone, with a half dozen murderers, and they didn't try to kill me when they had the chance.

"These men are studying to become the first certified alcohol and drug addiction counselors in the country who are incarcerated," Claire-Elizabeth says. "The state of California requires counselors working in drug and alcohol treatment programs to be certified by a professional association. They just took a three-hour exam, one of the final steps to getting their associate credential. That man who just walked out"—she glances at the back of Bryan Smith, on his way to get a glass of water—"he's been found suitable for parole. We're all hopeful. He might be the first man in the program to get out of prison on parole."

Perhaps it is the blur of adrenaline, but my brain can't seem to process "might." This inmate, Bryan, has been found suitable for parole—and even so, he still *might* not be set free? What would it take to clear it up? Will there be a phone call? From whom?

Before I can sort out the ins and outs of parole, Messick returns. "Well, that took longer than I thought. You okay?"

"Sure," I say with a nod, and follow him out. It's the end of my first visit inside a prison and I'm leaving with more questions than answers.

two

RESULTS

JULY 2007

Bryan Smith walks over to the American flag holding his gilt-and-ivory certificate just below his face and motions for me to take his picture. *Click.*

Even before my initial news story on the cost of California's prison system aired, I had already pitched another: how a group of San Quentin prisoners were trying to become the first inmates in the nation certified as addiction counselors. My editor at National Public Radio was interested, but on the condition that at least one of the inmates passed the exam. Otherwise I wouldn't have a story.

Three weeks after my first trip inside "Q" (as they sometimes call San Quentin), I'm back inside the prison's Protestant chapel, watching as nine of the eleven inmates who took the exam receive the paperwork certifying their status as addiction counselors, a rare skill marketable outside of prison, should they ever get parole—a subject that is clearly on at least one prisoner's mind.

As I pull the camera down to show him the digitized image, Bryan grins. "You know, I might be going home in a month."

"That's great!" I say, then pause. "Claire-Elizabeth mentioned you *might* be getting out. But I don't understand. What does that mean? You might?"

The process of imprisonment and parole is fairly simple . . . right? A person is sent to prison for committing a crime. When the prisoner has reformed and is ready to get out, he appears before officials on a parole board authorized to determine whether he is rehabilitated, reformed, no longer a threat to public safety, and ready to be released back into society.

"You see," Bryan says, his grin fading, "the parole board found me suitable for parole, but I still have to wait for the governor's decision. He could take my date."

Looking at his face, up close, I notice he doesn't really look happy. He looks miserable. And in that split second, the anxiety and strain tugging at his mouth and eyes all makes sense. Of course. After years in prison, Bryan doesn't know if he's nearly out, or not out at all. I wonder: How and why does the governor take parole dates away from prisoners? Does he know something the parole board doesn't?

The other men gather around as Bryan himself fills me in on the details. People convicted of murder who are serving a sentence of life with the possibility of parole automatically go before the parole board after they've served about 75 percent to 80 percent of their sentence. If the parole board finds them suitable for parole and no longer a threat to public safety, the lifer has to wait five more months or 150 days for the governor to decide whether to let him out of prison on parole. This is Bryan's situation: "I was found suitable on March 15, so I'll find out on August 12th, my 150th day. If the governor says okay, then I'm going home."

Lieutenant Eric Messick, the prison's press officer, is standing halfway down the aisle, hands on hips. It's time for me to leave. Realizing their photo opportunity is passing, the other men in the group who have not had their Kodak moment quickly form a half circle, encouraging me to click: "Take the photo! *Please*."

I lift my camera and take one final shot.

As we walk back out the sally port, Messick muses on what just happened. "That's the phenomenon about convicts," he says. "They all want their picture taken."

I think about that for a bit. I too would want my picture taken if I were in danger of being forgotten.

In prison movies, the plot often turns on a last-minute phone call from the governor staying the execution of a murderer sentenced to die. But there are no movies made about governors withdrawing parole. Back at my office, I dig into why Bryan Smith's parole hangs on word from the governor.

The fact is, it's no simple matter to get parole. First, a prisoner sentenced to life with the possibility of parole has to serve at least 80 percent of his sentence: twelve years of the standard fifteen-to-life sentence for second-degree murder, or twenty of the twenty-five-to-life for first-degree. When the prisoner reaches his minimum eligible parole date, he automatically sits before a panel of two or three of the twelve commissioners on the state's Adult Board of Parole Hearings, many of whom are former corrections officers, police officers, or district attorneys. If the commissioners decide the inmate is suitable for parole, the prisoner is told right there and then he is suitable. Then his official file is sent to Sacramento. That's when the 150-day countdown begins.

The California Department of Corrections and Rehabilitation then has four months or 120 days to review the prisoner's file. For a lifer to get past the CDCR's review, he must have a job and a safe home waiting for him on the outside. To verify what the inmate has promised, the CDCR sends parole officers to check references, to be sure there aren't any inconsistencies. If things don't add up, the CDCR can rescind the inmate's parole. If the inmate makes it past the CDCR's review, only then is his file sent to the governor, who has thirty more days to decide whether to honor the parole board's decision or to reverse it. Proposition 89 was the referendum voters passed back in 1988 that gave the governor this power.

That's why Bryan Smith is waiting for the governor's word: it usually comes on the 150th day. If the governor reverses the parole, the lifer has to wait until his next scheduled parole hearing—in seven more months—to try again. And there is no guarantee that if a lifer has been found suitable once he'll ever be found suitable again.

The more I learn, the more I realize I don't know. Do all prisoners have to go before commissioners on the Board of Parole Hearings to be found suitable for freedom before getting out of prison? Do all prisoners need the governor's final approval?

The first thing I piece together is something I'm pretty sure I already knew: not everyone convicted of a crime goes to prison. If a person is found guilty of a misdemeanor, the maximum sentence is a fine and up to one year in the county jail. But if a person is convicted of a felony, he is sentenced to a state prison to do time. That's where things get a little confusing.

Before 1977 all people convicted of felonies in California faced three kinds of sentence: the "death sentence," "life in prison *without* the possibility of parole," and for everyone else, an "indeterminate life sentence—or life *with* the possibility of parole." That's right: prior to 1977 *everyone* who committed a felony in California—whether robbery, larceny, assault, rape, or murder—got some kind of life sentence, whether it was six months to life, twenty-five years to life, or the rest of his life. Every prisoner who got life *with* the possibility of parole had to go before a parole board where he had to prove he was rehabilitated and was ready to reenter society. If the board found the prisoner suitable for parole, he was back out in society in two or three days. If parole was denied, the prisoner had to wait and try again at his next annual hearing.

No matter how many years the inmate had served—say, ten years on a five-to-life sentence—if the board found the prisoner unreformed and still a danger to society, the prisoner would go back to his cell and wait.

In some respects, it was a troubling system—I can imagine many circumstances in which an indefinite sentence might violate the Constitution's provision against cruel and unusual punishment—but one that assured that all prisoners released back into society had made some kind of effort to rehabilitate themselves and that all prisons had given them some sort of chance to do so through programs and counseling. Then, in 1977, the purpose of imprisonment and the process of releasing inmates from state prisons was fundamentally altered.

In that year Jerry Brown was serving the first of his nonconsecutive terms. In what he has since referred to as an "abysmal failure," Brown attempted to get tough on crime by abolishing indeterminate sentencing for all crimes but murder and replacing it with "determinate sentencing."

Determinate sentencing policy left it up to judges to impose exact or "determined" prison sentences from a selection of "low-term," "mid-term," and "high-term" choices. Beginning in 1977 prisoners given determinate sentences—for all felonies other than murder, including rape, robbery, child molestation, and drug dealing—would *no longer* have to appear before a parole board to prove rehabilitation as a condition for getting out of prison. After an inmate had served his determinate sentence, such as three years for a rape and sixteen months for incest, he would be taken outside the prison gate, handed $200 in "gate money," and released, no questions asked. No longer would there exist the slightest expectation that he had reformed while he was in prison. It was the beginning of the popular *do-the-crime, do-the-time* philosophy of incarceration.

The ripple effect of Governor Brown's determinate sentencing reform was almost immediate. Following the governor's lead and looking for ways to cut the growing cost of prison reform, state lawmakers enacted legislation clarifying that the purpose of incarceration in California was punishment, not rehabilitation, and that it was not society's obligation to reform a criminal. This eliminated the need to continue funding the rehabilitation and counseling programs that had been haphazardly offered behind prison walls. By 1980 the state legislature had all but eliminated the words "rehabilitation" and "treatment" from the state penal code.

But in 1977, when the determinate sentencing law was enacted, some 2,600 prisoners were still serving indeterminate life sentences in state prisons for murder. Now that education and counseling programs were being cut from the state's prisons, how would these prisoners get access to the classes and programs they needed to document their rehabilitation efforts and achievements when they appeared before the parole board?

Society's attitudes toward prisoners made parole even harder to achieve. By the mid-'80s, Californians began seeing and feeling the effect of the determinate sentencing law. The recidivism rate nearly doubled from a forty-year average of about 40 percent, to a new high of nearly 75 percent. Increasingly, bold newspaper headlines reported the arrest of yet another parolee for a violent crime. Politicians responded to the headlines with renewed cries to get tough on crime and tougher on prisoners, ignoring the statistics indicating that growing recidivism had been caused by "tough on crime" laws in the first place. Meanwhile, a political and cultural shift was about to change the system anew.

Everyone who was paying any attention to politics or the television set in the late '80s remembers the name Willie Horton. A convicted murderer sentenced to life without the possibility of parole, Horton was released from prison under Massachusetts's weekend furlough program for prisoners. Outside the walls of the Concord Correctional Facility, Horton fled to Maryland, where nearly a year later he raped a woman and viciously assaulted her fiancé. I know what Horton did is what most people expect from paroled prisoners. But Horton wasn't supposed to get out. He was serving a life sentence *without* the possibility of parole.

The fault couldn't be laid entirely at Governor Michael Dukakis's feet. The state's furlough program was signed into law in 1972 by Republican governor Francis Sargent. However, under the law as it was first written, people convicted of first-degree murder were excluded from the program. Four years later, in 1976, the state supreme court ruled that the right to the furlough program extended to first-degree murderers as well. When the legislature tried to get a bill passed that would have limited the program, Governor Dukakis vetoed the bill, allowing the supreme court's ruling to stand—unwittingly setting the stage for Horton's crime.

Oddly enough, governors all over America in those years were engaged in very similar programs. So I learned from Jonathan Simon, Adrian A. Kragen professor of law and a criminologist at the University of California at Berkeley. As governor of California, Ronald Reagan had overseen just such a furlough program. As Simon told me, "The permanent parole of prisoners was a normal course of business for state criminal justice systems all over America." Yet Dukakis was the one who paid the price along with every governor thereafter.

The elder George Bush's astute 1988 presidential campaign staff was charged with beefing up the reputation of the slightly effete vice president in his race against Dukakis. Thanks to an infamous commercial they produced, Horton became a household name.

This phenomenon collided with a series of social and economic trends in a perfect storm of sorts. According to Simon, "I believe, and other people who have studied the history of mass incarceration believe, that the emergence of seemingly strikingly high homicide rates in the 1960s and '70s at the height of American affluence, and at a time when Americans were being encouraged to view sort of privatized personal security as the top goal, the American Dream as it were, created a very peculiar commitment to a War on Crime."

In other words, the twentieth-century rise of private property ownership and the middle class made America a more prosperous nation, but also a more paranoid one. More of us than ever had possessions and dignified livelihoods, and therefore, more of us had something to lose from crime. We also had less compassion for Americans who committed crimes.

With the advent of the Horton ad campaign, the calculus of parole was forever changed. "After the Willie Horton controversy of '88, every parole decision made by a state about its murderers became a potential political liability with a governor," maintains Simon.

Wanting to appear tough on crime, then–California governor George Deukmejian and a group of allied politicians supported Proposition 89, which brought the fate of prisoners closer to the political whims and vulnerabilities of the governorship and thus the control of the electorate.

The citizens of California voted their fear in 1988. By a 55 percent majority they passed Prop 89. The legislative constitutional amendment gave the governor the authority to affirm, modify, or reverse any decision made by the Board of Parole Hearings (then known as the Board of Prison Terms) regarding the parole of a person sentenced to an indeterminate life sentence for murder. Governors in Oklahoma and Maryland began implementing similar laws.

The original authors of the proposition intended it as a final check or veto to be used sparingly—evident in the wording of the referendum, which stated that the governor would assess prisoners' eligibility for parole "on the basis of the same factors which the parole authority is required to consider." But that's not the way governors have used the proposition.

Parole suddenly became a rarity. Governor Deukmejian paroled only about 5 percent of the eligible lifers—and that's a high number compared to today. Deukmejian's successor, Pete Wilson, allowed the parole board's decision to stand for far fewer inmates—closer to 1 percent—and despite the widely noted decline in homicide that occurred in California and across America in the mid- to late 1990s, the next governor, Gray Davis, paroled virtually no one. (Compare this with the number paroled during Jerry Brown's first term in the 1970s: nearly 20 percent.)

Parole decisions have *always* been under the governor's power, since the governor is the one who appoints the seventeen commissioners who ultimately sit on the state's Board of Parole Hearings. But once governors felt the political spotlight of the board's decision, most prisoners incarcerated with the hope of parole lost their chance of ever seeing the light of a free day again.

No wonder Bryan Smith is nervous.

—

By law the governor is supposed to have 150 days to decide whether to reverse the board's decision about Bryan's parole. That decision is supposed to arrive in the prison by fax no later than five p.m. on that 150th day. But there's no real oversight keeping the governor on schedule, and by day 155, a Friday in August, no fax has arrived and nobody at San Quentin has any idea whether Bryan will be released.

I make a call to Messick, then to the warden's office. No fax yet.

My editors at NPR can't run the story until we know whether Bryan is getting out. Good thing I already recorded two endings: one reports that he is getting out of San Quentin; the other, that he is not. All the producers in Washington have to do is mix in the right one—and all I can do is wait.

At 1:45 in the afternoon, my phone rings. It's Claire-Elizabeth. She's calling from inside the prison chapel.

"Nancy! Bryan got parole," she gushes over the phone. "We've been celebrating! Everyone is hugging and cheering. Bryan's a little numb. I'm a wreck."

"May I speak with Bryan?" I plead.

"Sure." I hear her call for Bryan over the sound of yelps and laughter. Then a voice higher and lighter than I remember is on the phone.

"Hi, Nancy!"

"Bryan, congratulations! What's the first thing you want to do when you get out?"

A slight giggle escapes over the receiver. "Take my shoes off and then take my socks off and walk on the carpet. Then I want to go to the store and buy all different kinds of salsa. Here at the prison they have one kind of chips and one kind of salsa. I want to buy all kinds of salsa!"

"What happens now?" I ask him. It occurs to me that I have no idea when I'll have another chance to speak with him. While he's an inmate, he is a captive subject. After he gets out, he can choose whether to continue telling me his story.

"I'm not sure," he says, struggling to stay focused amid the euphoria swirling around him. "I think I'm going home tomorrow or the next day, but you never know for sure."

I call my producer in DC. "Go with the first ending. The governor has declined to review the board's recommendation. After twenty-four years in prison, Bryan Smith is going home."

Governor Arnold Schwarzenegger didn't reverse Bryan's parole. *The system works!* We don't need to worry about Proposition 89. Apparently Schwarzenegger is willing to be a little more reasonable than his predecessors. Right?

Wrong. But it's going to be a while before I figure that out.

I'm dying to follow Bryan, but I don't get the opportunity. First of all, I'm not waiting at the gate when he gets released. Still a little new as a prison reporter, I haven't quite realized just how much journalistic doggedness it takes to get access to the real-time release of a lifer. It's hard to explain to free people how closed off from the outside world prisoners actually are. Prisons are a part of our open, democratic society, but just as prisoners lose many constitutional protections when they commit their crimes, prisons limit the ability of America's citizens to really know what is happening behind those walls.

Additionally, Bryan doesn't seem too eager to have a journalist around as he reunites with his family. That's understandable. He'd have to be almost a martyr to let some reporter trumpet his status as a paroled murderer just as he's about to rebuild his free life.

I understand Bryan's hesitation, especially after I talk with criminal defense attorney Laurie Saunders, who represents some of San Quentin's lifers at their parole hearings. "It would be really a lot to ask somebody in that position . . . to make themselves a guinea pig, to make themselves the first person who would come out and say, 'This is who I am, this is what I've accomplished, let me start making the effort to change your mind.' Because what it would mean is they would suffer," she says. "Their ability to melt back into society and become normal or viewed as normal would be destroyed because nobody would let them. Who's going to ask them to make that sacrifice?"

Not me. Not now, at least. But that's when it hits me. The reason I've never met a murderer before is that from the moment they are arrested until, if ever, they are released from prison, they are locked-away invisible. And if, as Saunders says, the only safe thing a person paroled on a murder conviction can do is fade as seamlessly and anonymously as possible back into the fabric of American society, it begs the question: Why, after decades in jail, would he consent to having his life and crime made public?

I hold out hope that once Bryan has had a chance to settle into his new life, he'll give me a call. I am terribly curious about his first hours and days of freedom. He hasn't taken a casual free walk or private shower without an armed guard watching since 1983, back when Madonna released her first album and *Flashdance* was a new hit movie. Instead of witnessing twenty-four years of slow, seismic cultural spins and shifts, Bryan Smith is waking from a long, unplanned night of incarceration. I'll simply have to wait. After all, he just got out of prison.

In the meantime, I'm going to hold out hope that someday a prisoner will make the sacrifice, to go public with his post-murder story so others can understand. I want to be around when and if that ever happens.

Even so: it's a long shot.

three

TIME AND SPACE

SEPTEMBER 2007

Past the chapel courtyard, Lieutenant Messick turns right and heads down a single-lane road that banks left along a forty-foot-high wall. I struggle to keep up. Since no running is allowed inside the prison, most people seem to settle for walking at a brisk clip at all times.

That's when I realize that an inmate directly in front of me and another behind are keeping pace. The man behind moves closer and raises his voice just above a whisper: "Don't worry, we've got your back."

Messick smiles and keeps walking, a few steps ahead of me and my self-appointed bodyguards. Why do they need to have my back? Whom are they protecting me from, if not their own?

Just as I'm about to ask the question, we reach the end of the canyon of walls, and there, stretched out before me, is the San Quentin lower yard filled with hundreds of men, a shifting mosaic of prison-issued clothes in blue, gray, and white. "Not all of the inmates on the yard today are lifers," says Messick, looking back at me, "Many are what's called 'determinate sentenced' inmates and they're a whole different breed. Be careful."

Standing at the top of the yard, I stop and stare at the locked-up sweep of blacktop and grass, a bright wedge of blue sky hovering overhead. So immense and so closed off. For decades this has been the entire world the men around me have seen with their naked eyes. It is all many of them will ever see again.

Straight ahead, about seventy-five feet across the blacktop, a dozen or so men hunched over thick wooden picnic tables play chess. Others with hard, round biceps lie on benches lifting barbells over their heads. Beyond the weight pile, inmates holding tennis rackets race to lob bright yellow balls back and forth, and a little farther to my left, men shout and grunt over a serious game of hoops. But it's the enormous grassy athletic field that takes up the lion's share of the yard and the men pacing the oval track at its edge that makes it all seem almost normal. Until, that is, I look up at the guards on the walls and their rifles trained down on them all. Nobody seems to notice, or mind.

A screech of feedback cuts through the air, followed by the first grinding notes of an electric guitar. A band begins to play. The first-ever San Quentin National Addiction Recovery Month celebration has begun.

One of my self-appointed guardians tells me the band is called Cold Steel Blues. "All but one of the musicians are inmates," says the taller one. "The bass player, the one in street clothes, is Dewey Wooten. He's a retired associate warden but he comes back to play with the band."

Just as the lead singer in the band launches into Jimi Hendrix's "Voodoo Child," I hear a voice calling my name over the slashing chords. It's Bobby Brown, the tall black man who took (and failed) the CAADAC test on my first day visiting San Quentin. He's standing next to Don Cronk, the white guy with the wire-rimmed glasses.

We talk in loud voices about our surroundings on the yard: the sun, the grass, the sky. I peer up and over the high walls where cottony clouds bounce over the tops of massive purple humps in the distance and ask which mountains I'm looking at.

"That's Mount Tam!" Don says with a laugh. "It's probably a side you never see 'cause it's only observable from this angle. For over twenty years, it's just been an inspiration to me. It changes every day with each sunset and sunrise, and maybe it's fog or clouds or the color of the sun. It's what keeps me feeling not so incarcerated or lost or thrown away."

"Have you ever been to the top?"

"Nope. Before my crime I lived in Sacramento. But when I get out," he says, looking up at the craggy peaks, "you bet I'll climb it."

I try to smile encouragingly, but I'm afraid my eyes reflect some skepticism. I already know a little too much about how parole works to assume that he'll be getting out of prison anytime soon.

We stare together at the mountain for a moment before I attempt to change the subject. "Speaking of getting out, have you heard from Bryan Smith?"

"I haven't personally," Don says, "but through other people and the chaplain. Apparently he's just taking it slow, getting acclimated. When he called, I think it was in his second week. He said he just had to lie down on the couch and put an ice pack on his head because it was overwhelming. It had caught up with him. Your body's changing; the hours you sleep, the food you eat, the water. Everything. We know by no stretch of the imagination is walking out of this front gate the end. It's not over. It's just beginning and we're not going to be accepted in some circles."

"Don't you want to know whether being in the counseling program and earning a certificate has made a difference?"

Don has to raise his voice to be heard over the sound of Cold Steel Blues. "You know, addiction and alcoholism are the root cause of all crimes in some fashion. Dealing it, selling it, robbing and burglarizing to get money to buy it. When people are under the influence, they do crazy things.

"I'm working on my twenty-sixth year inside. I did a horrible crime against society, and I was sent to prison to be punished. Rightly so. And my first four, five, six years, I didn't get it yet. I was acclimating to a new culture, a violent culture, and a negative environment. But through the Lord Jesus Christ, I began to realize there was more to life. So the past twenty years I've worked diligently discovering why I did what I did and who am I really and as the years went by I began to understand the role I played in the victimization of society: not just the man I killed, but his family and their friends and their children and their friends and my family and on and on. It's countless."

I am skeptical at first. This all sounds a little scripted. But I keep listening.

"What a waste. What a tragedy," he continues. "I thought, 'If I can do anything, I can change my life and hopefully help turn other people around so that they don't harm society anymore and end up in prison forever.' But as the years go by, I cry out so much that after a while, it doesn't even have meaning to my ears anymore and society looks at us like, 'So what?' I don't know if anyone else experiences this, but for me, it begins to blur, the punishment and what society sent us here for.

"How long? How long can I continue to pay? I don't know. There is a point where even we say, 'What more can I do? Do you just want me to rot in here and die? Is that it? If so, please say that.' You keep telling us we're suitable or eligible for parole but it never happens and oftentimes it feels like it's the carrot dangling. But we can't give up. We can never give up. But it's my hope that one day I can reenter society and make people more aware of what's going on. We need prisons. Crime is a reality. People need to be punished, but to what extent and when is it over?"

I don't have the answer. But I want to know whether Don is for real about all this. I'd love to see more of his life here in San Quentin.

"I don't know if this is even possible," I say, thinking as I'm talking, "but I have a request. I want Messick to show me a cell. Unless I see a cell, I don't really know what life on the inside of prison is like. If Messick agrees, would you show me your cell?"

Don looks away. When he finally speaks, he says bluntly, "You will be horrified. When you really see the cells and you step inside one and you realize your whole life has to happen right here, it puts a whole new perspective on our accomplishments and what we're able to do. If Messick will let you come inside North Block, it's fine with me. I just have to check with my cellie." I find myself hoping the inmate Don shares his cell with will say yes. Somehow that seems more improbable than getting Messick to agree.

From all around, the crackling sound of a voice abruptly blares from loudspeakers. "Attention on the yard. Attention on the yard." Immediately the band stops playing, the pulsing sounds of R&B replaced by the broken static of a prison alarm. In a matter of seconds, all of the hundreds of prisoners on the yard crouch down, one of their knees touching the earth. "Attention on the yard. Attention on the yard. Stewart 488. Stewart 488."

Still standing and sticking out like a female sore thumb, waiting for the sound of a rifle, I start to bend down to the ground. Messick catches sight of me. "No. Not you," he says. "The alarm is just for the inmates."

From high up inside one of the box-like towers propped on top of the walls connecting one end of the razor wire to another, an officer leans out and yells at one of the prisoners who isn't completely "down on the yard." All eyes follow to see who it is. By the look on their faces, it must be serious. A man sitting on a low bench near the weight pile slides off and puts his butt flush with the blacktop. Later Don informs me that if that prisoner is a lifer eligible for parole, that one infraction could end his chances of ever being released.

A minute passes. No one moves. Then, just as suddenly as the alarm blared, a sharp buzzer sounds over the speakers. The prisoners rise and resume their business, pacing around the track and playing basketball as if nothing at all had happened. Apparently the alarm sounded just so the guards could find a prisoner.

Cold Blue Steel's set ends. I approach Dewey Wooten, the former associate warden, to congratulate him on a great performance. "When you play with inmates in a band," I observe, "it's almost like you're an equal with them."

"Nothing wrong with that!" Wooten replies. "People are people. You know, thirty-five years ago I was a drug counselor at another prison. One of the clients I had was a marijuana user and he messed around with drugs. He kept coming into my program, and I got to know him rather well. Many years later I came to San Quentin and one day I was walking up on Death Row and there he was. And I go, 'What happened to you?' And his response was, 'I had a really bad day.' For me, that sums it all up. These are regular people who some of them had a really bad day, or a bad week or a bad month or some bad luck. They're just people."

A week later Messick agrees to take me into North Block, home to the prison's lifer population, to let me see Don's cell. Pulling open the heavy glass door to the Protestant chapel hallway, I'm relieved to see Don standing outside one of the offices talking to another inmate. I stop to look at some photos taped on one of the security windows outside another office door. Men in street clothes are sitting in trucks, walking on the beach, and standing around a barbecue, wide smiles on their faces, their arms wrapped around the shoulder or waist of a woman.

"Who are these people?" I ask.

"Oh, these are men I did time with," Don says, "lifers who have been released. Hopefully we're not too far behind 'em. Except for one, they all got out on court action. So the governor didn't release 'em, the courts did. Which is a real big political story."

Don goes on to explain that when the governor reverses the parole board and "takes a lifer's date" on the 150th day, a lifer's only recourse is to file an appeal in the courts. Lawsuits take years and lots of money, especially if you have to take your fight all the way to the federal courts.

"How long has it been since the earliest date you could have been paroled?"

"I was eligible in 1998. So almost ten years. I've never had a write-up in twenty-five years."

"What's a write-up?"

"If I were to break the rule, like the guy did out on the yard that day. That's a discipline thing. And when you do something like that, you not only get more time added to your sentence, but it also removes any good-time credit you've earned. I have one hundred months of good-time credit. But what good is it? I'm still here."

Walking out of the chapel, Don takes the lead: "We'll go this way." As we pass prisoners on their way to the yard, many nod or lift a hand to say hi, much like when I walk on the sidewalk in my neighborhood. There are casual greetings, nods of acknowledgment.

Not all inmates have the same range of movement inside the prison. As we reach the entrance to North Block, one of four massive cell blocks built on the southern nib of land jutting out in the bay, an inmate in an all-white jumpsuit passes us escorted at both elbows by two corrections officers. The inmate's hands are locked in steel handcuffs attached to a thick leather belt cinched around his waist. His entire head is covered in a netted veil much like the sort beekeepers wear to protect themselves from being stung. As they pass by, I try to catch a glimpse of the inmate's face through the veil. The two officers holding him by the elbows pick up their pace, practically lifting the gangly man off the ground. He turns and looks back at me, his dark eyes untamed.

"He's a spitter. He spits on people," Messick explains, his voice laced with disgust. "It's a health hazard to the officers and everyone else, so he has to wear that head covering whenever he has to be moved."

I follow Messick and Don past a guard outpost, down a cement ramp, and through an opened solid-steel door into North Block. It's *loud.* The sounds of men's voices, sprays of water from a bank of showers hitting the tiled floor, cell gates clunking open, others closing, officers' walkie-talkies mumbling static conversations: all of these noises and more fill the moist, warm, stuffy air bouncing up and down the block's five-story, chalk-colored walls.

Bright afternoon light filters through dirty windows high up on the walls, illuminating the specks of dust floating in the air. Looking down the full length of the first tiers of cell gates, one no more than a foot from the next, I'm surprised at how close together they are. Are there two doors to one cell? Nope. Looking hard through the steel mesh–covered bars of the first few cells we walk by, I can barely see the outline of two bunks, one directly on top of the other. It may be an illusion, but it seems the three-foot-wide door just about covers the face of the entire cell.

While Messick gives me a minute to get my bearings, I watch an elderly man push open his cell door, sweep the narrow space directly in front of it, and with a small dustpan, collect the imperceptible flakes of dirt that have sifted down to his front door from the four tiers of cells overhead.

About halfway down the first tier, Don points out a bank of old-fashioned telephone booths lining the wall opposite the cells. "Making a phone call is a very expensive proposition, but it's all we have. Those of us that are responsible try to limit our collect calls to several a month." Every fifteen-minute collect call an inmate makes to someone costs the receiver $4.85. A few calls each week can add nearly $100 to a person's monthly phone bill. And then there are the care packages, which have to be ordered through state-approved suppliers. The cost of having an incarcerated loved one can add up.

"I'm on the third tier on the other side," Don says, leading me along the corridor at the end of the tiers. "We'll go around. Just didn't want to go by the showers. Be embarrassing for you and them." As we make our way along the end of the cell block, a few men wearing only briefs and towels slung over their shoulders pass by, staring hard at me, their eyes filled with question marks.

"Open showers?" I ask, trying to avert my face from the sound of running water nearby.

"Like in high school," Don says.

We climb up and around on steel stairs that bookend the tiers. Over the loudspeakers, a guard's voice calls out, each word bouncing around inside the cell block, "Attention . . . attention . . . in the unit.

Attention in the unit. The following inmates need to report to North Block 6: Biel, Baker, Ballard . . . "

"Listen to that," Don says, his voice drowned out by the guard's. "I hear that in the morning. It will wake me up. I hear this all day and night long. It's terrible. Then I look through the bars and screens, then through more bars. You're looking at the dirt and filth."

As we walk out onto the third tier, to our left a waist-high rail prevents anyone from accidentally falling to the ground floor thirty-five feet below. On the right we pass cell after cell, the jet-black steel bars covered in thick sheets of steel mesh.

Don stops in front of a cell door, midway down the tier.

"Certain times of the day they'll call an 'in-and-out.' An officer standing down at the end pulls the long steel bar that runs over the tops of all the cells, and it moves this mechanism," he says, pointing to a short steel bar hanging over the top of his cell door, "and then you're allowed to go in and out."

"You can't get out unless an officer comes up to the tier and pulls that long bar? Then you can get out?" I ask, shuddering.

"Not until they call another in-and-out and pull the bar."

"That would make me claustrophobic."

"You get used to it. I was here in '89 for the earthquake, and it was surreal. You could see the steel moving and the bars were all rattling and shaking and you could feel the floor moving. We thought, 'This place is going to crumble on us.' It was terrifying. But thank God, this old place has really stood the test. We've had a fire. There've been reports of smoke. They've gotten us out, evacuated us quickly. A medical emergency, if someone has a heart attack or a seizure, it's pretty quick. It's surprising. So I guess you lose that fear."

As if on cue, from the end of the tier a corrections officer lifts a large key from a ring of them, unlocks a box, and wrenches a lever that pulls the long steel bar running along the top of all the cell doors some four inches, disengaging it from the shorter steel bars in front of the cell doors.

"Now, I want you to know I didn't do any special preparations," Don says, fingering a single combination lock on his cell door and pulling the gate open. "It's kind of stagnant. There's really no fresh air."

Don walks into the cell, his shoulders nearly touching the rail of his top bunk on the left side and the cell wall on the right. Tugging the white sheet on the top bunk, he quickly straightens the place up.

"So this is it?"

"My cellie and I live here. Two men. You can see how only one person can be on the floor at one time."

From outside the cell door, Messick adds, "San Quentin and Folsom have the smallest cells in the state." Apparently new prisons have more room.

"So if I need to do something, my cellie either has to step out if the door's open, or he has to stay on his bunk." I step inside. It feels like a low closet.

While I look around, mouth agape, Don continues explaining how he and his cellie share what looks like about a nine-by-four-foot space. "We each have a television," he says, pointing to the mini-TV anchored to the ceiling, right where his feet would go if he were lying on his bunk. "We're allowed to have a radio or CD player."

Near where he would have a pillow if the prison allowed them, a crate-like shelf is attached to the wall. Every inch inside the foot-square cubicle holds something. "This is some of my property," Don says. "What I keep on the shelves is stuff I use every day, like laundry, cosmetics, my Bible, some books, a lot of CAADAC reading. The other stuff—clothes, legal materials, mementos—things I don't want to get rid of, we keep in boxes."

"But you can't sit up on your bunk and dangle your legs over the edge. Your head will hit the ceiling. . . . "

Don agrees, but then he sits on the bottom bunk to show me it's not much better. He has to lean out and hold his neck at an odd angle. "It's a little better on the top bunk. Now I have degenerative disc disease. I've had one surgery already."

Not sure what to say, I pat the mattress. "It looks like a nice soft bed," I say.

He tells me to lie on it. It's harder and narrower than it looks. "When we're on lockdown, we only get out to eat a meal for a half hour. We can be locked in here for twenty-three hours a day for weeks or months. We never know when a lockdown starts how long it's going to last." A lockdowns happens whenever there's a security concern on the block.

"Do you ever think of painting the walls?" I ask, gazing at the putrid gray around me.

"We could. One guy's got a whole universe with Saturn and moons. He painted it black, of course, but then the stars. The planets are fluorescent. It looks pretty cool."

"How do you deal with living in a space this small?"

"I wish I knew the formula," Don says, looking around, the walls so close. "You just slowly acclimate to it."

"Do you have compassion for people when they first come in and they can't deal with it?"

"Yeah. There are men with claustrophobia. Another thing I will never do is have a pet that I have to put in a cage. Never again." Looking down at the floor, he adds, "Speaking of animals and floor space: if you were to measure this, the Society for the Prevention of Cruelty to Animals and federal rules say this is too small to confine one dog."

Officially, by measurement, a double-man cell inside San Quentin's North Block is forty-four inches wide. The cell door takes up twenty-four inches. Inside the cell measures seven feet, seven inches high by four feet, six inches wide (wall to wall), by ten feet, eight inches long. The beds measure two feet, six inches wide by six feet, five inches long. There are thirty-six inches from the top bunk to the ceiling and thirty-four inches from the bottom bunk to the top bunk, and twenty-two inches from the edge of the bunk to the far wall.

Don reaches up behind his bed and pulls down a photograph to show me. "Here's a picture! The latest of my fiancée."

"Your *fiancée?*" I ask, trying not to look stunned. "You're engaged?"

"Yes, that's Kathleen."

He hands me the photo. Holding it in the shadows of the cell, I study the woman with the bright smile, trim body, and short auburn hair.

"When are you getting married?"

"As soon as I'm out this door. We've been together for fifteen years and we live as if we are married. We love each other deeply. We do business things together. We confide in each other. I consider myself married, and she does too, but there's no benefit to be gained being married. We're not allowed family or conjugal visits. There was a time when we had them, but not anymore."

Don tells me Kathleen manages a travel agency and owns her own home in San Anselmo. I know it as a small über-white, upper-middle-class village of a town nestled in the Marin hills twenty minutes west of San Quentin. "We're both Christians," he continues. "I led her to the Lord in '95, and we just hope to enjoy whatever days God gives us together."

Am I shaking my head or just imagining it? Don is locked up in prison for murder. He's not bad looking, trim and clean-cut, but really, who would want to marry someone convicted of murder?

I take another good look at the photo. She looks normal enough. There must be a backstory, something I can't tell from the photo.

"What's this?" I ask, changing the subject again, picking up a ball of wire all curled up in a mass.

"Stainless steel to clean the sink and toilet," he says. Don pushes his body flush against the stone wall opposite the bunks so I can squeeze past him to get to the back end of the cell.

"There's the toilet and sink. They're all stainless steel," Don says. "This is our bathroom, our sink, our kitchen. We have to do everything in here. If there's a death in the family, we grieve in here together. We celebrate accomplishments or victories, holidays. If you're sick and you're throwing up and diarrhea? Right here with another person. You just have to get over the embarrassment and do it. But it is humiliating. It's all you have. So you try to make the best of it. Keep it as clean as you can. The dust is really bad. I'll wipe my television off Monday morning, do a general clean"—he reaches over with his finger to wipe the top of his television—"today it's covered with dust again."

Don falls silent, then turns to Messick. "I think it would be a good thing if Messick and I just stand outside the cell and you stay in and we shut the door. That way you'll really get a feeling for what it's like to be in the cell. Alone."

"If you promise you won't close the door all the way," I say, embarrassed.

Nearly in unison Messick and Don say, "The bar's pulled back. We can't really lock you in."

Don walks out and slowly closes the cell door until it is open just a sliver.

"It's morning and you're waking up," Don says, setting the scene, standing next to Messick against the rail. "We'll just be quiet."

I sit down on the edge of the bottom bunk, close my eyes and listen to the sounds of the cell block: the rhythmic clang of a machine far below, the echo of fans and conversations. A minute passes, then two. Opening my eyes, I look through the black mesh of the gate. I see the outline of Don and Messick's backs, their bodies leaning over the railing. I stand to walk around. There's really nowhere to go.

Immobile in the middle of the cell, I face the door and stretch my arms out to the side; my fingers nearly touch the two walls. I lift my arm. At five feet seven, I'm average height for a woman. With my elbow still bent, my hand touches the stone ceiling. Now that I've explored the edges of the space, the walls seem closer.

Sitting back down on the edge of the bottom bunk, I can't sit up straight. The bottom rail of the upper bunk hits the back of my neck, so I lean forward and put my elbows on my knees, my hands cupped around my face. It's been about five minutes since Don closed the gate. If I could just sit up straight, push my shoulders back, I could relax a bit. And Don has to share this space with another guy. Oh, God.

I'm done with this experiment. Rising, I shove the gate open. Even the dust-choked, sweaty cell-block air feels refreshing.

"I'm fine," I say, breathless. "It wasn't too bad. I knew I was walking out."

Messick smirks the same way he did when he left me in the chapel that first time. "Lesser minds don't adapt," he murmurs. "There are some who spend their whole time in mental health care in prisons, or they're in Ad Seg and they never adapt. The confinement is more than they can handle."

"What happens to them?" I ask, the back of my neck beginning to itch.

"They'll act out," Messick says, "deteriorate mentally. The security gets tighter and tighter as their condition gets worse and worse. Inside Ad Seg, they're behind solid doors. A little peephole like that." He wraps his forefinger against his thumb to make a small hole. "Much less property. Much less privilege. No work. No school. No contact visits. No phone calls. Some have been in there twenty years. Then it's the question of the chicken or the egg. Bad behavior got them in there, but sometimes I wonder if the methods employed, the custody levels, don't perpetuate it. The guy's not going to get any better. Some of them do. Some of them are like, 'Let me out of here.' Some guys just get worse and worse and more dangerous. We've got some really dangerous guys in there. We couldn't let them out on the yard. Nobody would be safe."

"I wouldn't want them out," Don says with a nervous laugh.

I'm curious about whether Don has ever tried to reach out to inmates who might be sliding down that slippery emotional slope. "When you hear about someone having difficulty, do people ever reach out to them and say, 'It's going to be all right—calm down'? Do they try to help?"

"Sometimes," he says. "I think it would depend on the situation. If someone were suicidal or in ill health? That way? Oh yeah, there's a lot of people around here who are compassionate and willing. But a lot of guys get into messes they shouldn't get into, and you don't want to be part of it. And like Messick said, sometimes a person will deteriorate. I've known men that were pretty good, stand-up guys, five, ten, fifteen years. And then all of a sudden, one day you notice they're slipping."

"Then it's hard for them to come back?" I ask.

"Usually it's a pretty psychotic event. It's beyond us. What you felt in the cell just now. Try and repeat that in your mind, thousands of times, day and night. This is hell."

Standing out on the tier, I look at Don again, hard. I study his face, his eyes and mouth. How is it possible this man killed a person? I remember what Dewey Wooten told me down on the yard about lifers being regular people who had a bad day, week, month. Is that even possible: that murder happens when a regular Joe, a neighbor, friend, stranger, hits a rough patch?

I don't yet know the story of Don's crime, but the man standing in front of me is no sociopath. Isn't that what the court's sentence, life with the possibility of parole, reflects? That he's no Night Stalker, no Dating Game Killer—that he's capable of rehabilitation.

If so, why has he been in here so *long?* What am I missing?

It's time to go. I thank Don and head over to the sally port with Messick. "I've known Don for almost twenty-six years," he muses as we leave. "My emotions have run the gamut over the years, of how I feel about prisoners. Now, after more than a quarter of a century, I'm . . . confused. I don't invest myself too much in whether these lifers get out or not, because it's hard for me. If I get too invested emotionally on individual cases and how they turn out, it's not healthy for me. It would be a lot of disappointment. It's a huge weight."

Standing together in the sun just outside the warden's office, I ask whether he's ever wondered what it would be like to end up inside, locked up.

"I've experienced incarceration in my dreams, where I've been on the other side of the bars. I wouldn't call it a nightmare, but it is a surreal sort of dream. I don't know why I'm there, but it seems natural that I'm locked up. I don't know if it suggests there's a small separation between the feeling of incarceration and working inside the prison."

I remember the image I saw through Don's door: Messick and Don together, leaning against the railing of the tier, looking down at the cell block below. How hard it must be for both of them to have spent half their lives together, to know and even respect each other, and yet feel the chasm of circumstance between them. What a tremendously isolating experience for both of them—not just Don, but Messick, who's been working in the prison since he was twenty-one.

Driving away from the prison, I flash back to Don's cell. While I was sitting on the lower bunk, unable to sit up or lift my head erect, I didn't panic. I observed, measured, took notes. But now, as I drive along the bay, a deep, unnerving sadness rushes over me.

The light skips off the bay. Children are playing on the beach, practically in the shadow of Don and all the men in their cages. In just a few hours the sun will set gloriously over the water, but the walls of the prison will hide that from view. Who knows whether any of those men will ever see the sun set again.

When I realize I am sobbing, I slowly pull my car off the road.

four

WORLDS APART

OCTOBER 2007

The feeling of confinement in Don's cell has so seared me that it is a relief to hear from Bryan Smith, now fresh out of prison on parole. He calls out of the blue to say that his parents are throwing him a little party to celebrate, and he invites me. As a journalist, I can't wait to see how he's adjusting to freedom, and what life on the outside is like for someone just released from prison after serving more than two decades in prison for murder. On the flip side, I'm nervous: parties full of strangers are awkward enough when you're not playing "guess which guest is a paroled murderer." I say yes.

My first surprise is the location of the party: a ballroom at a local Marriott. I half expected the party to be in a fourth-floor hotel room, a couple dozen people standing around a king-size bed, the door to the minibar open. I can't imagine a cotillion's worth of guests have been waiting for Bryan's release these past two decades. But I'm swiftly learning that my imagination falls short of prison reality.

Peeking through an open door at the end of the hall, I see balloons, streamers hanging down from the ceiling, and tables decorated with colorful plates and napkins. It looks more like a blue-and-white-themed wedding or graduation party than the celebration of a prisoner's release. Just as I'm about to turn and leave, I catch sight of Claire-Elizabeth waving from one of the round tables on the far side of the room.

Midway across the crowded floor I run into Bryan. "Nancy, I'm so glad you could make it!" he cries, opening his arms wide for a quick hug.

"Bryan, who are all these people?" I ask.

"Oh, they're family and friends. Some old school pals and some people I met inside. Do you want to meet my parents?"

Grasping my arm, he works the room, accepting hearty congratulations and kisses on the cheek.

"Mom, Dad, this is Nancy. She's the reporter I met inside."

Looking into Sue and Jack Smith's eyes, I search for signs of twenty-four years of devastation. More than two decades ago, their son was convicted of murder and sent to prison. As they hold out their hands to welcome me, I see parental caution in their eyes. Now that it's over, do they really want to be publicly exposed? Up until this moment, Bryan's party and his release from prison have been private affairs shared with good friends and close family. Everyone in the room knows who he is and what he did and they are all happy he is out. They don't want a reporter to upset their still-fragile relief.

Even so, they seem genuinely glad I have come. "How nice to meet you, Nancy. Be sure and get some cake," says his mother. The rest of the room is just as friendly. Women sit at tables, leaning in to chat with one another; men hold drinks of some kind and stand talking like men do about sports and such. No one appears outwardly concerned about sharing the room with men convicted of murder.

Turning back to look out on the festivities, balloons, and music, Bryan says, "Hey. Didn't you want to meet some of the guys I did time with, inside San Quentin?"

He steers me toward a group of five men standing together, a little apart from everyone else. One at a time, Bryan introduces me. There's Eddie, Richie, "T," Rico, Pat, German, and Kevin. They look anxious, skeptical, just like the men in the room inside the prison chapel office looked before I cut the tension with Claire-Elizabeth's name. At the same time, they look like everyone else at the party: middle to working class, ordinary people. If Bryan hadn't pointed them out, I never would have been able to identify them as parolees.

Looking at the nervousness on their faces, I wonder whether any of these men will ever talk to me on the record. Aside from their parole agents, whom they meet with regularly, no one on the outside has to know they've served more than half their adult lives in prison for murder. Their criminal pasts are hidden from neighbors, coworkers, fellow churchgoers, and strangers they meet on the street.

Responding to his friends' obvious discomfort, Bryan vouches for me. "She's okay," he assures them. "I met her inside San Quentin. She's a reporter, but she's okay."

Each of the men scans my face and eyes and calculates the risk. Eddie, a Latino with dark eyes and enormous shoulders, is the first to reach out his hand, tattoos etched across the length of his forearm, a thin smile breaking over his face. "If Bryan says you're okay, you're okay."

Richie, a quiet Latino who looks white, is next.

So it will be. From Richie and Eddie, I will attempt to learn more about the ins and outs of life on parole—but first I'll have to convince them to open up their lives to a journalist.

five

RICHIE'S STORY

The Good Son

DECEMBER 2007

A few days after Bryan's party, back at my desk, the real weight of what I'll be asking these men to do hits me. If I do call, I will have to tell them, come out with it, no holding back. "I want you to tell me everything."

They could say no. That would be the end of it. The secret life of paroled murderers buried beneath the risk inherent in the exposure. I'll never know until I ask the first question, a journalist's wedge.

I leave messages for Eddie and Richie. A day later, Richie is the first to return my call. His voice sounds young, tender, eager to please.

"Would you have time to get together next week?" I ask, trying not to scare him.

"Oh, um . . . sure," he says. "How about Friday? I have plans every other day. I get off work at four and need a little time to change and clean up, so how about if we meet at five at my parents' house in Newark. That's where I'm living."

Newark is one town away from Fremont, the site of Bryan's freedom party. I quickly calculate a trip on three freeways at five on a Friday afternoon. Ugh.

"Richie, I live in San Francisco. Do you know how long it would take me to get there on a Friday afternoon? Can we do it any other time? Maybe over the weekend?"

"Oh, Nancy." Richie laughs a little. "I've never been stuck on the freeway on a Friday afternoon before, and after twenty years in prison, I've got patience. I could come where you are after work. Or I could come over next Saturday morning. . . . I've been meaning to visit San Francisco. It's within the fifty-mile limit of my parole."

"Sure," I say, relieved. "I'll just meet you at my house next Saturday morning."

I hang up the phone only to second-guess myself: *Wait. Did I just invite a convicted murderer over to my house? Was that a good idea? What if it goes badly?*

Saturday morning, a little before eleven, Richie pulls up in front of my home in an electric-blue Chevy Colorado pickup truck. He parks parallel across my driveway—the only legal option. From the loving way he looks at his car, I half-expect him to pat it as he walks by.

"Nice truck," I call out.

"Yeah," he says, bobbing his way over to shake my hand. "I really needed it for work. I have payments, but I hope to pay it off early."

I look around my block, a bit self-conscious. I don't know this man, not yet, and I can't help but worry that I am exposing my neighbors and their small children to risk. Too late now. At least he's wearing nice clothes: a button-down shirt, khaki pants, and white athletic shoes. (But what did I expect him to be wearing? A Freddy Krueger mask?)

"I was thinking it would be nice to talk up on my roof deck," I say, directing Richie to a set of stairs at the side of the house that lead up to the privacy of the wide open sky. Sitting down at a small round table, the sun on our faces, Richie pulls his chair up. "What do you want to know?" he asks, with a "let's get on with it" look on his nearly line-free face. How is it possible a man who has spent more than two decades in prison has such a youthful face?

"That was quite a party. How long have you known Bryan? Were you ever cellies?"

"I thought you knew," Richie says, leaning in, his eyes growing wide. "Bryan and I grew up together. We were best friends. Twenty-three years ago, he was my crime partner. We were together the night of the murder."

I had thought we were going to take our time and slowly work our way around to talking about the murder. Sitting before me, his hands clasped in his lap, Richie has brought up the M-word so quickly that it seems he wants to get something out in the open, off his chest.

"I got out of prison on September 16, 2006," Richie says, then immediately changes tack, dialing back the pace a little: "Are we forever *bad* because of our crime? I don't believe we are. We're human beings. We did something bad, but we've also been able to grow in our lives and in our experiences in prison and come to a point where, 'Hey, I did the crime and I've forgiven myself over the crime,' and from that point on, I can go forward. From there, it's just a growing process. A lot of the guys in prison, I believe they shouldn't even be there anymore. Some have done crimes a lot worse than mine, or just as bad, or even less. But . . . they've outgrown the prison system. I'd outgrown the prison system eight, nine years ago. There was nothing there for me except my existence of being there."

Before I can process Richie's crime or his years in prison, I need the basics. "Let's begin by you giving me your name."

"My name is Richard Rael. My dad's name is Richard Jr., so I'm Richard the third. Do you want my CDC [California Department of Corrections] number, too?" he asks, with a little chuckle.

This seems like a detail parolees would want to put out of their minds. "Do you remember it?"

"Sure. C47374. It's the same backwards. In prison you have to say it every time you want to go somewhere, like the library, church, the yard.

"So where do you want to start with me? Birth?" Richie asks, jumping enthusiastically into his story with so much good feeling I wonder how it's going to turn bad.

"I was born into a Mexican-American family. I'm the third of six siblings and I was raised Catholic. I had my communion and confirmation."

Richie's mom, Alice, is from Arizona. His dad, Richard Jr., is from Escabosa, a little town high up in the mountains southeast of Albuquerque where the roots of the Rael family reach back to the 1600s. Alice and Richard Jr. met fifty-four years ago in a small central California town before moving to Newark, where his father got steady blue-collar work as a welder. His stay-at-home mom took care of the kids and did all the housework. "Now I see she is the rock, the glue," he says. "She keeps us all together. When I got home from prison, my dad said, 'I'm so glad you're here because now your mom will make tortillas again.' She had stopped making them when I was inside.

"I had two older brothers, two younger sisters, and a brother who was the youngest. His name is Rod and he plays into my life because he was with me the night of the crime. He was thirteen when it happened. I was nineteen."

Richie had a pretty good childhood. "In elementary school, which was right around the corner from my house, I had a core group of guys I hung out with in the neighborhood. My parents always knew where I was. When I was a kid you could get on your bike and ride for miles and your parents never had to worry about you." Then in 1970 it all came apart.

Richie was nine years old when his father was seriously injured in a welding accident. "He was thrown thirty to forty feet. They took him to the hospital. He was all busted up. All of his bones, his face, everywhere. I vividly remember him walking into the house like this"—Richie gets up and walks around the roof deck, his arms out, stiff—"with his arms out, like you see Frankenstein. He was in a cast from his head down to his waist because of the explosion. I didn't know how to react to the situation. When he first walked into the house, I cried and ran out of the room. Before that, he was never sick."

After he spent six months in the body cast, the doctors retired him for life. Now, with a mortgage to pay and six kids at home to feed and clothe, the family quickly tumbled from steady middle to working class to barely surviving.

"Up until the point when my father had the accident, I felt equal to the kids I hung around with. I had a lot of the same things they had. Then, when the explosion happened, the money changed in the house and I didn't get new clothes anymore. I really noticed it because now I wasn't as equal as the kids I was with, because of them coming with new clothes and I would get hand-me-downs from my cousins or I'd get my brothers' clothes. I guess it did affect me. I remember that. It made me feel less than they were. A lower class than they were."

In high school Richie began experimenting with marijuana, hanging out with a different crowd. "That's where I met Bryan. We'd known each other for a while 'cause when I was an eighth grader at McGregor Junior High, he was a seventh grader. We played Little League, but we really met when I was sixteen and he was fifteen, during football. We did things teenagers did. We both had older brothers and he smoked weed and I smoked weed. So we started hanging out together."

Eventually Richie's dad recovered enough to build a business of his own as a maintenance man, bringing on Richie as unpaid, part-time help. "I look back now and realize then I felt obligated to go to work with my dad. Maybe that's why I never said no to him. Rather than him just being disappointed, I felt obligated. If I asked him if he could pay me for my work, he said he didn't have it. So I didn't make any money in high school."

By his senior year in high school, Richie was smoking so much marijuana, his grades had slipped from a strong B average to a D. "School wasn't important to me. I didn't put effort in anymore and no one at Newark High School reached out to me. I just barely had enough credits to graduate. They gave me a diploma to get rid of me. I didn't even go to my graduation ceremony. I lied to my parents and said I couldn't go because I cut school on a senior cut day. I used that as a lie, because I wanted to get high. That's the way it was."

After his graduation no-show, Richie went to work for a painting company. "College didn't seem like an option. My dad couldn't send me to school. He had too many kids. I was nineteen and making $10 an hour working as a journeyman for a painting outfit. That was good money back then. So I wasn't really going anywhere. I didn't have any goals. That was going to be my life."

"What about your brothers and sisters?" I ask, wondering whether their lives were also derailed by their father's tragedy.

"Henry, my oldest brother, passed away in 1997 while I was in prison. He actually did a little time in prison. He was going to burglarize a house with a friend. They didn't know the people who lived there were there. So they took the people from one room to another, which turned out to be kidnap. He ended up doing seven years in Vacaville state prison [California State Prison, Solano] and in Norco prison [California Rehabilitation Center, Norco]. I must have been fifteen, sixteen when it happened."

The rest of his siblings are doing well. Ronnie, his other older brother, owns a window and door company and is now Richie's boss. His younger sister Lorraine calls him all the time just to ask how he's doing. His younger brother, Rod, who was in the car the night Richie and Bryan committed their crime, is a little more closed off. "He doesn't talk about it," Richie says. "I've talked a few times with him about it since I've been out, and he brushes it off. But, yeah. He's seen a very bad thing."

We realize hours have passed since Richie began telling his story, and he leaves with that ominous thought unresolved. The next time Richie and I meet, I will find out exactly what that very bad thing was.

A week later, in the hour after work and before dinner, I pull up in front of Richie's parents' tract house, just inside the lip of the cul-de-sac. So this is where he grew up: the house he left to go to prison more than twenty-five years ago.

As I step on the doormat, digital voices sing out, "Merry Christmas! Jingle bells, jingle bells . . . " Before I can locate the source of the electronic carolers, Richie appears from behind the screen door. "Hey, Nancy, come on in," he calls out, immediately following up with, "I know. My dad likes to kid around with the holidays. You should have seen it on Halloween!"

In a reclining chair centered between two sectional couches, Richie's father rests in an almost horizontal position, his eyes closed, the twinkling lights of the Christmas tree behind him adding to the soft natural glow of the late afternoon sun humming through the sliding glass doors. "Poppa," Richie says softly, hoping to wake him, "this is Nancy Mullane, the reporter I told you about."

Half-waking, Richie's father slowly shifts his aged weight to sit more upright in the chair. "*Bueno.* Good to meet you," he says, a smile crossing his deeply lined, light brown face, his words accented. Richie smiles nervously, looking back and forth from his father to me.

As if on cue, the front door just down the hall opens, and a small, compact woman with gray hair, a welcome smile, and busy eyes makes her way toward us. Her feet are tripping over the grandchildren who are following her, holding onto her arms, which are filled with bags of groceries, "*Hola,*" she calls out as she approaches. "Rich told me you were coming. I'm his mother."

"Good to meet you," I say. "It must be so good to have Richie home." Instantly I worry that I may have just put my foot in my mouth. Is it polite to openly acknowledge a prison sentence to a parolee's mother?

"Oh. It is God's blessing," his mother says without hesitating. "I prayed and prayed, and God answered my prayers."

I'm a little embarrassed when I ask Richie whether he'll show me his bedroom. It's an important part of his life post-prison, but I can only imagine what it might sound like to his parents.

"Sure," Richie says, walking ahead of me down the short hall to his bedroom door. Pushing it open, he steps in to show me around. A double bed with a simple blanket pulled smooth over the sheets fills the center of the room, leaving just enough space on three sides for Richie to get around to the far side to adjust the slatted blinds covering the narrow horizontal window high on the far wall. He reaches to turn on a lamp on the nightstand next to his bed. Filling the little remaining space, a small wooden desk is pushed up into a narrow piece of wall between the door and an open closet, where a few plaid shirts, spaced neatly, dangle from wire hangers.

"It's not much, but it's private," he says, all but closing the bedroom door. Sitting on a wooden chair at the end of the bed, he reaches over and picks up an acoustic guitar. "It's busy here at my parents' house with kids in and out all the time, but I can close the door and play my guitar. I'm not very good, but I'm learning."

"This must feel like a huge improvement over the past twenty-four years," I offer, flashing back to Don's cell.

"Oh my, yes," he says with that wide, sort of surprisingly innocent look on his middle-aged face. He reminds me of Brendan Fraser's character in the movie *Blast from the Past,* emerging from a bunker with the birth date of a middle-aged man and the soul, and skin tone, of a teenager.

He picks out a few songs while talking about his life back at home with his parents. "It's only been fifteen months. I'm not in a hurry. I want to take my time. My brother, Ron, gave me a job. It isn't paying me much, but it's a job and I'm lucky to have it. I know some guys who get out can't get work for years, so even if it's not a lot of money, I can save nearly all of what I make living here with my parents. I pay them some rent every month and I bought my truck, so I have car payments. Maybe in a year or so, I'll get my own place."

But after twenty-four years, doesn't he want to get together with a woman, maybe have sex? A thin wall is all that separates him from his parents' master bedroom. "What if you wanted to bring friends or a woman back here to your room? That's not a problem?"

"That's not even on the table right now. I'm not ready to date. If I want, I can bring a friend or two home. We can sit in here and talk or take a drive. It's fine for now. Really. Not in a hurry."

"Speaking of driving, want to show me around your neighborhood? I'd like to see where you went to school and where you used to hang out. I've never been in Newark before, so it'll all be new to me."

"Sure. Let's go," he says, carefully laying his guitar back on the bed.

As we make our way back out into the hall, Richie calls, "Mom, we'll be back in a while."

"Okay, *niño.*"

Walking out the front door, past the Christmas lights that dangle from every point of his family's single-story roof and the tips of shrubs separating his house from the neighbors, we jump in his shiny blue truck. Again, I feel a little twinge of worry. I don't really know Richie all that well yet, and it's getting dark out.

A few blocks later the tour begins. "So, I went to this elementary school right here," Richie says, driving slowly past a long, low complex of buildings, the name of the school posted over the administration wing, a flagpole anchored out front. "The high school is around the corner. So everything was really close. I didn't have to go far. The junior high is right down this street, Cedar. All this area," he says, with what's left of the setting sun shining across his face, "is the same. This shopping center and these gas stations. They're the infrastructure of Newark. This Home Depot used to be a Kmart when I was a kid. We're going to go right by the shop where I work."

"When you came home fifteen months ago, how did it all look to you?"

"The trees were bigger. That's what I noticed. And here's one of the houses I'm working on. It's a three-day job. We're putting in ten new-construction windows. We pull the whole frame out and we nail new windows in. You know, in 1980, when I went to prison, this place exploded with development. This mall right here, it was built in 1980, the year of my crime. All of this to the left was field."

So that's how the world looks to him, a before-and-after snapshot of his hometown. I ask him where we are going next, and he responds, "I thought I'd take you to Mowry School Road, where my crime took place."

"Where the crime happened?" I watch his face. "We haven't talked about that."

"No. We haven't," he says. Unflustered, he keeps his eyes on the road and tells the story of the night it happened, twenty-seven years before.

"It was August 26, 1980. My thirteen-year-old younger brother, Rod, was going to an Oakland A's game at the Coliseum with Raymond, my next-door neighbor. They were going to go on BART [the local heavy-rail public transit system here in Northern California]."

Richie was nineteen at the time. Raymond, the next-door neighbor, was twenty. "He wasn't somebody I hung around with. His parents and my parents were really good friends from high school. Raymond was getting in trouble, arrested, so my parents helped his parents find the house next door to us so they could move out of San Jose. They had just moved in, so this was the first time my dad arranged for Raymond to do something with us.

"I had a job and I came home and my dad said, 'Rich, you go to the game with them.' I didn't want to go because I didn't trust Raymond, but I couldn't say no to my father. So I said, 'Okay, I'll go.' And then Bryan walked in, and I said, 'Bryan, let's go to the game. I'll drive.' So we all went to the game together."

To this day, Richie says his father holds a lot of guilt, and a deep burden for asking him to take Raymond to the game. If his father had never asked, "it" never would have happened. But that's not the way

Richie sees it. "It was my fault because of what I was doing—my actions. I could have prevented it. I didn't.

"It all started with the Reggie Bar." Before they went to the game, Richie says, they stopped off at a liquor store and bought a twelve-pack of beer and some candy—some Reggie Bars. Rod had seen on TV that people threw quarters onto the Yankee Stadium field when Reggie Jackson was up to bat. "So Rod wanted to sit in right field and throw Reggie Bars out on the field.

"Then, at the game, when my younger brother throws the candy bars onto the field, the people that were sitting in front of us said, 'Hey, that's not cool. You're not supposed to be throwing stuff onto the baseball field.' And we said, 'Okay.' But Raymond took offense to what they told him and he opened his jacket and made a comment to them: 'Hey. Don't even mess around with us,' and he showed them a three-inch buck knife he had on his belt. I remember me and Bryan looking at each other, saying, 'What do you got a knife for?' And Raymond said, 'I never come to Oakland without carrying a weapon.' And we're like, 'Wow.'"

It's getting dark. Driving around Newark in Richie's truck on this cold December night, I have no idea where we are. Every few minutes I turn to look out the window, to make a mental mark of a building, a street sign, an intersection, then back at Richie's face illuminated by the lights on the truck's instrument panel and the rhythmic flashing of overhead street lights.

Driving away from the baseball stadium, Richie says, they got stuck in bumper-to-bumper traffic on the freeway overpass. "Our windows were down, and these two guys walked up to the passenger side of my car and said, 'Hey. We parked our car down the freeway and took BART. Could you give us a ride back to our car?' I said, 'Sure, where you going?' They said, 'We're going to Stevenson.' I actually said, 'That's close by where I live. I'm going to Jarvis, that's three exits [before]. I'll drop you off there.' They said, 'Fine,' and they got in the backseat of the car and we left down the freeway. I'd been drinking at the game, and so were my codefendants, except for my younger brother. So we were in the car laughing. I could sense they'd been drinking, too."

Driving down the freeway, there were six in the car. Bryan and Richie's younger brother, Rod, were in the backseat next to the windows. Joseph Catton and Robert Sabertino were sitting in the back in the middle. Richie was driving. Raymond was in the front passenger seat. A few miles down the freeway, Raymond turned and asked Joseph and Robert if they had any money to go buy some beer. They said no.

"I believe Ray was offended by it," Richie says. "At that point Ray leaned over and kind of mentioned to me, 'Let's do them.' Meaning beat 'em up, rob 'em. Something to that nature. When he said that, I thought, 'I'm not going to get involved in something like that,' and I just brushed it off. But I clearly remember thinking I'm not even going to get off at Jarvis [our stop]. I'm just going to take them to Stevenson [three stops farther, where their car was waiting]. I thought it seemed like the safe thing to do, that maybe I could prevent trouble by taking them to their car. So I asked the guys, 'Where do you want me to drop you off on Stevenson?' and they said, 'Right here.'"

"They wanted to get out right then?" I asked.

"They wanted to get out right then," Richie says, his voice hitting the word "then" with a punch. "They wouldn't let me take them to their car. I don't know why."

It's not hard to imagine what must have been happening. The two men were getting scared. They wanted to get away but were trapped in the middle of a backseat on a freeway.

"So I got off the freeway," he says, "and I made a U-turn so after dropping them off I could get back on the freeway and leave."

By now Richie and I are headed down a mostly dark road near a freeway.

"Now, keep in mind this whole area is all field," he says, pointing to the back of a hotel in the distance and an adjoining nearly empty parking lot, talking about the night in 1980 in the present tense, "so there's nothing here. From here all the way to the bay is all field. I believe Joseph Catton and Robert Sabertino felt we were taking them somewhere we shouldn't be taking them."

Richie pulls off the road running along the freeway embankment high overhead, and into the empty parking lot, the dark trunks of winter trees lit by the glow of a few overhead streetlamps. "This is where it all happened," he says, his voice shallow, a little spooky. I look out the front and side windows. Other than Richie and me, there are no other cars or people to be seen.

"I faced this way," Richie says, turning off the car. "And they got out right here. Raymond Gonzalez had to get out of the passenger side to let them out, and Bryan had to get out because they were sitting in the middle, in between Bryan and my brother in the backseat. I was going to get out and let one of the guys out on my side, and one of the guys said, 'No need for you to get out. I'll get out on the other side.' So I stayed in the car."

Richie's voice is anxious, the words higher in his throat, his face alert. He's telling me the story, but he's telling himself, too. It's all happening before his eyes. I'm watching, wondering how this memory is going to end.

"My brother was sitting right behind me in the backseat. And, um, at that point, Raymond immediately attacked one of the guys. With his fists. But I knew from what happened at the game that he had a weapon, the knife, on him. Then Bryan attacked the other guy. Bryan didn't know what Raymond had said to me, because they were in the backseat, but his instinct was to attack the other guy. My mentality at that time, as a teenager, was if we went places, we would look out for each other. That's when I got out and got involved in what I thought was a fight. I didn't believe Raymond would pull out a knife. Even though he showed it, in my youthful mind, I didn't think that would happen. I got out of the car and the melee was already going on, right there."

"What did it look like?" I ask, hoping if I ask him now, he'll tell it as he sees it, instead of how he wants to see it. How many times has he played this over in his mind?

"It looked like seeing people fight. They were throwing fists. It was dark. Imagine there's no lights. There's nothing. My car lights were on. I didn't even turn the car off. The car was still running. When I got out of the car to get involved in the fight, I turned around to my brother and said, 'Rod, stay in the car.'"

To illustrate the moment twenty-seven years before, Richie opens the car door, steps out, and walks to the front of the car. For a moment I sit and watch him walk slowly in front of the headlights, his face down like he's looking for a mark on the blacktop. He stops, his shoulders slumped over, then looks up, back into the lights, at me. His face has changed. He doesn't look young anymore. Now he looks haggard and worn, even afraid. I open the door and follow him into the beam of the headlights.

"I came around here," he says, looking down at the ground, "and they were fighting right here. On the side of the car. Pushing. Over there, on the side of the road, there was a little embankment and a cyclone fence. There was nothing here. Just cow pastures. The road led to nothing. No one was getting off the freeway here. So we're fighting right out here, and I thought Raymond was slugging people. I didn't know it then but he was stabbing. I know that now. It's just obvious. So the fight's happening, and I'm involved now, and I get thrown, pushed to the ground, and when I got up, I realized my brother Rod had gotten out of the car. When I seen him, 'cause he walked to the back here and was watching and I got up and said, 'Rod, get back in the car,' and the fight moved."

Richie is turning, moving around, watching it all happen in front of his eyes.

"One of the guys, Robert Sabertino, took off running. It may have been this fence." Richie points to a line of crippled chain-link fence about two hundred yards to the east, up against the steep freeway embankment.

"Robert Sabertino went to the fence, and Raymond chased him to the fence. . . . I stayed right here, and Rod got back in the car, and the other guy, Joseph Catton, ran that way." He points away from the freeway. "Bryan chased him. Joseph Catton fell into the road . . . and Bryan pursued him and Bryan was on top of him hitting him in the face. At that point, I ran up to Bryan and Joseph Catton and kicked Joseph in the side of the head. So he was laying this way, right here. I kicked him right in the side of the head. And I remember saying, 'Bryan, he's not moving. Let's go.'

"Bryan got up, and we went back to the car and we were standing at the car and Raymond had chased Robert Sabertino and was pulling him off the fence."

We both look over at the freeway embankment, to the fence. I can picture it happening. How a young man could run for his life, and how he could be pulled back down, stabbed. It is horrible, desperate.

"Joseph [who was on the ground] had already been fatally injured by Raymond Gonzalez, and we didn't know it. So when we got back to the car, we called Raymond, 'Come on, Raymond, let's go,' and he was beating the guy while he was trying to get on the fence, and that motion"—Richie pulls his arm back and thrusts his hand forward, over and over, like he's hitting someone from behind—"he was actually stabbing him. You think he's slugging the guy who's trying to get over the fence, but I know now he was stabbing Robert Sabertino.

"Raymond heard us and he came back, and we got in the car. At that point, I still thought it was a fight, and I didn't think anyone was seriously injured, and that's when Raymond said, 'I stabbed both of them guys.' At that point, we fled the scene. The first thing I wanted to do was get my brother Rod back home. I took Rod to the house and he went inside."

"What were you saying to each other?" I ask. "That's a good five-minute drive to your house."

"Yeah," Richie says, sounding empty. "That's a good five, ten minutes. We weren't saying anything. We were all quiet."

"Did you see if there was any blood on your hands?"

"I didn't have any blood on me. Nothing. Bryan had blood on him. He mentioned it in the car going back. He said, 'I got blood on my pants.' Raymond had a little blood, but he didn't say anything about blood.

"At that point, we decided to go over to our friends' house where we used to hang out. It was kind of like a place to smoke weed. The parents didn't care. We went over there and waited for our buddy to show up because he worked swing shift. He wasn't there, but his father was there. So we walked in and everything was pretty normal and he said, 'What happened to you guys,' 'cause he'd seen the blood on Bryan. 'Well, we just got in a fight in Fremont.' That's what we told him.

"We went into the bathroom all together, all three of us, and I told Raymond, 'You better get rid of that knife. If anything, get rid of it, because that's evidence against us.'"

Is Richie saying he wanted to hide evidence? That he wasn't going to go back and see if the two men were all right? And he wasn't going to call the police and report the knife or Raymond?

"I didn't have no consideration for Joseph Catton or Robert Sabertino at the time. I was more concerned with getting in trouble. That's how messed up I was." He looks down, then slowly up. "I'm getting chills right now.

"Robert Sabertino lived. He had three stab wounds. Twice in the stomach and once in the kidney. Somehow he made it to the street. From him testifying, he said he crawled to the street, and a car came by and seen him and helped him. They took them both, and Joseph Catton was already dead in the street. So my last scene was right here. I left and Joseph Catton was laying right here. He was on his back. His face was pretty bloody. He was also stabbed in the abdomen several times. Raymond was pretty vicious and we didn't know it. I wish we would have."

"If it had been a fight," I say, "and you had just used your fists, what would have happened?"

"They would have got up," Richie says, energy returning to his voice, "and they would have had bumps and bruises."

"But when you fight, isn't that what people do?" I ask. "Kick, hit?"

"Growing up here in Newark," Richie says, "you get in a fight with somebody, you beat them up or they beat you up. That's it. It's over. Everybody goes home. It's not like you're going to come back with a weapon or you're going to try and get revenge. It's over. That's the way it was. But Raymond came from a totally different neighborhood, and he took his show on the road and brought it over here to where we lived. That's what I call it. He took his show on the road."

"Where's Raymond today?"

"Raymond is still in prison. I believe he's in New Folsom. He's not gotten out. He was convicted of attempted murder on Robert Sabertino, murder in the first degree on Joseph Catton, and robbery charges."

But Richie was there and he didn't go back. How could a good son make such a bad decision?

"I never thought something like this could happen to me, but it did. And I believe it happened because I was putting myself in risky situations. Twenty-seven years, four months ago. Right here."

"Your life took a huge detour."

"It took a detour, but a lot of people suffered from what I did. I look back, and I can only imagine what Robert Sabertino and Joseph Catton's families went through. The night of the crime, when policemen had to go to their door and say, 'Hey, your son Joseph Catton is dead. He's been brutally beaten and his friend, Robert, is in the hospital in critical condition.' I can see it. The shock his parents went through. Sad. And everybody that suffers along with what I did. My family. Bryan's family. Raymond's family. The post-traumatic stress my younger brother went through and wasn't able to get any counseling because my parents didn't know. The community was shocked Bryan and I could be involved in something of that nature. They didn't believe it. It was tragic. It shouldn't have happened. I should have did something, but I didn't. I didn't care enough."

For more than a half hour, I've been standing in the dark, staring at Richie. I don't know what to think. "I'm freezing," I call out, suddenly feeling the bone-chilling cold of the night. We both jump back in the cab of the truck, rubbing our hands together to get warm.

"When did you know you were in trouble?" I ask, trying to put myself back in time.

"I don't think we understood the seriousness until the following day."

When Richie got home from work that next afternoon, his younger brother Rod was outside the house, waiting for him, holding a newspaper. The article said, "One killed and one seriously injured in a vicious slaying robbery." Richie read the article and knew it was them.

"Bryan came over, and I showed it to him. He was just getting off work and hadn't seen it. We knew we were in a lot of trouble. But the paper's description was totally off of who we were, so we said, they don't even know who did it. They had the description of my car wrong and the description of us wrong. They got all the information from Robert Sabertino. He was probably heavily sedated.

"Somehow Raymond showed up, and we kind of said, 'Well, we just should keep quiet about it because they don't know who did it.' And we did. I think Bryan said, 'Maybe we should turn ourselves in.'"

But Bryan and Richie decided not to turn themselves in and not to see Raymond again—ever.

"How did it happen?" I ask. "Your arrest?"

"Five days later, on August 30, I got up to go to work," Richie says, sitting back in the cab of the truck, the heater warming our feet.

It was Labor Day weekend and his parents were going to Merced. Richie was going to be home by himself. He went outside to start his car, to warm it up, and he noticed an unmarked police car down the street.

"It's a small town. You know who the cops are and who the unmarked cars are. There was someone sitting in it. I was kind of curious. I wanted to know if he was actually waiting for me."

"How would you know?"

"I would know, because I had done something terribly wrong. I passed him, and I looked at him, and he looked at me. I knew who he was because I went to school with his son. We played football together."

At the intersection, Richie turned left, past the school and the steak house, and right there, in the middle of the street where he used to ride his bike, he was surrounded by police, four or five patrol cars in every direction.

"They asked me to get out of the car. I got out of the car, and they asked me to lay down in the middle of the street, facedown. The guy in the unmarked car came up behind me, and he had a pistol, and he said, 'Richard, you're under arrest.' I knew who he was, and I was taken in."

Turns out, their friends' father who saw them with blood on their clothes the night of the murder put two and two together and called the police. "He was reading the same paper we were reading," Richie says. "He was doing the right thing. I don't wrong him. He was being a citizen. That's what you're supposed to do. When I bailed out, I even went to his home, 'cause his son was my friend. His son was furious at his dad for what he done, but that's the way it goes. He had to live with it, and I knew I was coming to prison—because of what I'd done."

Under questioning, Richie says, he told the police he was there and that he participated in a fight. "They said, 'Well, you know they were stabbed.' I said 'I didn't know that. I never seen a knife.' That's what I stuck to. But me putting myself at the scene of the crime and saying I was involved, there was enough evidence to charge me and convict me."

At first the police also charged Rod with the murder, but Richie told them his brother didn't have anything to do with it. "The detective who was interviewing everyone came to the conclusion all our stories matched as far as Rod, that Rod didn't get out of the car. He went back to Robert Sabertino and said, 'We arrested all four of them. The fourth is a boy.' And Robert Sabertino said, 'All I know is there was four of them.' The detective asked, 'Do you remember all four getting out of the car?' And Robert said, 'No.' And at that point, they released Rod, let him go."

The district attorney charged Richie with first-degree murder with special circumstances, which carried a possible death sentence; robbery; attempted murder with robbery; and assault with a deadly weapon, for using his foot to kick James Catton in the head. (First-degree murder means an attack was willful, deliberate, and premeditated; second-degree murder means it was a "crime of passion," a split-second terrible decision; and manslaughter means it was a killing that was inexcusable and unjustifiable, but unintentional.)

"They could have given me death," Richie says. "When we went through our municipal court hearings, we were bound over to Alameda County Superior Court and the judge in the superior court weighed the odds and said, 'No. Bryan and Richard are not charged with special circumstances.'"

Richie pleaded not guilty to the charges of first-degree murder, robbery, attempted murder, and assault with a deadly weapon. His parents hired a private attorney to represent Richie, put up their home as a property bond, and posted bail. "I went back to work, kept the same routine as before the crime. Bryan and I would see each other and do the things we used to do. We were getting high and drunk."

A year later, Richie and Bryan went to trial with the naive notion they wouldn't be convicted of murder. "I thought I could easily be convicted of manslaughter and do four, five years, seven years and get out. But that wasn't going to happen."

It took the jury almost a week to deliberate. "That last day, Bryan and I went out to lunch while we were waiting, and it was in downtown Oakland," Richie says with a little laugh. "We were up on the top of a parking lot, him and I, and we were smoking a joint. It seems funny, but it's stupid. We knew we were going to be convicted and we figured, 'Well, maybe we can just make it through this weekend.' It was a Friday."

When they got back in the courtroom there was hysteria. "Cops all over the place and my family was, 'Where you guys been?' We said, 'We went out to lunch.' And on top of that, we were loaded. They said, 'They're coming back with their decision.' I had weed on me, and I didn't know what to do with it, so I said, 'I got to go to the bathroom.' And I flushed it down the toilet.

"The jury convicted me of a second-degree murder for the death of Joseph Catton, attempted murder for the assault on Robert Sabertino, and assault with a deadly weapon, because of my own admission when I said I ran up and kicked Joseph Catton in the head. The assault was with my foot. It all happened in a minute, a minute and a half at most. It was fast."

A minute after the jury found him guilty, Richie was taken into custody to begin his life sentence.

"Twenty-two years to life," Richie says with a choking sort of laugh. "Fifteen years to life for the second-degree murder and seven years for attempted murder and the assault with a deadly weapon. They ran them consecutively, which means I had to start my seven years and complete that sentence before I started my fifteen to life."

Richie's first stop inside the California Department of Corrections was the California Medical Facility at Vacaville, then the state prison reception center in Northern California. "When Bryan and I walked off the bus into Reception and Release at Vacaville, my brother Henry was waiting there with his buddies. So, walking into the prison, we had status. Everyone getting off the bus saw my brother walk up to us. He handed us shopping bags full of food and said, 'We already have it set up to where you'll transfer from the reception center to the mainline.'" If Richie had been an ordinary prisoner without family connections already inside the prison, he would have had to wait days, even weeks before joining the mainline population and getting access to the prison canteen and the food his brother handed him. A month later, Henry left Vacaville, and for the next fourteen years, Bryan and Richie were family to each other behind bars.

"Bryan and I did everything together. We worked together, looked after each other, and cared for each other. Everybody knew we were codefendants. Usually they separate them. But the administration knew we weren't a threat. Sometimes they understand that, 'Okay, these guys did something as kids. They were stupid. They did it. Now they're doing what they need to do, they're functioning in prison. They're stable. They're not sociopaths.' So we hung out together for a long time. We played sports, soccer, softball, football, basketball. We did it all. We even lived together for a year and a half."

"Did you have to work in prison?"

"You don't have to. You could rebel. But if you do [rebel], you're not going to have the privileges of going to the yard or the store. You need to work to be a privilege A. Privilege C doesn't work at all. You're just there and you don't do anything. Privilege A is what you want to be if you're in prison. That's what I was."

Initially Richie got a job working in the maintenance shop, then about a year later he took a vocational trade class as a cabinetmaker, passing the test and earning his certification. "I remembered outside, when my father needed to remodel a kitchen, he had to go to cabinet shops to get cabinets for the kitchen. So I decided to build cabinets in prison. I was pretty good at it. My boss would take me into the administration building, where you have to have an escort, and he would take me into offices and we would remodel them. I would sketch out what the secretaries wanted, and I would take it back to the shop and do all my drafting. I would present my design and if it was a go, I would go back and build it and install it. That's what I did for fourteen years. I was making my boss look good."

It wasn't all good. Richie admits to some early stumbles behind bars—a missed work shift here, a smuggled joint there—but after a few years in prison, he says, it all came down to self-respect and trying to do something more with his life.

Having been raised in Newark as a Catholic and going to catechism, Sunday school, Holy Communion, confirmation, Richie says he always felt God but distanced himself, because of what he had done.

"At the moment I committed my crime and I was in the county jail, I honestly thought God had turned away from me. I was just going to leave it like that. I'm thinking, 'I go to church every Sunday morning. I do what's told of me and I thought I was doing all the right things. I wasn't doing anything to get myself in trouble and this happened to me. 'God, how could you let this happen to me?' That's what I was thinking. I was mad. Upset. I felt that because I believed God was there for me to watch over me and to protect me, he wouldn't let me do this. So I was steered away from God for a long time, but I knew a lot of Christians at Vacaville and oddly enough, they would always ask me, 'Read me verses,' and I could tell them exactly what it meant. And they would say, 'Rich, how do you know this stuff?' 'Cause they saw Rich as a guy who smoked weed and was going to work and not going to church, and I said, ''Cause I'm Catholic. I went to school for this.' Bryan noticed and said, 'Rich, why don't you go to church?' I said, 'No. I'm not going to do it,' because I just wasn't ready. I was still caught up with my friends who were smoking marijuana, and I worried about what my peers would think. I hadn't grown up yet."

But when Richie left Vacaville in 1996, fourteen years after going to prison, he says, he knew his whole life was going to change. For the first time since the crime, he was leaving everything, including his best friend, Bryan, behind.

"I figured, I'm going to take the opportunity and run with it. I'm going to do everything I can, get involved in all the programs. I had made a decision to change my life."

Inside San Quentin, Richie joined Alcoholics Anonymous, Narcotics Anonymous, and Kairos, a prison ministry program offering an intensive three-day workshop to inmates in search of their spiritual roots. "Kairos breaks you down mentally and spiritually and leaves you really vulnerable. And that's when I realized I had never forgiven myself for my crime, and at that moment, I had a lot of guys there supporting me and I felt loved. I didn't actually let it go until I was able to understand who I was, and I was able to forgive myself for what I had done. That's when I knew I was going through a big transformation."

"If you had it to do over again: You're sitting in the car. Raymond gets out. The two guys get out. What would a different Rich have done?"

"If I had to do it over again? I can't, I can't, I can't even do that. No way. I can look at every different angle and say, 'I could have done this. I could have done that. But I didn't.'"

"If you had been paying attention, what was the first thing . . . "

"I wouldn't have been with Raymond Gonzalez that night," Richie says definitively. "I woulda had better discernment about knowing who people are and what their capabilities are. That's what I look for today. What are they capable of doing? You don't know, but I can judge character a lot better now than before as a kid. That's just from experience of being in prison. I could easily have said no when my dad asked me. I was just so afraid to say no to my dad." When Richie says the word "dad," he slows, adds weight to the word. "Whatever he said, I pretty much did."

"But with the mind you have right now, if the scene were played again with the mind-set you have now, and your dad says, 'Take Rod to the game with Raymond,' what could you do?"

"I'd probably say okay. And as we were getting ready to leave, I would say, 'Raymond, you're not going.' That would be my way of doing it. That way my dad doesn't know and I walk out the door with everybody."

"And Raymond goes and tells his parents, 'Richie didn't let me go.'"

"That's fine. Because I know who Raymond is, and I know what he's capable of. But these scenarios don't matter. These questions are so off-the-wall. I've played all this out. What if I would've done this? I always came to the conclusion it doesn't matter to me, because I was involved, and I can't change that. I can only change who I am, and I have to move forward.

"But looking back, I knew something could happen. I didn't think it would happen. I've played it out: as soon as Raymond got out of the car, I could have just taken off, before anybody got out of the car except him. Or when I knew Raymond had stabbed them, I could have told him to get out of the car, and I could have gone for help. But I've played it all out and bottom line is, I did it. I was part of it. There's no changing that. How can I go through these things and keep beating myself up, over and over again, role-playing a different situation? It doesn't work for me."

He stops.

It's getting late. "Want to drive me back?"

"How'd it feel to come to this place?" Richie asks, starting the truck.

"To me, it's a parking lot," I say, fastening the seat belt, "How'd it feel to you?"

"This is the first time I've been back since the night it happened. Coming back here? Some people would do something like this to have closure, and it does give me a little bit of closure. But wow. I've already had closure, so it's not that stressful to be here. It made me think a little bit more about when we were right there in the spot where I kicked Joseph Catton. It made me think about him. That's always sad."

We drive for a while, neither of us talking before he pulls into his cul-de-sac, the Christmas lights on his parents' house the best on the block. "When we were in prison," Richie says, turning off the engine, looking up at the bright colors, "we used to break a little branch of a tree so we had a little Christmas in our cell. No ornaments."

I ask if he remembers the day he got out of prison.

"I got notified on a Thursday. I was in the shower, and my next-door neighbor ran up to me, 'Rich. They're calling for you. . . . There's two counselors waiting for you.' I'm like, okay, this is it. They're either going to deny me or they're going to approve me. Can't be anything else.

"I take my time. Take my shower. My friend was with me the whole time. He walked me back to my cell, waited while I got my clothes on. He was, 'How can you be so calm? They're waiting!' I went over there, and I walked in and they asked me, 'Are you Richard Rael? Well,' they said, 'we have a piece of paper for you, and it's good news.'

"Right then and there, I lit up. Big smile on my face. They showed me the paper, and I read it and behind me there was about ten or twelve guys waiting to see what was going to happen. I showed them the paper and gave them a thumbs-up, because they like to see people go home. Everybody wants to go.

"I thought I'd have 'til Monday to say good-bye to everybody. My parole officer showed up on a Saturday to pick me up. He did it on his own time, which was really cool. He was really playing hardball with me in R&R [Reception and Release]: 'Are these your boxes?' he said. 'You carry them out to the car.' He didn't smile or talk to me. And R&R is right out there on the yard, and being there as long as I was, I know a lot of people, and all my buddies were saying bye to me and waving, and I got in that car and he drove real slow through the yard, and I'm waving to people and this is all races, black, white, Mexican, gang members. They're all happy for me, and he's just absorbing all this.

"When we got off the grounds, he stopped the car, and he said, 'Richie, you're a popular guy. I've come in here before to pick people up, and I've never seen so many people saying good-bye to one person.' I said, 'They're my friends. I talk to everybody. I don't just stay with my race. I'm everywhere.'"

After a stop at the parole office to review the terms of his parole and take some photos, his parole agent took him straight home. "He said, 'Rich, I'm not even going to get out of the car. I'm just going to let you be with your family.' Which was really cool. My dad was standing out in the garage. He was pretty much the same. His demeanor hadn't changed much. My niece was there, and my nephew. They were hysterical. Then I seen my mom. She walked into the garage. It was the first time I seen her really. She didn't cry but she broke down. I just held her. She was shaking. I'd never seen her like that before. My mom is really, really strong, and she was vulnerable right then, and I just held her. That was the best thing right there."

The day Richie was released from prison was his little brother Rod's thirty-seventh birthday. "So they were having a birthday party for him, and I was the best present he ever had. Me coming home."

Driving home that night and in the days and weeks that follow, I re-examine Richie's crime, pick it up in my mind, turn it around, sifting through his words for inconsistencies, half-truths. If I believe his version of the night, he didn't stab, shoot, strangle, or poison anyone. He was there when a young, innocent man was robbed of his money and his life. He could have tried to stop it, but he didn't. He didn't turn himself in to the police, nor did he report the blood on Bryan's clothes and Raymond's hands. He was guilty. But murder? He was arrested, convicted by a jury of his peers, and sentenced to twenty-two years in prison. He was by fact and name a criminal who had committed the absolute worst of all crimes.

Maybe the other murderers, the ones still locked up, are a different kind of killer. Maybe their crimes were worse, more violent. After all, the parole board found Richie suitable for release and, in the end, Governor Arnold Schwarzenegger agreed to let him out. Did that make him different? What about Eddie? Was he a different sort of murderer, too?

six

EDDIE'S STORY

Midnight Run to Hell

DECEMBER 2007

I ring the bell to the two-story suburban townhouse and wait. A yappy bark snaps a warning and growls louder as the door opens. "Hi, Nancy," Eddie says, bending over to grab a black and white Chihuahua wearing mini reindeer antlers. "Spunky!" he says to the dog, pleading. "It's Nancy. She's all right." He adds almost apologetically, "We thought he should get dressed up for the holidays."

It's been a little over a month since I met Eddie at Bryan's coming-home party and I'd nearly forgotten: Eddie Ramirez is a big man, a big, dark bear of a man with thick tattoos shooting up his forearms, not to mention the deepest-set eyes I've ever seen.

Stepping over the threshold, I turn in a circle on the wall-to-wall carpet and inventory his private world. I'm here, and if all goes well, Eddie will take me into his confidence and, like Richie, tell me the secret about his past.

"You have to meet Lupe. Lupe?" he calls softly up the stairs.

Appearing at the bottom of the stairs a moment later, Eddie's wife, Lupe, is equal parts warm and cool, accepting and skeptical. It's then

I realize I'm just as curious to get to know Lupe as I am Eddie: a woman who willingly married a man pulling a cargo ship's worth of criminal weight behind him. But first I need their permission to be interviewed. Talking to me is a risk, and I bring no guarantee the short or long ripples can be managed.

"Would it be all right if we sat around the table?" I ask. "I want to record our conversation, and I can't do that sitting so far apart on the couch."

There. I've said it: "record." Their eyes connect in an *I told you so* moment. Eddie is the first to speak: "I'd like to hear more about your project before we record anything."

I start by telling them about my first surprising visit to San Quentin and the men I met inside. With each name Eddie smiles, nods. Don, Bryan, and now Richie.

I explain to them that as a reporter, I can't just go inside the prison and talk to the men I want to, when I want to. I have to wait and hope for access. When Bryan introduced me to Eddie and the other men who had gotten out, I thought this might be a way to really find out, without a prison official looking over my shoulder, what it's like to commit murder and live with it. Americans don't know what happens to someone who commits murder ten, twenty, thirty years after the crime. "I was hoping you might be willing to tell me."

Silence. We sit together for a few minutes. No one says anything. Eddie and Lupe are having a conversation with their eyes.

"Okay. Let's get started," Eddie says, a deep tremor in his voice. "But I want to leave it up to Lupe to decide how much of her story we share. She's an educator at a local public elementary school, and she has to be careful. If people connect her with this, it might make it difficult for her."

"Absolutely," I say. "I'll follow your lead. Here we go. If there's anything I ask that you don't want to answer, you can either say no or just don't answer it. You decide how much you want to say. Let's start with your childhood."

Eddie smiles a little and takes a deep breath. In a voice as warm as butterscotch, he begins, "I was born here in San Jose in 1961. . . . "

Later I'm able to match Eddie's story of his crime to an official report. It's a report prepared back in 1982 by the probation officer based on witness testimony, the arresting officer's report, and the defendant, in this case Eddie's testimony following his arrest. The probation officer's report is considered a summary of the case presented to the court before a plea deal of guilt is accepted or a trial date is set. As in most crimes, not everyone remembers the incident exactly the same way:

> PROBATION OFFICER REPORT December 22, 1982
> *Name:* Edward Ramirez
> *Date and Birthplace:* 9-18-61: San Jose, CA
> *Race/Ethnic Origin:* Caucasian/Mexican American
> *No. of Brothers:* 1 [my correction: 2]
> *No. of Sisters:* 3

Eddie's father, Ralph Edward Ramirez, was a barber with three shops. "He was the perfect dad. He went fishing with us and played baseball with us. He disciplined us but always gave us a reason why." His mother, Alice Ramirez, took care of the home. "I had two older brothers, two older sisters, and one younger sister. My mom was always there when we came home from school. We used to go on vacations every year. Never missed a year at Disneyland. Never missed a year up at Lake Tahoe, camping."

If his idyllic childhood had stretched out, through puberty and even into young adulthood, with a dad going to work and a mom waiting for him at home after school, maybe things would have been different in Eddie's life. But it didn't work out that way. When Eddie turned nine, his mother, then thirty-nine, died from kidney failure.

"That's how I gauge my age. If my mom was there, I was at most nine. Any older than that, ten. My mom was gone."

After his mother died, things fell apart. His father tried to keep the family together, "but when she passed, his life died and he fell into a deep depression." Then one day a little over six months later, Eddie's father told him to go into the attic to get his rifle.

"No one was home but him and me. I'm a kid. I don't know what's going on. But I know a rifle is somethin' dangerous. I handed it down to him, and he pulled me down from the attic and told me to 'go downstairs, and if anybody calls, tell them everything's okay. After, you can tell them to come over, and they'll take care of you.' I went outside and put my fingers in my ears 'cause I'd never heard a gunshot and I'm thinking it's going to be a bomb or something."

Instead of a boom, Eddie heard the phone ring. It was his aunt calling to see how things were. Eddie broke. He told her about the gun and his father locked in his room. "My two aunts and my uncle Joe came over in a heartbeat and the police took him away for three months."

Eddie stops, his voice evaporating, his eyes filling. "Sorry," he says. Lupe gets up and comes back with a box of tissues. Before sitting back down, she puts her hand on his shoulder.

After his father was taken away, Eddie and his little sister Kathy went to stay with relatives but returned home when Ralph, their older brother, came to take care of his siblings. "It was strange. All us kids living together in our house without our mom or dad."

Three months after his dad was driven away, he came back home and for a while, Eddie says, "he tried to make things normal. Ralph even took him out for a beer now and then. He was trying to do the social thing. But he was always depressed and drowned his life in work, work, work."

Kids at school sensed Eddie's new motherless vulnerability. They began stealing his lunch money. "No one was talking to me, and everyone was at a distance. I think that's when I put up my defenses with everybody. I stopped letting people get close to me. I remember the first time I got in a fight with a guy. This kid said, 'Ha. Your mom died.' I went over and just laid it on him. I wouldn't get off him. One time I beat up this one boy pretty bad. The school called the cops, and they came and got me. I was handcuffed right there in front of the other students. First time they took me to juvenile hall. When I got out, I was rebellious. That's when I began burglarizing."

A few weeks later, after he got out of "juvie," Eddie came home from school and found his father upstairs in a heap against his bedroom door with blood on his face. His father had suffered a heart attack. "When my aunts and paramedics came, they pulled me away from him." At forty-two, his father was dead. Eddie was twelve.

PROBATION OFFICER REPORT December 22, 1982
FAMILY INFORMATION:
Father's Name: Ralph Ramirez (Deceased)
Mother's Name: Alice Ramirez (Deceased)

"My brother Frank would give me weed and PCP or crystal meth. He was probably trying to fight a lot of his own pain. It helped me forget for a while. I started bringing it to school. Because I was loaded, I mixed with the wrong people."

With no one to look after them, his two brothers moved out and Eddie and his three sisters were again farmed out to relatives. This time, it was supposed to be for good. "My Aunt Carol sent me to a new middle school but I started fighting again and burglarizing houses. Every bit of money I would get, I would give to my brother Frank to get me weed or PCP."

Eddie's aunt called his older brother Ralph. "She said, 'I can't control him. Will you come get Eddie?' They found me at the cemetery."

From across the table, Lupe, who has been watching and listening, breaks in. "Eddie didn't have a chance."

Again, it's silent at the table. Eddie lowers his head, then lifts it, looking Lupe in the eye. "My Aunt Carol came to see me in San Quentin after I'd been in prison eighteen or nineteen years and the first thing she said was, 'I'm sorry.' I asked her what she was sorry for. And she said, 'When you were living with us for that short time . . . '" Eddie's voice starts to break. "She said, 'I went to check on you and you were curled up, no blankets on the bed, with your back towards the door, crying. I should have went in there and hugged you. Instead, I closed the door.' She said, 'I think if I'd have went in there, it would have changed your life. But I shut the door.'"

Now Eddie is crying in broken, nearly silent sobs. Lupe reaches over and puts her hand on his thick forearm. "I've met his Aunt Carol," she says. "She's a very nice, nurturing person. I just don't think she knew how to handle it. You were already in trouble and she just didn't know how to handle it."

A few minutes pass while Eddie finds his way back from the still-raw memory. "That's when I moved in with my brother Ralph, who was twenty-one with two babies," Eddie says. "He followed the law except for selling drugs."

That was the least of it. If he wanted to get high, Eddie could reach into his brother's stash and get high. If he wanted to drink beer, he'd have a beer. Girlfriends slept over. If he didn't want to go to school, it was a no-school day.

> PROBATION OFFICER REPORT December 22, 1982
> PERSONAL DATA:
> *He began drinking alcohol, mainly beer at the age of 13. The defendant stated he began using crystal PCP at approximately 10 years of age. He stated he has previously used angel dust, marijuana and hashish.*

As corrupt as his new life was with Ralph, it wouldn't last. At the age of twenty-two, Ralph was shot and killed trying to break up a fight between two women. At fourteen, Eddie was homeless. Walking away from his brother's funeral, with nowhere to go, Eddie ran into his Uncle Roberto, known to everyone as Beto. "As close as we are right now," Eddie says, "he looked at me and asked, 'How you doin'?' I said, 'I don't know.' I wanted to cry, and he seen that, and he pulled me and hugged me and said, 'You want to come home with us?'"

Now Eddie and Lupe are both crying.

"He's such a wonderful man," Lupe says, reaching for a tissue.

"He had nine kids!" Eddie says, wiping his eyes.

"You were number ten," Lupe says.

PROBATION OFFICER REPORT December 22, 1982
FAMILY INFORMATION:
The defendant stated that after his parents died from natural causes in 1971 and 1972, he was sent to live with an uncle in Northridge in 1974.

Eddie moved in with his uncle and his family in a big five-bedroom home with a pool and rules. He enrolled in the local school and got close to his cousin, Robert. But one day while he was out drinking with friends, he got in a fight with some white guys, stole their car, and forced them to take him on a long drive.

While Eddie's talking, I recall Richie and the story of his crime. He stopped to get alcohol and there was a fight. I make a mental note: pay attention when the words "alcohol" and "fight" are mentioned in the same sentence.

Eddie was found guilty of three counts of false imprisonment and robbery, and at the age of sixteen, he began his first stretch in the California Youth Authority, or YA.

PROBATION OFFICER REPORT December 22, 1982
CRIMINAL HISTORY:
Information provided by the Los Angeles Probation Department indicated the defendant and a codefendant, who was armed with a knife, robbed five victims and forced the victims to drive them aimlessly in the victims' two vehicles while the defendant, who was

armed with a tire iron, rode in one vehicle and the codefendant, who was armed with a knife, rode in the second vehicle.

Locked up in juvenile hall, Eddie found a new family: gangs. "I embraced the family structure of the gang. But because I was originally from San Jose and they don't like northern guys in Los Angeles, I was constantly fighting. My pride wouldn't let me go into protective custody."

Eventually he was transferred to the California Department of Corrections Department of Juvenile Justice Facility in Stockton, "where I was accepted as a northern gang member. When they got in a fight, I fought with them, side by side."

Eddie was also attracted to the culture of the gang family. "In YA, there are guys who have been there for two, three years, so there's a structure. There's somebody who's a boss, someone they call the 'shot-caller,' and he didn't get there by the luck of the draw. He's a fighter. He worked his way up. So that's another reason you fought, because you wanted to be that guy. Like, if somebody disrespects you, you're supposed to get up and beat 'em. Beat 'em down. Don't negotiate anything. The mentality is so twisted that you have to become violent to get respect."

Inside Stockton YA, Eddie got close to the institution's shot-caller, Mumbles. "He was a nut. In my eyes, I wanted to be close to the nut, because he'd have my back. All the stuff that hurt in my life got covered up by the fighting and tattooing and drinking pruno, the homemade wine."

There were constant fights. After one particularly vicious riot, Mumbles was transferred out to Preston, a more secure youth facility, leaving the shot-caller position vacant. A few days later gang members slipped a note, a "kite," under Eddie's cell door. He was the new shot-caller. It didn't last. After six months of "craziness," Eddie, too, was transferred to the Preston facility. "It's like a youth prison. They play with knives. Guys stab you."

At the time, a war was being waged between the northern Mexicans, the southern Mexicans, and the whites against the blacks. Eddie had gotten into weight lifting and was getting big. "I walked into the drama," he recalls.

On the day of a planned fight, Eddie saw the Bible his uncle had given him. "It was lying open to a scripture my uncle always used to tell me, Deuteronomy 30:19. 'I set before you life and death. Blessing or curse. Oh that you would choose life.' And it, oh, stung me. It never made much sense to me before and it hit me. I just wanted to do right and go home. I never told anyone about it. I still went with the flow. The riot happened. It was really big. Really ugly."

A few months after the riot, at the age of eighteen, Eddie was found suitable by the parole board to go home. "It didn't feel real. I went from my cell to flying in a plane to Burbank. My uncle came to the airport and he hugged me and cried and said, 'It's over. You're home.' He thought it was over. I thought it was, too."

PROBATION OFFICER REPORT December 22, 1982
CRIMINAL HISTORY:
Paroled (out of the Preston Youth Facility) 2-11-80

A year and a half after getting out of the Youth Authority, Eddie was living with his uncle in Northridge, going to church, working as a punch press operator. Wanting to do something more, he went back to school, got a Class A license, and began driving diesel trucks cross-country. A few months later Eddie decided to channel some of his father's entrepreneurial spirit by investing in a long-haul truck with a partner. "We had a mortgage on the truck and we would drive together. I'd drive, then he'd drive to keep the truck moving, hauling." But when his partner's wife got pregnant, he wanted out of the partnership so he could stay home. Eddie couldn't afford the $1,400 truck payments on his own. "As much as I tried to hold onto the truck, I lost it."

The feeling of failure and the frustration of losing his first business put him at odds with his uncle. Eddie was griping and complaining about the rules: "I don't need to listen to this counseling and stuff." His uncle had had enough as well. He told Eddie, "If you want to go, go," and on his aunt's birthday, Eddie walked out.

With little money and nowhere to live, Eddie's life slowly and utterly collapsed. "I started delivering newspapers in the middle of the night, picking up cans, trying to make a living. I was looking like death because I never slept. One night in Hollywood—I've never told Lupe about this—I went and robbed a pimp. The money would only last for a little while, before I'd be back in Hollywood, looking for another pimp. It was dangerous. I was desperate, trying to maintain my dignity." Eddie laughs. "It was crazy. I saw guys on the street who knew me from the Youth Authority, and I started tattooing a lot of the local gang members. Making $20 here, $40 there. It paved the way."

To what, I wonder.

"My girlfriend was afraid of me because I was rude, yelling at her, breaking and throwing things. One time she slapped me, just from the heat of an argument. I slapped her back and she fell. It scared me that I could do that. She was terrified and said, 'I don't know who you are. I don't want you around me.' It was an ugly night in 1982, and things were falling apart quickly."

Then he begins to tell me the story. When things went from bad to worse, from the edges of crime to the bull's-eye.

After he left his girlfriend's, Eddie went to a gas station to wash up. Coming out of the bathroom, he saw a guy he knew. "Roger and couple of people jumped in my car and said they wanted to go to a party. I didn't have anything better to do. No one noticed how dirty I looked. I hadn't showered in a week. I was still a kid. Just nineteen. There was food, drink, music, dancing, girls. There was arm wrestling in the kitchen. I was skinny, but I won a lot."

In the middle of a winning streak, "another group of a dozen guys came in. They looked like gang-bangers," Eddie says. "They looked like trouble, crazy. One guy told Roger, 'These guys are rivals. There's going to be trouble. Get out of here.'"

PROBATION OFFICER REPORT December 22, 1982
CIRCUMSTANCES OF OFFENSE:
According to the transcripts of the preliminary hearings, . . . the following is a summary of facts and circumstances in this matter. Also based on a consensus of the defendants' statements, it appears that prior to the commission of the crimes, the defendants and [victim] were at a residential party in Simi Valley, and that they left the party together in order to purchase more alcohol.

STATEMENT OF DEFENDANT:
On the night of July 10, 1982, he and codefendant Roger Yepez had driven from San Fernando Valley to a party in Simi Valley. He stated that codefendants Francisco Chapa and Arnold Herrera were at the same party. The defendant stated that he had been drinking beer since about 5 p.m. and at the party he continued to drink. He had also taken two Quaaludes. He recalled that at one point, a money collection was taken and he was going to the nearest store to buy more beer. He and Yepez went to his car where Chapa was standing. The three decided they would go, and Arnold Herrera who had followed them from the party to the car went along. The defendant explained that codefendants Chapa and Herrera were friends and he personally did not know either one very well.

"Right then a girl said, 'Someone needs to do a beer run.' That was our chance to get out. She gave us the basket with the pool of beer money. A guy named Chapa and his sixteen-year-old cousin, Arnold, came along. I said, 'Okay, just get in back. Don't say nothing.' He bugged me. He was a little kid. He was sixteen but he looked fourteen, a little bugger."

It turns out that none of the four in Eddie's car knew where to buy beer in Simi Valley. They couldn't find a store, but they found a restaurant, Rube's Valley House of Bar-B-Que. They decided to try to get the cook to sell them a case.

"Roger went in first, directly to the bar. As we came in the door, I saw all these bikers. Everybody looked big. We're kids. They're walking towards us and I'm backing out of the door. They're getting closer and closer. I'm the first one out the door. One of the guys grabbed Arnold. I ran to the car 'cause I knew I had Roger's sawed-off shotgun in the car."

"When did you put the shotgun in your car?" I ask, incredulous at the word "shotgun."

"Roger had cut off the barrels of his dad's shotgun with a hacksaw and he broke it. He was going to buy his dad another gun. I thought it was cool, and he gave it to me and I threw it in my trunk. It didn't work but it looked scary. I grabbed it out of the trunk.

"By that time, they were all out in front of the restaurant, and Arnold's pulling and pulling to get away. I cock it at them and they all duck. When they did that, Roger ran through, too, and we all ran to the car. I jumped in the driver's seat and plowed over all their bikes. Boom, boom, boom, boom. At first it wasn't intentional. But once I hit the first one, I ran over as many as I could. In my mirror, I could see them running to a white truck. Some of them jumped in the bed. It was full and they were chasing us all over Simi Valley. We ended up way up on some hill in a residential area, parked my car in somebody's driveway, jumped out, and hid in some bushes."

PROBATION OFFICER REPORT December 22, 1982
CIRCUMSTANCES OF OFFENSE:
At approximately 1 a.m., witnesses at Rube's Restaurant [at] Simi Valley, observed three "Mexicans" as they entered and walked toward the bar. Witness testified he could identify only one defendant, Edward Ramirez, and stated that Ramirez carried a "sawed-off shotgun." He saw the three walk around the bar and after approx-

imately three minutes, they walked back to the exit. As Ramirez left the restaurant, the witness stated he displayed the shotgun in plain view and pointed it toward the ceiling as he backed out of the door. The manager had also seen Ramirez with the shotgun and had told the owner to call the police. When the police arrived, the manager gave them a description of the defendants' vehicle.

STATEMENT OF DEFENDANT:
Upon driving out of the residential area, he stated Rube's Restaurant was the first place they saw and they decided to stop there. He stated he was not carrying a shotgun and they decided not to stay because the restaurant appeared to be crowded with "bikers." They simply walked in, looked around, and because of the noise and crowd of people, they turned and walked out almost immediately. However, once outside, customers from inside the bar had followed them out. He recalled that since they did not get any beer to drink, he went to the trunk of his car where he had put a couple of six-packs in an ice-chest before leaving the Valley. While getting his beer, the defendant noticed that about ten or 12 customers had come out of the bar and someone who was with him, possibly Herrera, was grabbed by some of the men from the bar. Realizing there could be some trouble, he recalled that he had codefendant Yepez' shotgun in the trunk of the car. He knew it was not loaded, but he pulled it out in plain view hoping this would intimidate or scare the men back into the bar. The defendant stated he personally never carried or kept any type of weapons. When the men finally backed away from them, they all re-entered his car and drove quickly from the area because they were being followed by some of the same customers. Though they were chased, they managed to elude them by driving into a residential area.

STATEMENT OF VICTIMS:
Mr. Ruben Donabedian, owner of Rube's Restaurant, was contacted. Mr. Donabedian stated, "Anytime anybody walks in a

> *restaurant with a loaded shotgun they should get the maximum. If it had discharged (they) could have blown five people apart or seriously injured some. There's no need for that. No excuse to walk into a lounge loaded with customers with a shotgun. (They should get) the maximum prison according to the law—the only way to learn." On balance, Mr. Donabedian stated that his opinions would be tempered depending on the circumstances surrounding the defendants' life situations. He stated that many times, people become desperate in order to feed their children or some other life crises. Finally, he stated that the sentencing decision is "up to the Court."*

"We got back in the car and down the road, and the first opening in the road there's a Stop 'N Go store. 'We got money, let's get beer.' I had $165 on me and a little extra I earned from arm wrestling. Plus, we had the money we had collected for the beer.

"We stopped at the Stop 'N Go. I'm sitting in the car. Roger gets out and Arnold gets out. I stay with Chapa in the car. While we're sitting in the parking lot, here comes this white truck full of bikers. We're facing the street, and here they come around the corner. They spot the car and they start to make the left turn to get in the parking lot. I run to the back of the car to get the shotgun. Right when they pull into the parking lot, I point it at them and cock it. They pull out of the parking lot and head down the street to the right. They're going to turn around, and obviously they're going to come back, but there's a center divider they have to go all the way around.

"I ran in the store to tell Roger and Arnold, and they're behind the counter and they have the lady's [the clerk's] hair in their hand and they're at the cash register taking the money. I say, 'What the hell are you doing? These bikers are back. We need to get out of here.' They're saying they're trying to open the register. She's crying, saying, 'I can't open the register.' He's yelling at her, 'Give me the f-ing money.'"

"Who's saying that?" I ask.

"Roger," Lupe says.

"Arnold is in the front taking money from the Jerry's Kids thing," Eddie says. "He's opening that plastic donation thing. He's filling his pockets, and he's getting candy from the candy rack.

"They're struggling with this lady. I can't remember exactly, but I think it was Chapa who was behind the counter with her. I think Roger stayed in the car with me. It was Chapa and Arnold who went in. Roger stayed in the car with me. When I jumped out, then he ran in the store with me, and he was standing at the counter getting the beer off the counter, 'cause they had already got the beer. Chapa was with the woman, and he hit her with the tray once it opened, and there was just a few dollars. I yelled at her, too. 'Just give him the money and we're out of here.' She was saying, 'I can't open it. I can't open it.' Finally it opened, and he grabbed the money and then he hit her with the tray and just like that, she went down to the ground."

I'm a little shaken by Eddie's confused memory of the crime. First it was Chapa who stayed in the car, then Roger. Isn't that something you would remember even years later? But maybe not. As I sit here across from Eddie, it has been twenty-seven years since the night it all happened in a haze of drugs and alcohol.

"Did he hit her hard?" I ask.

"Just, like, hit her. It was hard enough to hurt her. He ran around giggling."

PROBATION OFFICER REPORT December 22, 1982
CIRCUMSTANCES OF OFFENSE:
At approximately 1:30 a.m. Melanie McVey, age 20, the victim and store clerk, was working at the Stop 'N Go market, Simi Valley, when Arnold Herrera, age 15, and defendants Edward Ramirez and Francisco Vidal Chapa entered the store. Herrera went to the cooler and got two six-packs of beer and walked toward the counter. Ramirez held the shotgun and told the victim, "This is a hold up," while Chapa walked around the counter and stood behind her. Herrera watched and laughed as Chapa punched the victim in the back with his fists and took approximately $90 from the register and

stuffed it in his pants pocket. Chapa took the plastic money tray from the register and hit the victim with it. After Ramirez told Chapa to "hurry up," he left the store and Chapa grabbed several packages of "M&M" candies before he left and followed Ramirez outside. Herrera asked the victim for 12 boxes of Marlboro Cigarettes and left the market.

It should be noted that Melanie McVey's testimony on July 26, 1982, conflicted with her testimony given at the second preliminary hearing on October 14, 1982. She stated on July 26 that defendants Chapa, Ramirez and Yepez had entered the store and that Chapa had carried the shotgun rather than Ramirez and that Ramirez was the one who hit her and took the money. Her ability to identify the defendants was based on seeing them in court since she was unable to identify any of them earlier from a police photographic lineup.

STATEMENT OF DEFENDANT:

After they decided it was safe, they drove down a street and saw a Stop 'N Go market where they decided to stop to buy beer. However, once in the parking lot, he noticed that a truck and two or three cars pulled up and the occupants of these vehicles appeared to be the same people who chased them from the bar. The defendant stated that when Herrera and Chapa went into the Stop 'N Go market, he pulled out the shotgun again and cocked it one time so that the people from the bar would see him. When they realized he had a shotgun, they immediately left the parking lot. Ramirez stated that at this time, he turned and realized that Chapa was behind the counter of the Stop 'N Go market, committing what appeared to be a robbery. His explanation was that Chapa and Herrera must have seen him with the shotgun and assumed that they were going to rob the market. He denied that any prior discussion had taken place regarding the robbing of the store. He denied ever saying to the store clerk, "this is a hold up," and though he was still holding the shotgun, the defendant stated that at no time did he point it or threaten the victim with it. He simply stood in the doorway of the market. He explained that he did not leave the area because he felt a sense of responsibility toward Herrera and Chapa even though what they were doing was wrong. He stated he would have felt a lot more guilty if he had left them and something happened to them. He realized that it was a dumb thing and added, "we all took part." The defendant emphasized the fact that if he had left Herrera and Chapa in the market, he "wouldn't last long if he had." He stated it would be "better to serve time than leave them."

STATEMENT OF VICTIMS:

First contact was made with Mr. Jeff McKnight, store representative for Stop 'N Go market. Mr. McKnight estimated that his store's losses were $98. Further, Mr. McKnight expressed his personal feelings that persons who perpetrate such crimes should be punished. Mr. McKnight emphasized that the instant offense has resulted in both physical and emotional problems for victim Melanie McVey. He went on to explain that immediately after the instant offense, he spent a number of hours counseling Ms. McVey inasmuch as she was suffering from nightmares, fear of leaving her house, and suffering tremendous physical pain. He stated the instant offense had a great impact on her life and she has since moved from the area. He stated, "We shouldn't mess around with people who pull this nonsense. (There have been) surveys in the industry . . . people leave because of fear . . . This is changing retailing, there are social costs to be paid."

On November 15, 1982, Deputy Probation Officer Marsha Engel spoke with victim Melanie McVey. Concerning sentencing, Ms. McVey stated, "I wish they'd (the defendants) get put away for life. I didn't appreciate being hit in the back with fists." Ms. McVey went on to say that she is still having back pains and occasionally takes medication. Although Workmen's Compensation paid for some of her expenses, she is no longer covered. When she inquired about payments being made for the cost of counseling, however,

> *Workmen's Compensation does not pay for this. At this point, during the interview, Ms. McVey was advised about her possible eligibility for the Victim's Indemnity Fund. Ms. McVey also related that she did not work for some time after the instant offense and "it put me financially behind." In addition, she moved from the state after she discovered that one of the defendants was out on bail. She is still fearful of all of the defendants inasmuch as she was threatened during the robbery. She said, "They said they weren't joking. That they'd use it (the shotgun.) They punched me in the back to show me they weren't fooling around." Ms. McVey related that she still suffers emotionally from her experiences during the robbery. Even now, in her present job, she has a problem dealing "with Mexicans," becoming fearful even at their mere presence. Finally, Ms. McVey reiterated her physical and emotional trauma, saying, "It does bother me still. It's (the instant offense) changed quite a few things."*

"We were getting ready to go and that's when I turned around and saw an old man standing behind me. He said, 'What the hell you guys think you're doing?' I said, 'Man, get in your car and mind your own business, old man.' He said, 'No. What are you doing?' I could see his wife in the car, screaming, probably telling him to get back in the car. He's not going to do it. He's standing outside the store.

"Chapa comes out, and he still has the silly grin, laughing. I get the shotgun and put it to the guy's belly and I told him, 'Get in your car or you're going to get hurt. Matter of fact, give me your wallet. You want to act like a hero.' He gets his wallet and gives me one. But he has two, and Chapa grabs the other one, looks in it and says, 'Man, there's no money in here.' He says, 'The money's in that one,' the one that I have. I told him, 'Now just get in your car and mind your own business.' That's when he finally got in his car. I yelled at him, cussed at him, whatever. We wouldn't have even paid attention to him if he'd been in his car. We probably would have got in and just took off, but he was right there and he came up in our face. He was brave. Brave. Or stupid. We got in my car.

"Roger was in the driver seat and he has it running. He's yelling, 'Come on. Come on. Let's go.'"

PROBATION OFFICER REPORT December 22, 1982
CIRCUMSTANCES OF OFFENSE:
Outside the market, Sidney and Beverly Holtzman, ages 60 and 58, had just driven up and parked. Mr. Holtzman was standing outside his car when Ramirez and Chapa approached him. Ramirez had a smile on his face as he told Mr. Holtzman, "Let me have your wallet." When the victim replied, "You're kidding." Ramirez pointed the shotgun at him and stated, "Give me your wallet, you son-of-a-bitch. I'm not kidding you." And racked the shotgun. Mr. Holtzman turned over two wallets, one of which had $80 in cash and the other contained various credit cards. Chapa threatened to kill him when he saw there was no money in the wallet he had been given. After the victim explained that the money was in the wallet he gave Ramirez, Chapa left and joined the other defendants in their vehicle. Mr. Holtzman recalled that the defendants drove from the parking lot at an accelerated speed.

During subsequent investigation, Mrs. Beverly Holtzman was able to positively identify Ramirez as the man who held the shotgun and removed Mr. Holtzman's property. She also positively identified Roger Yepez as the result of a police photographic lineup as being seated behind the wheel of the defendants' vehicle at the time of the robbery at the Stop 'N Go market. In addition, witnesses who observed the robbery in the Stop 'N Go parking lot stated they saw Ramirez and Chapa exit the store and turn the gun on victim Holtzman. They further stated that they saw Ramirez "pump the shotgun level three or four times" and reach into the left rear pocket of the victim's pants and take a wallet. They also heard Ramirez say to the victim, "Give me your wallet or I'll shoot you." They saw two males sitting in the back seat of the defendants' vehicle and watched as Chapa and Ramirez ran back to the car to leave the area.

STATEMENT OF DEFENDANT:

Regarding the robbery of Mr. Holtzman, the defendant stated when they left the market, Mr. Holtzman was standing in the parking lot and questioned them as to what they were doing. He recalled being annoyed by Mr. Holtzman's questions because he felt he was involving himself in something that had nothing to do with him. When he approached him, he did tell Mr. Holtzman to give him his wallet but he did this because "the old man was getting smart." The defendant explained that while the robbery of the Stop 'N Go and of Mr. Holtzman was taking place, he did not understand the seriousness of what was happening because he was loaded and drunk and at the time did not really care about what was going to happen to him. He explained this feeling had a lot to do with his personal life in which he was having problems with his girl friend and was having difficulty with steady employment. He added he remembered feeling some fear, but considering the people who were robbed were "an old man and a girl" his concern was not great. The defendant stated he was not thinking about what he had just done and in fact, had forgotten all about the men from the bar who had been chasing them.

STATEMENT OF VICTIMS:

On November 10, 1982, Mr. Sydney Holtzman was contacted. While initially saying that his feelings were mixed, Mr. Holtzman stated, "I'm not very happy about having a shotgun stuck in my stomach. I'd like to see them get what's coming to them. They frightened the hell out of me. I was frightened to death. I was told two times by each individual that I was going to be killed. They told me if there was no money in the wallet, they were going to kill me. My personal opinion, I feel they should be punished to whatever the extent of the law allows." In addition, Mr. Holtzman related that although he had no prior history of cardiac illnesses, he has subsequent to the instant offense, suffered two heart attacks. Mrs.

Beverly Holtzman, witness to the instant offense, reiterated her husband's statements.

"Roger was so wasted, driving over the center divider, the curbs. Finally we stop on the side of the road and he said, 'I can't drive.' I came around and I got in the driver's seat and we took off.

"They're opening cans of beer. Celebrating. So we're headed back to the valley, and we stop at a light. For some reason we just stayed there."

"You're wasted," Lupe says.

"We're wasted. And the stoplight's turning green. Red. Turning green. Turning red. And I remember sitting in the seat just like this." Eddie slouches down at the kitchen table, looking around like he's peering over the edge of the car door. "Everybody's laughing and drinking. We're not even paying attention to the wallet and the money. Arnold's eating some candy. Next thing I realize, I remember seeing something from the side. Somebody running. I looked. That's the first time I noticed there was cops around us. There was cops laying in the street. I said, 'Man. Look at all these cops.' Everybody snapped to, and everybody looked around and said, 'Man.' There's three cop cars behind us and cops laying in the front on the street with shotguns out at us.

"We're looking around, and I heard the cop-car announcer say, 'Driver, turn off your car and throw out your keys and put your hands on the roof of your car.' It got kind of weird. It got quiet for a minute. Then somebody, I don't know who it was, said, 'Fuck them. Let's go. Let's go.' I know my car, and I know it's not going to outrun these cops and I remember telling them, 'We can't get away with this car.' I'm in my Pontiac LeMans, and even though it's a fast car it's not a *fast* car. This car is a piece of junk. And I said, 'We're not going to get away.' And they're like, 'Let's go. Let's go. Go. Go. Go,' everybody just like that. Chapa grabbed the shotgun and wanted to shoot it out. I grabbed the gun and slammed it down and said, 'What the hell's wrong with you? This thing don't work.' Roger's laughing and said, 'That don't even work.'

"I said, 'Man, what are we gonna do?' I'm holding onto the keys 'cause they're telling me to throw the keys out and they're saying, 'No, no. Don't throw it out. We can get away. Let's run until we have to stop. Let's go, man.' So I didn't turn it off, and I put it in drive. And when they seen the lights that's when they all started crawling away to get to their cars and when they got out of the way, I just floored it. I floored it."

PROBATION OFFICER REPORT December 22, 1982

CIRCUMSTANCES OF THE OFFENSE:

In response to the silent alarm at the Stop 'N Go market, police obtained information regarding the robbery and a description of the defendants' vehicle was broadcast. On July 10, 1982, while on routine patrol, at approximately 1:45 a.m., Sergeant Mark Labew and Lieutenant Rich Terborch observed the defendants' vehicle eastbound on Los Angeles Avenue. A pursuit followed and assistance was requested. Officer Hostettler took over the pursuit and attempted a felony car stop. At the intersection of Los Angeles Avenue and Tapo Street, he activated his emergency equipment and attempted to make a traffic stop. The vehicle refused to yield and continued in an eastbound direction, eventually coming to a stop in front of a red traffic signal at the intersection of Stern and Los Angeles Avenue. When the vehicle pulled to a stop, a felony car stop was initiated and Officer Hostettler gave orders for the ignition of the vehicle to be turned off and for the keys to be thrown out. However, defendant Ramirez, who was driving, did not comply and rapidly accelerated away after the light changed.

STATEMENT OF DEFENDANT:

When he and the others returned to the car, they drove away at a normal speed and had resumed drinking beer again in the car. He recalled Herrera and codefendant Yepez were in the back seat and he thought they had all the beer, but he could not remember too much after this. He did recall that at one time, they stopped at a light and he put the car in park and turned off the ignition. He was not thinking clearly and did not concern himself with the possibility that the police might be looking for them.

"We took off, and we started going and going and going. My car got up to 110. We're going down California Street in Simi Valley. I was so surprised my car was going at that speed.

"We're flying and curve like we're going to flip. There's a train track that ran crisscrossing the road, and when we crossed it, it made us spin a little bit and almost lose control. I remember looking in the mirror and seeing the lights of the cop cars getting smaller and smaller and smaller and I said, 'Man. We're getting away from these guys.' And everybody's laughing. And no sooner had I said that than I looked at the front and there's this center divider coming, and it has trees right in line, and we hit them things so hard the car went airborne. *Boom . . . boom . . . boom . . .* " With each "boom," Eddie is there, in that moment, the sound of the car flipping in the air and hitting the dirt, over and over again, alive.

"We flipped five times, and the car rolled and rolled and rolled and rolled and rolled and then it hit a wall. *Boom.*"

PROBATION OFFICER REPORT December 22, 1982
CIRCUMSTANCES OF THE OFFENSE:
He drove eastbound on Los Angeles Avenue at an estimated 102 miles per hour; and after failing to negotiate a sharp turn, the vehicle hit a large cement median, became airborne, and eventually rested against the east curb lane of Kuehne Drive, south of Los Angeles Avenue.

STATEMENT OF DEFENDANT:
The defendant stated he recalled driving very fast because he was trying to see "how fast my car would go." He also recalled he was

almost out of gas, and though they were trying to return to the Valley, he knew they probably would not make it. He remembered he was almost at a stop sign, when he first became aware of sirens from police cars. He was not paying close attention, but noticed there was a police car behind him. Prior to this, he had no idea that the police had tried to stop him at an earlier point when he was at a red traffic signal. He remembered he had turned his head around, saw the police car, and said something to the effect that the police were behind them. When he turned his head back, he saw the turn, but was unable to slow his car. He saw a telephone pole which he hit and he remembered the front window shattering, and the next thing he recalled was when he hit the ground as he fell from the car.

"Everybody was ejected. The doors were shaved off. The front tires were gone. The roof was down like a convertible. The car was so beat up and we're just out of it. I remember thinking just when I thought it was over, that's when I felt the ground. I was still airborne when I realized what happened. I was still airborne because all of a sudden, *boom.* Then all this pain. I felt so much pain. I thought I broke my back. I thought about running, and I went to get up and I felt this screech down my back and, *ahwwaa.*

"I started throwing up. I remember feeling the ground and the ground was so warm. It was so warm and I could hear the sirens real far and I could hear the engine going, *vooooooom.* . . . It was still running, then it started to die. I could hear the back tire, just scraping on something, *vfff, vfff, vfff, vfff, vfff.* It was crazy sounds. I'm kind of waiting for the sirens to come, and it took forever. I wanted them to hurry 'cause I felt so much pain. I didn't know where I was or what happened. I could smell the steam and the oil and the gas.

"I think I might have passed out, because when I woke up, they were there. I could see people walking right in front of me. One guy came and was checking on me with his lights."

"A police officer?" I ask.

"I don't know who it was. All I could see was their shoe. They were checking the other guys, and I could hear them say, 'This guy's gone. This guy's dead. Check that guy over there, he's bleeding pretty bad.' I don't know who they're talking about. Then they came to me, and the guy's looking at me and he says, 'This guy's not going to make it.'" Eddie's voice is cracking now. "I'm thinking, 'How did I get here? Now I'm going to die here.' They came and put a microphone and a little tape recorder on the ground in front of my face. I could see it. One of the guys—I later learned it was a cop—he said, 'Who was driving? Just tell me. Who was driving? What happened?' I tried to talk, but I was throwing up blood. He told me to speak right here and tell me who was driving. 'Were you driving the car? Did you do a robbery? You're not going to make it. You're gonna die. Just tell me who was driving.' I couldn't open this eye. It might have been just blood. I remember thinking I was going to die. I prayed right there, in my head. I knew how to pray; my uncle taught me how. I was praying, 'God. Don't let me die here in this condition. I don't want to die like this. If I could live I could get a second chance, I won't waste it. But don't let me die like this.' Then I passed out."

PROBATION OFFICER REPORT December 22, 1982
CIRCUMSTANCES OF OFFENSE:
Apparently, during the rolling of the vehicle, all occupants were thrown from the vehicle. From the positioning of the bodies after the impact, it appeared that defendant Ramirez had been driving the vehicle prior to the accident. The three defendants were advised that they were under arrest for armed robbery. Further investigation at the scene of the accident revealed one unloaded Harrington/Richardson 10 gauge shotgun. Serial number AU536036 which was found protruding from the rear seat of the defendant's vehicle. Items found at the scene of the accident consisted of property taken from the Stop 'N Go market as well as property taken from victim Holtzman. Also found in the parking lot of the Stop 'N Go market was

the multiple sclerosis bank tin can that had been taken from the market's counter by the defendants.

STATEMENT OF DEFENDANT:
He remembered he had trouble getting up, and he thought he had broken his back or a leg. He could hear Yepez yelling for him, and he heard an officer say he was going to die. Almost all at once, he sobered up and realized what had happened. At the hospital the defendant asked about the condition of his car and the comment he made to the officer was "we must have been driving too fast." He did not admit to being the driver of the car and decided the police would probably find out later who had been driving.

"I woke up days later in Simi Valley General. I was handcuffed to the bed feeling all the pain. There was a police officer sitting right there. I woke up and asked him, 'What happened?' He said, 'You guys had one crazy night.' I said, 'What about my car?' He said, 'You can forget about your car. Your car is demolished. And one of your buddies is not doing too good either. I think he's passed.' I didn't know who he was talking about, but I think he was talking about Arnold. Arnold died."

PROBATION OFFICER REPORT December 22, 1982
CIRCUMSTANCES OF OFFENSE:
Herrera sustained fatal injuries and was determined by the coroner to have died instantly as a result of a fracture that resulted in the separation of the brain and brainstem. The three defendants suffered only minor injuries.

STATEMENT OF VICTIMS:
Deputy Probation Officer Marsha Engel contacted Santiago Herrera, paternal grandmother of Arnold Herrera. When asked if she wished to express any thoughts, concerns or feelings concerning the sentencing of the codefendants involved in her grandson's death,

Mrs. Herrera replied, "I can't explain my feelings. It's kind of a shock to me. He (the victim) never was involved in anything like this. He never did give me any trouble. At school, but not like this." Mrs. Herrera went on to say that she had no knowledge of the activities which led to her grandson's death or the friends with whom he was involved. Although she did not know either Edward Ramirez or Roger Yepez, she did acknowledge that Francisco Chapa was known to her for quite some time. She explained that Chapa's family rented the second house on their property but had moved "a long time ago" during the time her grandson was still in elementary school. During the evening in question, her grandson had told her that he was going to the movies, then the next day, she was told of his death.

STATEMENT OF DEFENDANT:

The defendant stated that although he did not know Herrera, he felt very sorry for his death. He believed that what happened was a result of "God telling me to straighten out." He stated he did not understand why Herrera had to die, but recently found an explanation in the Bible. He mentioned that up to approximately a month before this incident, he had been leading a Christian life and had not been drinking. He felt this has been like a second chance to him since he did not die in the accident. He feels that God wants him to understand this and he believes that now he has a better chance at changing his life because of what has happened. He stated he is not guilty of murder and no matter what the Court decides, he knows that God knows what he is guilty of and if it is God's will for him to remain in prison for the rest of his life, he understands this now. He stated that what happened was no one's fault. At first he "blamed it all on God." But now he realizes that he did the wrong thing. He feels no anger and holds no grudges when considering the type of prison time he will be serving. He firmly believes that when he goes to prison, he will be going with God and he would rather do time and live as a Christian than return to the type of life-style he was living at the time of the offense. He explained that he realizes that though his prior record is not extensive, he can see that each time he has become involved with the courts, each incident has been worse than the one before. In any event, the defendant stated he has no intention of returning to an unlawful type of life-style and he will resume a Christian life. He believes that if he is to stay in prison, it will be because God wants him to help those who are in prison and the opposite will be true if by some chance, he is considered for parole.

"I stayed there in the hospital, and I didn't see Roger and I didn't see Chapa until we were arraigned in court for the death of Arnold and the two robberies, one in Rube's Restaurant. They counted it as a robbery because there was a gun there and they said we went in to rob them. It looked like a robbery. If I was there and I seen someone with a gun, I would say we were being robbed or they were attempting to rob us. The other was at the Stop 'N Go market.

"At first they were trying to give us the death penalty because of Arnold, and the judge threw it out. They tried again and the judge threw it out again. They finally came up with a plea bargain of fifteen years to life. They said only if everybody pleads guilty."

"So why wasn't it vehicular manslaughter?" I ask.

"It should have been, but being that the crime was committed during the felony offense, the robbery, it was a murder. That's why it couldn't be a vehicular manslaughter, because it was intentional. We were breaking the law when we committed this other offense, which makes it a felony offense. If I would have got shot by the cops, it would have been the same thing, murder."

"So if the police had shot one of you while you were driving away, you would have been charged with felony murder?" I ask.

"Exactly," Eddie says. "Everyone would have been responsible. Roger and Chapa were eighteen. Arnold was the only sixteen-year-old.

"I'm in the hospital being charged with this. We go through the legal proceedings. I feel bad because Arnold is dead. I'm grateful I'm alive. I remember my prayer in Simi Valley and my commitment. I didn't really care what my lawyers did. It didn't matter. They came up with the agreement of fifteen to life: 'You'll all be charged with this, but if one guy doesn't want to, then we're going to trial and you're going to get twenty-five years to life. It's an election year, and you're in a brand-new county jail. You're not going to win. This is Ventura County, and they need to pay for this jail, and you're not going to walk away from this.'

"They convinced us this was the best deal, and we all said okay. It came down to sentencing, and Roger had a top-notch private attorney that got his sentence reduced to thirteen months. Chapa ended up getting six years, and they gave me fifteen to life, and off to prison we go. They gave me that because I had a criminal record. They said I was the master planner, the brains of the operation. I had the gun, the car. I was the oldest, and everything pointed to me. They gave me the butt of it. Off to Chino [prison] we went from there. All of us."

PROBATION OFFICER REPORT December 22, 1982
EVALUATION—SENTENCING ALTERNATIVES:
The defendant has been convicted by his plea to two counts of robbery (Ca Penal Code 211) non-alternative felonies, punishable by two, three or five years in state prison. Further, the defendant has been found to have used a firearm in the commission of both counts, each punishable by an additional two years in prison. The defendant has been convicted by his plea to second degree murder, a non-alternative felony, punishable by imprisonment in the state prison for a term of 15 years to life.

RECOMMENDATION:
It is respectfully recommended that the defendant be committed to the Department of Corrections for the term of 15 years to life.

It is respectfully recommended that the defendant be committed to the Department of Corrections for seven years, concurrent.

"I wasn't mad at the authorities. They didn't do anything. Arnold dying said it all. Arnold was dead. Now we would all have to deal with this. I didn't realize what fifteen to life meant at that time."

"You said at that time, on a fifteen-to-life sentence, the state was offering parole at about seven years. Your public defender didn't make it sound that bad," Lupe says.

"He said, 'You'll do about seven and a half years and you'll go to board and most likely get a date and come home,' because Chapa got six, and that's how they sort of evened it out. 'Yours is different,' they said, 'because you're going to have to go to the board and you'll have to present yourself as being responsible to go home, but you'll go in seven and a half years. Half of fifteen to life, right? You'll convince them you're able to go home, you'll do good and you'll go home.' I remember the conversation. I thought, 'I can do this—get back on my feet and do right.'"

Before Proposition 89 was passed in 1988, people sent to prison for second-degree murder were serving a median term of five years.

"What did seven years seem like then?" I ask.

"It seemed like a lot, but it didn't seem like life," Eddie says. "When they said 'life,' it was scary. I didn't know what that meant."

"So seven and a half and you're nineteen, you're thinking twenty-six," I say, suggesting how Eddie might have calculated his time.

"Exactly," Eddie says, relief in his voice. "That's what I went into the system thinking. I'll go to the board in seven and a half years, and that's how it was at first. That's how it had been. Guys usually did half time, went to the board, and went home. Some states they still do that. I didn't know the law of California."

"This is '82," I say. "Six years later, one year shy of your seven years, voters pass Proposition 89, the law that gave the governor the authority to review and reverse parole board decisions."

"No one knew in '82 what was coming down the road in '88," Eddie says.

A few months after accepting a plea of second-degree murder, Eddie was taken out of the Ventura County Jail and put on a bus to the California Institution for Men in Chino, where he began serving his time.

By the time I leave Eddie and Lupe's, I'm exhausted. Driving home, it occurs to me that the man I was sitting with for hours just told me about robbing pimps and shoving a sawed-off shotgun in the belly of a Good Samaritan. I've met his wife and his little dog, and chatted with him in his house. I can't help but wonder what I would have thought of him if I were one of the victims on that crazy night decades ago.

seven

BLIND DATE

JANUARY 2008

Over time, Eddie and Richie tell me everything: how they adapted to prison and survived the hole, or solitary confinement, lockups and lockdowns; the quirky life skills and unspoken "inmate" rules; the process of parole hearings and denials; and for those lucky enough to get a "date" from the parole board, the agonizing 150-day wait for a fax from the governor notifying them whether they would go home in two days or remain locked up indefinitely. Both of them went into prison imagining that they would leave as young men; both worked hard to make that goal a reality. Their stories help make it easier to comprehend the enormity of what others, such as Don, are still going through.

The next time I see Don, it's early January 2008, a little more than two months since my visit to his cell inside San Quentin's North Block. The official purpose for my visit this time is to interview new inductees in the Addiction Recovery Treatment program. But stepping out of the sally port and into the prisoners' world with Messick, I see Don standing out in front of the chapel, a mug of coffee in one hand, a watermelon-wide smile stretched across his face, his wire-rimmed glasses shading his eyes.

Something's happened. Just the way he's standing, with his feet wide apart, his upper torso arched back a little, I can tell something has changed. He's confident, even a little cocky.

"Why are you so happy?" I ask with a smile, approaching him and a few of the other lifers standing around.

Like a swollen bubble aching to be burst, Don pops with the news. "I got a date from the board!" he says, practically giggling. "The board found me suitable for parole. They said I'm ready to go home, that I'm no longer a threat to society. It means for the first time in twenty-seven years and seven board hearings, I'm not a monster."

Later, when we can secure some time, Don tells me a little bit about how the hearing went down. That morning he dressed in his best prison outfit—washed and pressed prison blues, with freshly washed hair, a shave, and clipped fingernails.

A correctional officer escorted him to the parole board hearing room, just to the right of the sally port. His attorney since his 1981 arrest, Richard Fathy, was sitting on one side of a long table across from two commissioners from the governor-appointed Board of Parole Hearings and the district attorney from Sacramento.

Once the hearing got under way, Don had an opportunity to account for his crime, to show that he fully understood what caused him to commit his offense, to take responsibility for what he had done, and to show he was remorseful—in essence, to prove beyond a shadow of a doubt he had fundamentally changed and was no longer "a threat to public safety."

Don had done his work. He had a flawless discipline record. If he had smoked a cigarette—banned in California prisons since 2005—or refused to sit all the way down at one call of "attention on the yard," or even been caught smuggling an extra towel to his cell, that infraction could have cost him parole. He hadn't done anything to get a 115, or disciplinary write-up, but still hadn't been able to convince the board of his rehabilitation over the six previous hearings.

"After the review part of the hearing was over, before the guard escorted me back down the hall to the holding cell to wait," Don says,

"I looked at my lawyer. He gave me a small smile as if to say, 'Let's hope.' Then we went out and they deliberated."

Don's voice has grown heavy, and his vowels seem to stretch over tightened vocal chords deep in his throat. "You never really know until they announce their decision. Every time the board denies you parole, they also tell you how long you will have to wait before you can go before them again. My very first denial was for four years. Every denial after that was one year. One year, one year, one year. Then when I went to this hearing . . . they found me suitable." The word "suitable" practically jumps out of his mouth.

"What was different?" I ask. "This time?"

Don believes the district attorney simply no longer had the energy to keep him in prison. He tells me that despite his triumph, he's jaded with the whole process. "You go in there and you keep that flame of hope alive always, and you pray about it and you go in there with expectations. You have to sell yourself, and you also have to have the documentation to prove, to back up what you're saying. So you're prepared. You have hope. But in the back of your mind, you've been denied so many times, and we're aware of everyone else going. The statistics are very much not in our favor. They are against us."

He's not kidding. In all of 2007, out of 6,181 parole board hearings scheduled, just 119 lifers were found suitable for parole. As of 2011, of the more than 17,000 lifers in California prisons serving sentences similar to Don's, more than 10,000 have served enough of their sentences to meet their minimum eligible parole date. Yet just a tiny fraction of them are being found suitable for parole, let alone released.

This is true despite the fact that California state penal code encourages release. Each inmate serving a life sentence costs taxpayers a minimum of $50,000 a year, so Penal Code Section 3041 says, "One year prior to the inmate's minimum eligible parole (MEP) release date, a panel of two or more commissioners or deputy commissioners shall meet with the inmate and *shall normally set a parole release date* as provided in California Penal Code, Section 3041.5." (Emphasis mine.)

Some quick math reveals that the cash-strapped state could save up to $500 million—that's not a typo—*this year alone* by heeding its own law. Of course, not all 10,000 lifers who have met their minimum eligible parole date are ready for release. But think of the money the state (and others) would save by honoring its legal commitment to release truly rehabilitated prisoners.

Initial and subsequent hearings are expensive not just for the taxpayer, but for inmates' families, too, because like trials themselves, they go a lot better with a great lawyer. Don's fiancée, Kathleen, got so frustrated with the seemingly boilerplate denials, she shelled out thousands of dollars to, unsuccessfully, challenge the board's denials in court.

A corrections officer who regularly presides over parole hearings at San Quentin tells me that although inmates are entitled to a state-appointed or private lawyer who will represent them at their parole hearings, a private attorney is generally crucial to the inmate's victory. "Your attorney has to prepare you for the point at the end of the hearing when they ask you a basic question: 'Tell me why you're suitable for parole.' You should have rehearsed this in your mind about 2,000 times, in front of your mirror, in front of your friends, in front of whomever. It has to be so scripted . . . genuine but rehearsed. You can rehearse genuineness. Some attorneys just don't prepare their clients for that."

A private attorney named Johanna Hoffman confirms this statement. She tells me that state-appointed lawyers just don't have the time to advocate effectively for their clients. She began her legal career working for the state but quickly realized that wasn't the best way to represent prisoners' needs. The state "gives you sixteen parole board cases to handle in one week at one prison, and you're there from eight thirty in the morning until whatever at night. When each day's four hearings are over, you have to be back at the prison at seven thirty the following morning. The BPH [Board of Parole Hearings] pays $30 an hour with a maximum of eight hours per hearing, so you're capped at $240 to represent one lifer at one parole hearing. You can make $240 times four hearings a day for a total of $960 a day. But that eight-hour cap per life hearing includes not just the two hours for the hearing, which is often longer. It also includes your interview with your client, a review of the lifer's central file, travel to and from the prison, a review of the hearing packet that the BPH mails to you, and any research or any follow-up work you have to do. So you do the whole week. You're doing all sixteen people beginning Monday at one and three. Then Tuesday it's eight thirty, ten thirty, one thirty, three thirty. But often they don't finish the ten thirty until four, and we would be there until midnight and then have to come back at seven thirty the following morning, with a repeat on Thursday."

Hoffman quit this frustrating work so she could represent fewer clients at a time and win more victories. But that means she has to charge a lot of money. She charges $5,000 on average for a subsequent (rather than an initial) parole hearing, then $2,500 for a hearing after a one-year denial of parole. She tells me that inmates' families generally foot the bill—yet another expensive proposition in the course of caring for an incarcerated loved one.

Hoffman tells me that she receives twenty or more requests a day to help inmates serving life sentences with their hearings. She hates to turn down a compelling case, so she accepts a lot of clients pro bono.

"What do you look for in a client?" I ask.

"I look to see if they're serious about it. One of the things I tell people when I meet them is I won't work harder than they do. If somebody doesn't get that, if somebody thinks they're hiring me and I'm their golden ticket and I'm going to get them out, that's crazy. I tell them, 'You've struggled, suffered, done programs. You've been preparing yourself for twenty years. I'm just stepping in at the last minute to try and pull all that together to help you make a good presentation.' When people get that, then we work well together."

Clearly Hoffman is someone who expects much of her clients—and respects them, too. Young, blond, and beautiful, she possesses an earnest desire to help inmates that I haven't seen in many people who don't have loved ones inside.

"What don't we know about people who commit murder?" I ask.

"That they're human, fundamentally. They made mistakes. They got themselves into situations that I would say any one of us could find ourselves in. They're bizarre circumstantial scenarios that probably in each person's wildest dreams never would have happened. But they did. They happened a long time ago, and whatever caused them either to spend time with the people they were spending time with, to be in that environment, to normalize some of the things they were doing, it is very different today."

Unfortunately, that's not something that voters in California and across the nation understand. Most laws that have been passed about prisoners and parolees make parole hearings more, not less, doctrinaire, and less attentive to the details of an individual inmate's progress. Most new laws carry the name of a victim of some well-known crime, reflecting that the public's perception of its safety—and therefore its preferences for tough penal codes—continues to be shaped by high-profile tragedies, but also by anger and revenge.

Marsy's Law, referred to as the "Victim's Bill of Rights," is one such piece of legislation. Passed in November 2008, it is just a little too late to affect Don's parole hearing. That's fortunate for Don, because it might have resulted in his being sentenced to die in prison.

Named after Marsy Nicholas, a woman stalked and murdered by a boyfriend, Marsy's Law increases victims' rights to participate in prisoners' parole hearings. It also dramatically increases the time a prisoner must wait for a subsequent hearing after a board denial. Before the law was passed, prisoners could be required to wait up to five years between hearings, but usually waited one to two years between their parole hearings. Now the minimum denial is three years and the new maximum wait between hearings is fifteen years. So before, it was most common to wait one to two years but now it's common for a life inmate to wait five to seven years between hearings.

Laurie Saunders, a state-appointed lawyer for inmates at parole hearings, thinks this is hugely unfair. "A fifteen-year denial is often more than a second sentence," she says. "Many of these people, their original sentences were seven to life. Now they're getting fifteen to life after they've done thirty years."

Saunders says that parole hearings are "an extremely difficult emotional experience" for an inmate, no matter how often the prisoner goes before the board. "It's a huge, huge moment for them, even under the old system, before Marsy's Law, when they went up before the board every year. It was always a huge emotional experience for them.

"One of the main things people don't know is how difficult it is for somebody to actually get rehabilitated or get credit for being rehabilitated. A lot of the people I see went into prison on their life sentence when they were sixteen or seventeen years old. So by the time I see them, when they're coming up on their parole dates, they're forty and obviously they're a completely different person. Who isn't a completely different person? They've made amends, and they really would be able to function fine, but nobody understands that."

—

It's the parole board's job to look past public hysteria about crime and criminals and evaluate the true nature of the inmates who come before them. In California, twelve commissioners sit on the state's Adult Board of Parole Hearings. Composed mostly of retired district attorneys, corrections officers, sheriffs, victims' rights advocates, and probation officers, the board pays people salaries of $100,000 to travel to prisons throughout the state, sleep in hotel rooms, and conduct parole hearings that often start before nine in the morning and sometimes last until well into the evening.

Lifers' files, detailing their crime and their time in prison, are sent to commissioners weeks before the hearing. According to the Board of Parole Hearings handbook, published by the Office of Victim and Survivor Rights and Services:

> Parole hearings are not to decide guilt or innocence. The BPH accepts as fact the guilty verdict imposed by the courts. In general, some of the

> factors considered by the panel and which are discussed in the hearing include: Counseling reports and psychological evaluations; Behavior in prison (i.e., disciplinary notices or laudatory accomplishments); Vocational and educational accomplishments in prison; Involvement in self-help therapy programs that can range from anti-addiction programs for drugs and alcohol to anger management; and Parole plans, including where an inmate would live and support themselves if they were released. The purpose of the parole hearing is to determine if or when an inmate can be returned to society.

Two commissioners generally attend each hearing. If for some reason two aren't available, one of seventy civil-service deputy commissioners sits in on the hearing and casts one of the two controlling votes. In addition, victims and their families are welcome to come. According to the handbook, "The victim, or if the victim has died, family members may attend and speak at the hearing. Victims and their families may choose to designate a representative to speak on their behalf."

Not all scheduled parole hearings even take place. In 2007, of the 6,181 parole suitability hearings scheduled in the state, only 3,118 lifer parole hearings, or 50 percent, were actually conducted. The other 50 percent were either canceled, postponed, "waived" (meaning the lifer didn't want to proceed with the hearing), or "stipulated," meaning the lifer formally agreed with the board that he wasn't ready for parole.

Anthony Kane, a former chief deputy warden of San Quentin, is a commissioner on the Board of Parole Hearings. In 2008, of the 136 lifers who appeared before him at parole hearings, he found just nineteen, or nearly 14 percent, suitable for parole.

"Our responsibility is to assess the risk of dangerousness to society," Kane tells me. "We take that responsibility very seriously. I lose sleep at night wondering if my decisions are going to put somebody else at risk. So I'm going to be as sure as I can, if I make that decision, that the possibility they are a risk is minimized by certain factors. It could be their age, if they've matured. It could be the fact that they've showed from being incarcerated they've been disciplinary-free their whole incarceration so their potential for violence is now gone away because they got it, they know how to get along with people. I've had men who have come before me that came in with no high school education, and they leave with a master's, leave with double-A [associate of arts] degrees. They have job offers already waiting for them with high salaries because they got it. That makes them less of a potential threat, because they don't need to go back to crime. We take our job seriously because we're protecting the public."

Commissioner Hollis Gillingham is a little more optimistic than Kane; she finds about 15 percent of the inmates she reviews suitable for parole. After thirty-two years as a county deputy probation officer, she says she trusts her instincts.

Gillingham's standard for suitability is both simple and ironclad: "You could have them next door to you and you're comfortable with that, because you're not speaking for yourself here. You're speaking for the community and you have to feel comfortable with thinking about this inmate living next door to you. You certainly don't want to put them in somebody else's neighborhood, 'cause your job is to protect everybody. So wherever he's gonna go, you pretend like you're his next-door neighbor."

It isn't easy to prove rehabilitation to people like Gillingham and Kane. They've heard it all before, and they want absolute proof of everything. It takes more than attending a couple of Alcoholics Anonymous meetings inside the prison to convince commissioners a lifer has changed. If you haven't done some programs, you're out of luck. If the state hasn't *provided* those programs to you—and if you're in California, the state isn't required to do so—you're probably out of luck, too.

Fortunately, after ten years of trying, Don is finally in luck. "By the time I got back to the room, my lawyer was already sitting in his chair, across the table from the commissioners. I couldn't read anything on his face—nothing," he tells me. "Then one of the commissioners reached over and turned the recorder back on.

"There's a format that they follow. It's all recorded, and while the woman commissioner is speaking, she's making sure what she's saying is all on tape. She's reading from a piece of paper in front of her, 'We find the inmate, Don Cronk, suitable for parole.' And she keeps talking. I didn't know she said it 'cause I'm so used to . . . That's where they usually say 'not suitable.' My first thought is, 'I have to call Kathleen. I have to call home and tell them the bad news.' And the woman is reading on and on and no indication.

"I'm thinking, did she just say I was suitable? I look at my attorney to see if he's thumbs-up, smiling. No change on his face. I couldn't get any indication from him. I looked back at the commissioners. The woman went on to read for several minutes, and when she got done with that part, she went on to speak about my suitability, what was going to happen next. She was saying my documents would be sent to the parole board in Sacramento to be reviewed for the next 120 days by the board. Then my file would be sent to the governor for thirty days to review my parole suitability.

"And that's when it hit me. I didn't hear anything else she said. I began crying, sobbing like a baby. I couldn't stop. The commissioner reached up and grabbed a tissue from a box on the table and handed it to me. They'd seen it before. It was uncontrollable. I didn't know I would be so not in control of my emotions. Not that I was trying to fight it, but it had never happened before. You wait almost twenty-seven years. I had been waiting for this and when it finally hit me that it had happened, it's just an emotional release. It's kind of unbelievable. I was in shock essentially. They had found me suitable for parole. They said I was no longer a threat to the public. They believed me. And then it was over. I was leaving. I was walking out the door, almost a free man."

Within minutes of Don's finding out he had been found suitable for release, word spread throughout the prison with the speed of an uncontrolled burn. Out in the chapel courtyard, down the blacktop passage to North Block and across the lower yard, men in blues called out to one another, "Cronk got a date," followed by high fives, cheers, and questions. Even before Don walked out of the parole board hearing room and back out in the prison population, lifers were pressing for details: "Who were his commissioners?" "How long did the hearing last?" "How long did they make him wait before they told him?"

Don called Kathleen on the prison pay phone and shed more tears. Finally they could begin planning their lives together.

Not Kathleen, or Don, or his buddies on the North Block dared talk about the alternative, because—thanks to Prop 89—there was still an alternative, a real glitch in planning a welcome-home party. Don's hard-won suitability ruling was a ticket not to freedom, but to limbo. Now he had to wait four months for the Board of Parole Hearings inside the California Department of Corrections and Rehabilitation in Sacramento to review the commissioners' decision . . . and then it would be time to hear what Governor Schwarzenegger thought. On April 11, 2008, they would find out, one way or another, whether the board's decision was a first critical step to Don's freedom or just another mirage along the way.

eight

150 DAYS

JANUARY–MARCH 2008

As Don begins his journey through the 150 days, I make every effort to get back inside San Quentin to witness firsthand what it's like to sit and wait those five long months.

Claire-Elizabeth invites me back to meet the new class of addiction counselors, and Lieutenant Eric Messick waves me in. Don, who's there to welcome the new inductees into the brotherhood of certified counselors, tells me that for the first few weeks after he was found suitable for parole, life inside San Quentin was a bit euphoric, almost like he had won a lifetime achievement award. All the hard work, classes, programming, getting involved, taking responsibility, doing good time: it had all made a difference.

"Just the fact that I crossed the hurdle of the board is a validation that for twenty-five years, I haven't had a single write-up," he says.

Over and over again, he repeats the board's word: "suitability." He's holding it in his thoughts like a talisman.

Eventually Don admits that his heady first weeks have given way to a creeping apprehension. In those moments when he can push aside the fear that parole might not happen, he is content to enjoy his new, somewhat elite status, of lifers who have been found suitable.

When he can't push it aside, when the fear rushes over him like a rogue wave, he listens to the lifers he knows and trusts, the lifers of San Quentin who keep track of the board and the governor, and who calculate within a few percentage points the likelihood that on the day Don's file hits the governor's desk, he will rule one way, or the other.

"There's almost eight hundred lifers here in North Block," he says, "and they're all eligible for parole. They go to those hearings and they get denied parole."

Of the 7,073 lifer parole board hearings scheduled in prisons throughout the state in 2008, only about half, or 3,473, were actually held. Of those Don was one of just 274, or 7.8 percent, found suitable.

Since Proposition 89 was passed, the chances for men like Don of actually getting out of prison after being found suitable for parole have dramatically declined. Of the thousands of men and women found suitable for parole, two-term Republican Governor Pete Wilson (1991–1999) let out 131 people in his eight years in office. One-and-a-half-term Democratic Governor Gray Davis (1999–2003) let out only *eight* people during his six-year term. And although Republican Governor Arnold Schwarzenegger (2003–2011) has relaxed his office's grip on this process a little bit, in 2008, four years into his term, he's rejecting about 77 percent of the recommendations that arrive on his desk from the parole board.

As if listening to my thoughts, Don admits he knows the odds are stacked against him. "I'm aware," he says. "It's kind of like going to the hearings. You keep that hope. You keep that prayer. You keep positive thoughts and energy but you temper it with reality. You look at the statistics, and they're not good. So you try to balance all of it and carry on your normal routine, your normal life. It gets touchy sometimes. We've been through worse, and so you endure."

I wonder out loud, "But does it make it any more difficult to be incarcerated once the board has found you suitable?"

"What I've noticed that's happened is that I've become intolerant now. So I really have to put myself in check. For some reason, the very next day after the board found me suitable, the meals I've been eating all these years were disgusting. And the noise and the smell and the lines. Suddenly I've just become aware this is crap. This is no way to live. How in the hell have I been doing this all these years and not gone insane or become violent or acted out? It's terrible. I don't know how I've lived with this. And it's not over yet."

Don knows his chances aren't great, but hope keeps springing up. He says he'll be watching a show on San Quentin cable TV, and someone will be doing something that looks fun, like going on a trip, and it will hit him so fast the air escapes: *I could be doing that soon.* He feels like every dream he's ever had is now a carrot dangled tauntingly in his face.

In 2003, when Arnold Schwarzenegger took office after successfully leading a recall campaign against Gray Davis, he installed Peter Siggins as both his counsel and legal affairs secretary. By the time I catch up with him, he has been promoted to associate justice of the California Court of Appeal. But as the man who set up the governor's process for reviewing parole decisions, he must have a lot of insight into Governor Schwarzenegger's thinking process.

"The legal affairs secretary has a staff of several lawyers," he tells me. "And those lawyers help to tee things up for disposition and consideration by the governor. In particular, in respect to paroles, the staff is very active, and when the board makes a decision to find someone suitable for parole and the time period for the governor's review period kicks in, the board sends to the governor the board's complete file on that prisoner."

Siggins says that even though the Board of Parole Hearings was expected to send the prisoner's file to the governor 120 days after finding the prisoner suitable—so the governor's office would have a full thirty days to review it and make a decision—occasionally the file came with just fifteen or twenty days remaining to review it.

When his office did receive the file, Siggins says, "one of the lawyers in the legal affairs secretary's office would go through that file, abstract it, and write a memo that details the salient points and things for consideration. The criteria the board considers when it decides to grant parole are the same criteria that the governor applies when considering whether to approve a grant or reverse a grant.

"As legal affairs secretary, I would routinely get ahold of those memos. I would review them. I'd talk to my staff about the cases and then would essentially present them to the governor."

When it came time to sit down with the governor, Siggins says, they usually would handle twelve to fifteen cases in an hour, to an hour and a half. "It would be only me and the governor. If I wasn't there, my chief deputy would handle it. But it was one lawyer, either myself or my chief deputy, and the governor."

I asked if they always agreed on whether to approve a parole. Siggins says he doesn't want to say anything that would jeopardize the privileged discussions between him and his client, the governor, but "there could be vigorous discussions. There were occasions when I would disagree with my staff, but if that were the case, I always made it my personal practice to inform the governor there was a difference of opinion of our staff."

Siggins says he never listened to the recordings of the board hearings, and even though he recalls seeing photographs, he maintains that they didn't make an impression on his decision. "It was more a question of where would they live? Who was going to provide support for them? Did they have a spouse? Could they live with that spouse? I can't say that I ever had a strong desire to sit down and talk with a prisoner who was the subject of a parole proceeding. I never felt I needed that experience in trying to reach a resolution. It's just not the way the process is set up, nor is it the way the process could possibly function. There's too many cases and there's just too much to do. In feasibility and logistics, that kind of review is a practical impossibility."

So that's how Don's file is going to be considered. Two and a half decades of his life, reduced to salient bullet points on Arnold Schwarzenegger's desk.

Out of the blue, I get word. There's been a shake-up in the warden's office. Lieutenant Messick is now San Quentin's legal affairs coordinator. It looks like I'll have to start all over building a new professional relationship with San Quentin's new public information officer, Lieutenant Sam Robinson. I try not to panic. I call Messick's old number; Robinson picks up the phone. His voice is unfamiliar, but warm, almost encouraging. "Messick says you're okay," he says. Apparently San Quentin's staff relies on the same trust referral system as the inmates.

Standing outside the east gate, I'm watching for someone dressed in a suit to approach, hoping I make a good first impression. Right on time, from far down the frontage road, a black man in a dark blue suit walks right down the middle of the road. There's a clipped, confident step to his polished black shoes. That's got to be Robinson. He has inviting, wary eyes and a shake-every-hand personality.

Once I introduce myself, side-by-side we head straight for my latest entry pretext: a meeting of an organization called TRUST, short for Teaching Responsibility Utilizing Sociological Training. When do I ask him—now, or later? Until I do, it's impossible to guess how Robinson will feel about giving me access to lifers like Don Cronk over and over again.

"I was hoping to speak with Don Cronk today, if there's time. After the TRUST meeting?"

"We'll see," Robinson says. "Let's just go to the TRUST meeting and see how much time there is after that."

The interesting thing about Robinson is that whether he's walking out on the administration side, through the sally port, or inside the prison, he smiles at and talks to everyone, not just fellow corrections officers, more than a dozen of whom are blood relatives, but administrators and blue-clad inmates who know him and call out to him with a wave. Without skipping a beat he saunters over, shakes their hand, hears their concerns, checks in. When I went inside with Messick, the inmates nodded and shook his hand. But with Robinson, the men inside make an effort to walk over, reach out, laugh. He laughs with them, a lighthearted, inside-joke kind of laugh that cuts through the real-life tensions swirling around, enveloping every moment of every day inside the prison walls. I stand back a little and watch the easy interchange between the man with the keys and the men who are locked up.

"So, you all know Nancy Mullane?" Robinson says to a loose circle of men and volunteers standing around outside the Muslim chapel where TRUST holds its weekly meetings. "She's going to be joining the meeting today."

"Oh, yeah. That's great," says Nathaniel Ray Rouse, one of the lifers known inside by his Muslim name, Shahid. "We're just taking a short break. We'll be going back inside in a minute."

"Have any of you seen Don Cronk?" I ask to the inmates milling around. "I was hoping to check in with him. He's waiting to find out if the governor is going to let him go home." The inmates look at me with the kindest possible expressions that can read "duh."

"How's he doing?" I ask.

"You know, nowadays, when one of us gets a date, we try to help each other, to keep from getting too high," Shahid says, the sun bouncing off his deep brown skin. "'I'm going home.' Calm down, not yet. Calm down, calm down. So the impact of having your date taken from you isn't as severe as it would be if you totally invested your whole self into that. It's something you cannot afford to do, because it's devastating to spend thirty years of your life in prison after committing a crime such as we all have."

This balding man with a moon face, thin beard, and narrow eyes offers to quickly summarize his experience with the board. Shahid says he was nineteen years old when he was sentenced to life with the possibility of parole for murder. Over the past thirty-one years, he says, the board has found him suitable for parole three times. "I've been before the parole board eighteen times. Fifteen times denied parole." And since he's still talking to me from inside, that also means three times his parole suitability has been reversed by governors.

I ask some of the other lifers who have gathered around whether they've ever had a date reversed by the governor. All around the circle of men, hands shoot up.

"How many times?" I say.

One by one they look back at me and call out, "Three," "Two," "Five."

An inmate steps out of the meeting room just behind the circle of men to announce that the TRUST meeting is going to get back under way. We all head inside the linoleum-tiled room, where about thirty inmates and about half a dozen students from the University of San Francisco sit in a wide circle.

In December 2003 the San Quentin TRUST was recognized as an official organization within the prison. On September 20, 2004, TRUST fellows began facilitating intensive weekly group workshops in the Muslim chapel, pairing two dozen peer inmates with outside professionals.

The peer group/expert dynamic is essential to the program's success, says Kim Richman, a professor of sociology and legal studies at the University of San Francisco who, back in 2004, worked with the inmates to develop a curriculum for the program. "You have to have the perspective of a peer [another inmate] who has been through this, but it helps to have guidance from someone in the world you are transitioning to and someone with a professional background in the skills you need, whether it's criminology, sociology, psychology, or communication. We deal with anger management, self-evaluation, financial literacy, time management, and substance abuse counseling."

After the session I chat with Richman about her experiences in the prison. She says she has come to think of prisons as "two-sided locking." We lock people in and we lock people out. Most of the public doesn't see it as problematic that there's no vision in or out and that the walls are so high, physically and metaphorically. I think it is a problem.

"There's a functional element that a responsible citizenry needs to know, what they're voting for and where their money's going, 'cause it's their money. And there's a human element to it. Responsible human beings should understand the living conditions of their fellow human beings. That requires a leap, because it requires you to see people inside prisons as humans, which most people don't.

"It was a major challenge to my core beliefs when I found out that the majority of people I was working with inside San Quentin were in for homicide. I resist every single day thinking about them or calling them 'murderers,' because I think it reduces them to one horribly tragic act, but one act, and they are much more than that."

Before he escorts me out of the prison, Robinson says there's time for me to quickly visit Don at his job, inside the prison Protestant chapel. One hundred and six days into his wait, Don's not in a great mood; the anxiety and uncertainty are eating him alive. "This is the hardest thing I have ever been through," he tells me.

I ask whether it would be all right with him if I gave his fiancée a call. I'd like to meet her, to see who is waiting for him on the outside.

"Sure," he says, his eyes dancing. "She lives nearby, and she's a great lady. I'll let her know you're going to call."

The first time I hear Kathleen's voice, I have to reevaluate my mental image of who would love a man locked up for murder. Her voice is sharp, but also warm—not the voice of a troubled woman dependent on captive prey.

"I suppose we could meet somewhere for coffee," she offers.

"Um, well, you see, I'd really like to see where he will be living if he gets out. Don said if he is paroled, he is going to be living with you. Do you think I could come to your home and speak with you there?"

I hear her take a breath, pause. "Well, I guess that would be all right. But if my brother, who lives right next door, comes over while you're here, let's not talk about Don around him. I'll explain when we see each other."

A couple weeks later I pull up in front of Kathleen's early-twentieth-century bungalow in the precious town of San Anselmo, a community embedded deep in the sunniest part of Marin County. *So this is where Don will land if he gets out. Not bad.* Up on the far side of her front porch is a comfy swing. I can't help but imagine Don sitting there, rocking back and forth.

Kathleen opens the door like a rush of wind. "Come on in," she chirps. She's lovely: thin, compact, with sparkly blue eyes and styled auburn hair.

She takes me into a cozy, carpeted living room. There's a fireplace on the far wall. Framed family photos are propped up on all flat surfaces; beautiful handmade Easter decorations fill the gaps.

"I have lived here in this house all my life, born and raised," Kathleen says proudly, adjusting one of the standing frames on a polished side table. It's perfect. Every surface is painted to perfection: the moldings, walls, windows.

"I replaced the windows a few years ago," she says. "Don helped me decide which style to have installed." She moves down the hall. "This is the second bathroom. We're just about finished with the remodel. Don helped design all the changes. He picked out the color on the walls and all the fixtures. It's a split bath, and this half [the one with the toilet] never had a sink. Don figured out how we could install this little sink! Isn't it cute?"

An itty-bitty sink has been installed halfway down the skinny room. "It's small but it works," Kathleen says. "Don really wanted a sink in the half bath. I think it was a great idea."

He's never even set foot in this house. Yet as Kathleen frowns and drags her finger across a dusty surface, I'm haunted by déjà vu. While Don was showing me his cell, he wiped his finger over the top of the television and shelves over his bed, lamenting the dust in the air.

I can't help but think this is a sign—that even in this meticulously arranged and kept house, Don might just be one of the few men who could fit their body, their things into Kathleen's world. Is that possible? That a man locked up in prison for twenty-seven years could find a home here?

"So how did you meet Don?" I ask Kathleen as we sit at the table, a good first question between two women.

Kathleen motions for me to turn my tape deck off, which I do. She wants to go over some ground rules for the interview. She met Don in the visiting room of San Quentin while she was visiting someone else, whom she doesn't want to discuss. Okay. And if her brother comes in, let's change the subject. Fine.

Ground rules clear, I turn my deck back on. "So, while I was there in the visiting room," Kathleen says, "I met Don. I always thought he was such a nice guy, and I would look at him and wonder, what in the heck is he doing in here? He's so clean-cut, so upbeat. He's like a shiny penny. I thought they must have gotten something wrong. So I would go visit him, like, once a month, and they used to have banquets. A lot of them, like three a year. You could get dressed up. It was like being on a date, and every single time I went, Don would have a bouquet of flowers for me."

"Where did he get the flowers?" I ask. "Inside prison?"

"He said one time he went in a bush to pick them, and a bird attacked him. He said, 'You don't know what I had to do to get these flowers.' He always treated me like a queen. So special. He'd make me a place mat or a name card or give me flowers. One time it was just a rose. You don't see a guy with a rose in prison. His whole life he looked for this one girl he had in his mind. His dream girl.

We dated very, very slowly. This has been a very long process. It's been since 1995: thirteen years. So we started out as friends and it evolved into a deeper, deeper, deeper relationship. And now it's like—it's unbelievable."

"I guess when you start a relationship with someone incarcerated," I suggest, "you have to start slower."

"This is how I would do it. I would think about him during the day, like, 'Don would really like this' or 'I can't wait to drive here with him' or 'Wait 'til he sees this.' All day long it would be a joyful thought. If I was ever sad at all because he wasn't with me, it was at night, 'cause you get in bed and you settle down and you're quiet and alone. If there have been any tears shed at all, that's when it would be, or I would take a shower and the emotions would come out. But I didn't have much time to be sad about it because I work. I was taking care of my mother. But now my mother's gone, so I'm remodeling the house. You have to have a life. You have to have a life on the outside. That's my opinion."

"So has he asked you to marry him?"

Kathleen looks back at me, surprised. "I'm sorry?"

"Has he asked you to marry him?" I ask again.

"No."

"Don?" I say with a stammer. "You're not engaged?"

"Well, the words have not been said yet. It's like an understanding."

"He refers to you as his fiancée," I say.

"I know he does," Kathleen murmurs.

"But he hasn't said the words?" I ask. "And you refer to him as your fiancé? Maybe he doesn't feel he could . . . "

"Right," Kathleen says, finally giving me something I can chew and swallow. "Like he says, 'I don't have a pot to pee in or a window to throw it out of, so it's like, what am I bringing to the table? How could I have the nerve to ask her to marry me when I have nothing?' It's just not necessary right now. It really isn't. One thing at a time. Let's get him out. I would not marry him while he's in there. I made that very clear. For what? There's no conjugal visits for lifers. We're not married. We're not engaged. We're pre-engaged!

"He has nothing to hide," she continues. "He's like an open book. See, this is part of the reason why, in telling my family—like telling my brother—this is why I choose to do it the way I want to do it because I want him to see Don. Do you understand? You've seen him, you've met him, you know how he talks. Because I'm sure my brother, if I said to him, 'I really like this guy at San Quentin,' he's picturing a guy with tattoos up to here"—her fingertips brush her neck—"but he's not like that. I need to present this person to him and say, 'This is the guy.'

"We're very devout Christians, Don and I, and we believe Christ has got our lives in order, and some things are very, very clear to me that this is the way it's supposed to be. If you really, truly believe God is ruling your life or putting you on such and such a path, and you give your life to him, you're to follow his direction. You have to live it and breathe it, and that's what we do. We live it and breathe it. Sometimes it's really hard, but we reassure each other."

I ask if she remembers where she was when Don called back in November to tell her the good news. "When he would go before the board, there was always that cloud. Who knows what they're gonna pick on, or what they're actually gonna say. Nobody really knows. I was at work when he called on my cell phone. He said, 'Well, I'm out. I'm out of my hearing.' I was walking out the door of my office up the path to go sit on some outdoor chairs so I could talk to him. As I was walking, he said, 'They found me suitable.' I was in stride, walking, and I stopped. All I remember was thinking to myself, 'Okay, now put the other foot forward. Now put the other foot forward, until we get to the chair.' I sat down and I go, 'Wait . . . What?!' He goes, 'They found me suitable.' You talk about being blown away. Unbelievable." That was 141 days ago. In nine days, Kathleen will find out one way or another whether the man she met fifteen years ago in San Quentin's visiting room is moving in.

—

It's now the 149th day—the last day before the governor must notify the lifer of his decision. If all goes according to pattern, Schwarzenegger or someone from his Legal Affairs Office—perhaps Peter Siggins's successor—will send a fax to the warden's machine that sits in a short passageway near his secretary's office.

Lieutenant Robinson—fast becoming my ally on a level with Messick—brings me back into the prison for one last chat with Don before tomorrow. Don is standing outside the chapel doors with a fellow lifer, looking terrified.

"We're all very nervous," murmurs the lifer standing next to Don, in a slightly protective voice, as if to explain Don's unusually petrified state. "Tomorrow's tomorrow. We're doing the vigil."

"Tomorrow's tomorrow," I say.

"Oh, okay," Don says, letting out a sigh. "I thought maybe it was today. I looked at you and Sam and thought maybe. Sometimes they do it early."

The lifer standing vigil with Don says, "We used to think if you didn't hear early, it was bad."

While we're chatting, Pastor Morris Curry from the Protestant chapel walks up. "You know, I've been coming into San Quentin for twenty, twenty-five years, and let me tell you, no better administrator than Don Cronk. I'm going to be crippled when he leaves. Immensely." For years Don has been earning his prison wage of 30 cents an hour as Pastor Curry's assistant.

"Thanks, Pastor," Don says, patting the man on his broad, tall back. Turning, he opens the glass doors to move our conversation down the hall and into his office.

"So, how you doing?" I ask. "I went and visited Kathleen."

"She told me," Don says, his voice airy, hollow. "You know she's in the middle of remodeling her house."

"There's a beautiful south-facing deck," I say, maybe a little too enthusiastically. Am I dangling another carrot in his face? "I can just see you sitting on the deck. It's a beautiful neighborhood. Very nice."

Robinson shoots me a look: *Are you sure you want to do this?*

"Throughout the years, I've worked with her, the front of the house, the windows upstairs," Don says, like a proud homeowner. He's only seen pictures of the place. "Those weren't there. And the color scheme. That was my idea. But I guess it's more pink. It was supposed to look Spanish style, and I think she was kind of disappointed after they got it finished.

"The crown molding and the walls. We worked on it together. I can just see it. I can just picture it without being there. Often. And it seems to work most of the time. We'll see."

"So," I venture, hoping not to provoke too much more longing, "how's it been?"

"Well, since November, I told you about the drop in my tolerance, and that still persists. But I hadn't lost a night of sleep. And then, out of the clear blue sky, I was watching the Mayan history of the hieroglyphs on PBS at ten o'clock. I brushed my teeth, washed up, and went to sleep like normal. Went out like a light. Then around eleven thirty I heard a phone ringing. Just like a real phone. An analog phone, not one of your digital jobs.

"I heard it, and it disturbed me. I heard it ring again. It jolted me, and the phone call was they were telling me I was going home. My heart was pounding like I had just run laps and adrenaline. There were butterflies in my stomach.

"Where did that come from? I wasn't thinking it at all, and that's not even how they tell you. I'm spiritual. I believe God's hand is on this, so I don't know. Maybe he was giving me some assurance. It did keep me up until three thirty. I just couldn't shake it. I tried praying, meditating, breathing, and I could not stop the anxiety. I don't have that. I've never had that. I don't know. I want to take that as a message from my creator. We'll see. It's all we can do. We have it in prayer. Without the spiritual connection, without my pastor, I don't know how others do it. I don't know.

"It's monumental, the magnitude of this thing. If you try to imagine it, it would be on par with them telling you you have six months to live. You can imagine how you would react. You'd be broken at first, but then you'd be trying to live whatever life you had left in that short amount of time. But the seriousness of it, the reality of it, the finality of it. I can't think of anything that would be on the magnitude of it emotionally, spiritually, physically. Twenty-seven years of prison could be over with the signing of a pen, just like that.

"It's intense. Just going through one of those parole hearings is life-changing. And if they find you suitable, then they do 120 days of investigation. Actually I'm impressed. They contacted every person who wrote about me and supported me. The jobs and where I'll live. This is serious stuff."

"What *are* you going to do on the outside?" I ask.

"Well, the first thing, I don't know how long a time, but I'm not going to do anything," Don says, laughing. "We'll be in a position that I won't have to worry about that for a while. I just want to be reintroduced to life in society and just take it slow and not rush into anything.

"You know, I have two passions. One is counseling, and the other is audio. I do have some invitations to work in the field of audio, but my ears are changing. I don't have the golden ear as I had for a while. I just don't know. Maybe both. See, I'm out of sync. I don't know how much travel is required to get around, to accomplish things. I have to learn where I am and the traffic and how far is far, and that gas is at $4 a gallon. When I came in, gas was under $1 a gallon."

We pause, an easy intimacy in the silence. I feel it's time to ask the question I've been putting off for a long time. When I asked Eddie and Richie to tell me about their crimes, they reached back in their still-fresh memories and told me their stories. They didn't have to. But now that they had done their time and been released, whatever they told me on the record wouldn't return them to prison for the recounting, no matter how gruesome. The board that had found them suitable and the governor who eventually let them go had all the details.

But what about the thousands of people still locked up for committing murder? Is the fact that they are still locked up some sort of sign they are still unreformed, still a danger to society? Or are the board and governor playing with a politically stacked deck? This was my chance to find out, while he was still locked up, whether Don would tell the truth.

"I have a tough question," I say.

"Go ahead," he says. "Ask away." I can tell in his voice that he already knows what's coming.

nine

DON'S STORY

Seconds

APRIL 2008

For a brief moment, Don looks away. Then, lowering his head, he stares down at his hands. Taking a deep breath, he raises his shoulders, lifts his head, and looks me squarely in the eyes.

"I was a young man over my head in a big city. I came from Wisconsin, and I was in Sacramento. I had a great job working as a manager in a warehouse, and I was introduced to cocaine.

"I liked it—a lot. I liked it a real lot. Now I say that because I had tried almost every other kind of drug. I'm allergic to marijuana. I don't like alcohol: I'll drink it, a few beers, but I do not like that drunk feeling. Crank is too intense. Heroin makes you sick. LSD is a recreational thing once in a while when you were a kid going to concerts with Mickey Mouse ears. Other than that, I didn't really have any fascination with addiction. So I thought I was fine.

"When I was introduced to cocaine after a promotion, I instantly fell in love with it. I thought it was a wonder drug. It made me feel secure and confident, yet in control. There was a euphoria, and later that evening, I could go to sleep. The other drugs will keep you up all night.

"At that time, cocaine was very expensive. Guess who was doing it the most: wealthy people. So I associated it with the Porsches and the people like my boss: the millionaires, doctors, lawyers. That's who was doing it, and so I thought, this is great. Then I was told it wasn't addicting. Well, it's not so much physically as it is psychologically.

"Long story short, I threw everything in my life away to feed the addiction of cocaine, to the point where I had to commit a crime. I started dealing it and getting deeper away from the beautiful people to the ugly people, and I met some associates, like-minded. Two of them were ex-felons. They were charismatic. Nice fellows, not bad guys. We were using more than we were selling.

"Now we owe the connections and the dealers, and that's not good, and my newfound friends had done armed robbery in the past, so we could do some robberies. So we did some robberies. No one was hurt. We got some money. And then the night of the crime that I'm here for, it was to be a robbery.

"We had some inside information there would be a lot of money and jewels, and we were going to this man's home, wait for him, he would come in, tie him up, take the briefcase, take the money, and leave. We had the masks. We had the tape. The whole nine yards. We would surprise him as he came in."

The man Don and his crime partners were waiting to rob was a fifty-year-old man named James Allen, owner of the Allen Coin Shop. What they hadn't expected was that Allen had a .38 in a holster in his front pants pocket.

"Well, it didn't work out the way we planned. He got in without our warning signal going off, and when he opened the door and I came out of another room, I didn't know he was there. In those few seconds, when I walked out of the kitchen and saw Mr. Allen standing in the open door, my mind was going, 'How in the hell did he get in here?' While I'm standing there, I'm shot. He shot me three times. Emptied his gun on me. Hit me three, missed me three. Next thing I know, I'm on the floor in the corner of the wall and the floor and I reached in my pocket and shot right through my coat.

"He died instantly. Unbelievable. You couldn't do that again. You couldn't reenact that. Seconds. It all took place in seconds and you can't undo it. You can't change it. You can't ask questions.

"I didn't die. That's why I'm here, and rightfully so. I fell under the felony murder rule because it was in the commission of a felony. I fully intended to rob him and beat him into submission if we had to and tape him up and leave. Yet never once was there the intention or the thought to murder somebody.

"Of course, the law says if you have a weapon and you do a criminal act, then you premeditated it. Well, I understand that now, but at the time, it was just insurance in my pocket. I weighed about 150 pounds, and I wasn't intimidating. So if I were to say to you, 'Give me your money,' you'd look at me and say, 'Yeah, right.' But if I show you a pistol, you'll give me the money. So that's really why I had it.

"My codefendant, the ex-con, he was buff. He was a big guy. He was going to be the heavy. I was just there for support. He was the one who was going to grab him, and I was going to tape him up with duct tape and the masks. If we were planning on just going in to kill the guy, we wouldn't have mattered with all that. Just horrible, tragedy. Again, addicted thinking, immature thinking, selfish thinking, greedy thinking.

"Robbery, I would have done three years. I had no record or prior conviction. Nothing. So I was aware enough to know that I'm in trouble but not that much, versus killing somebody. The gas chamber? Life without parole? I don't know. It's just a horribly unfortunate turn of events that I'm responsible for. I caused it."

Silence. I look over at Sam Robinson, then back at Don. "What was the final conviction?"

"Twenty-five to life."

"First degree? Second degree?"

"First degree, and it's taken me a lot of years to get where I am now because of that. The robbery was sophisticated, but the shooting wasn't. If someone is looking at you and examining you and why you killed this human being, they want to understand what's going on in there. Was this a senseless thing? A psychotic thing? It wasn't an execution style: 'Oh, I'll take your money, and on the way out the door, I think I'll kill you.' None of those elements are there. This was a shootout that was unavoidable once it got going."

"Do you have a scar?"

"Well," Don says, rubbing his hand over his arms and chest, "they're just little now. It went through muscle there and came out there. I have a little mark."

"Was it a little bullet?"

"It was a .38, close range. About here to Mr. Robinson away, and the one that went in my chest collapsed my lung. Went through and ripped my intestines, and I still have a piece of a bullet down here," he says, pointing to his lower torso. "It went all the way through and came out. 'Course, you're bleeding profusely. You're in shock. Blood was coming out of my throat. I was in and out of consciousness. I was losing a lot of blood."

I ask him what he did after getting shot. "Ran," he says.

"How did you run with a bullet in you?"

"Shock. When you're in shock, the adrenaline and the whole nine yards, your body will do amazing things."

"Then what happened?" I ask.

"My crime partner was upstairs. He heard all these bullets firing, and he doesn't know what's going on. 'Cause like I said, this wasn't what was supposed to happen. He knew I wasn't a gunslinger thug. He figures I'm dead, and they're coming upstairs. I don't know how much time had passed, 'cause I heard nothing. Silence. So he came downstairs and saw a shoe, a foot. And when he looked around the corner he saw Mr. Allen. You couldn't tell anything. It just looked like he was asleep on the floor.

"My crime partner picked up the valuables and the gun and shut the door and got in his car and left, knowing I was out there somewhere. So he kept driving around slowly until he found me. He had all kinds of connections in Las Vegas, and I got a doctor and ID and everything was fenced. I was getting ready to leave the country."

"Where were you going to go?"

"I don't know. I had to convalesce for three months. My whole body was black and blue and yellow and blood underneath. But the doctor got the bullets out, and my lung reinflated. I was bedridden for a while."

"So you weren't arrested right away?" I ask. "How did they arrest you?"

"About six, seven months later, the third party got arrested for a DUI. He had his children in the car, and he was going to go to jail for a couple of years. He was the go-between between the Las Vegas people and my crime partner and I. We had gotten new identities, and they were the real deal, so he was the only person who knew who the new identities were attached to. He had put the whole thing together. I didn't know anything. But the third party knew. He had it all."

"So he's the one that gave you up?"

"Well, later, he's the one that gave us up. Now the FBI knew who they were looking for. They checked the vehicle registrations. After he told, it was only two weeks. I was in Idaho at the time."

"And that's where they found you?"

"Uh-huh. Easy once they know who they're looking for."

"Do you think you had a fair trial? Was justice administered?"

"I admitted I was guilty the first day. I admitted it. Now, twenty-seven years later, if in telling my story I can honor the life of Mr. Allen, then it is all worth it. But that was twenty-seven years ago. So much has changed. I've changed."

"When you talk about it, what do you see in your mind?" I ask. "What are you saying to yourself as you're telling me what happened?"

"I'm ashamed. I'm ashamed of the depth that I allowed myself to go to. It's with me forever, and that's my cross to bear. It's the damage I inflicted on the Allen family. I can't change any of those things. The damage I did to society. It's just shocking. So how does one do that? How does one go from a relatively normal person to a monster and then back to who you really are?"

I ask him if he's ever going to tell anyone his secret if he's released and meeting people on the outside.

"Each situation is different," he says. "I've never kept it private. When Kathleen and I started to get serious, we'd just visited for a long time—for about three years anyway, when it started to get serious. I had told her why I was here, but I said I want you to know because someday, somebody's going to ask, 'Well, do you really know? Those guys lie.' I had her meet with my attorney, Richard Fathy, and she did. They had lunch, and he told her and showed her everything. I didn't want it to be misrepresented. I wanted her to have the absolute truth. When I get out, depending on the situation, depending on where I am, I'll make that known."

Our time is drawing to a close. "Don, you know I'd like to be there tomorrow when you get word. Would that be all right with you?"

"Sure, that's fine," Don says without hesitation.

"Either way, I'd like to be there."

"Yes," Don says, "either way."

Walking out with Sam, I wonder if he knows how it's all going to go tomorrow.

"Sam, do you think Don's going to get released? Is the governor going to let him go?"

"Oh, I don't know," Sam says. "No one can tell."

"Do you get a heads-up?" I ask. "A warning? Can you call someone in the governor's office and check?"

"Nope," he says. "We don't have that kind of inside access."

"What do you think?" I say, pushing. "What does your instinct tell you? Is he going to go home?"

"I don't know," Sam says. "Really. I've never been the one to get the fax before, so this is all new to me."

"Come on," I ask, smiling, "what do you think?"

"I think he's going home," Sam says.

As I pull away from San Quentin's East Gate, I call Kathleen to see how she's holding up. Either way the governor decides tomorrow, it will have an impact on her life. She invites me to stop by.

"I think he'll be crying," Kathleen says sitting at her table, looking out the back deck where purple wisteria blooms are just beginning to cover the arbor, "if the governor says no. He'll be disappointed, obviously, but no matter what, he's going to get out because once they say you're suitable, it just becomes a fight. For Don, the hardest thing will be having to tell me."

If Don does get to come home, "he'll be a blubbering baby," Kathleen says a deeply satisfying laugh filling the room. "Pretty much. That's a given. That's what I love about him. He wears his heart on his sleeve."

"You'll get a phone call?"

"Don thinks the way it goes is the governor's office will contact his attorney. See we've never had this happen before. But Richard Fathy says he thinks they'll call me."

However it comes, if the word is good, Kathleen says, "it's going to be an adjustment. He's never seen an ATM machine. He's never used a cell phone. It's like that. All these things. Just think about checking out at Home Depot, where you do the scanning and stuff. He's never seen that. 'What do you mean check yourself out?' Oh and when we get in the car and turn the radio on and find a good station, and I'll just look at him and say, 'when was the last time you turned on a radio in a car? They don't have dial and slide,' you know what I'm saying? He'll see something like that, and wow."

"It must be exciting," I say.

"Oh God, yes. It's like bringing my cousins over from Italy and showing them everything. This is how we do it in America. It's like introducing someone foreign to your life."

It's quiet sitting in Kathleen's kitchen, the only sounds are the crows outside in the trees and her shaggy old dog snoring in his sleep.

"He calls me bird," she says, a wistful look in her ocean-blue eyes, "cause I fly in and fly out. I'm a travel agent. He'll say, 'Hey Bird, look at Mt. Tam. It looks beautiful today.' And I'll say, 'Hey, I never saw it look like that.' And I do that too. I carry him with me."

"How do you envision, that first day or that first weekend after Don gets out?"

"It's probably going to be a Tuesday. I'm going to have a bunch of food. I'm taking that whole week off, and it worked out perfectly. The following week, my boss is going to be gone so I'll have to work, but that first week, nothing's happening so I'm taking it off.

"I'm not asking him a lot of questions. I'm not asking him what he wants to eat or what he wants to do. I'm saying dinner's ready, not did you have a particular thing you want to eat. I think he's going to be so overwhelmed. It reminds me of my mother. 'Sit here. You're going to have this.' As he calms down and gets used to things, if he says, 'I'd like some barbecue chicken.' Okay."

Sitting there listening to Kathleen talk about her dreams for the future, I wonder aloud if she ever thinks about the fact that Don committed murder.

"The only reason I can deal with the crime is it wasn't a sick crime," she says. If it was really a sick crime, if it was rape or something, I couldn't handle that. I could not. But he was addicted to cocaine. I'm not saying Don wasn't wrong. He was totally wrong and to have a gun, that was just plain stupid. That's what got him. But it's like I can understand it. I can get past it."

It's time for me to go. Tomorrow's a big day. As we get up from the table, Kathleen says, "Don can help other people. We're getting into our golden years now, and I kind of look at things and say, 'what have I done for other people?' Well, Don is possibly saving lives and preventing guys from going to prison, and I love that. He's leaving his mark. Even though he is very quiet, he's planting the seed of Christianity. If we lead our lives as Christians, it's a good example for other people. He's living by example."

I start calling Sam at ten the next morning. "Have you heard anything?"

"No," he says, sitting at his office phone, thirty feet from the fax machine. "Nothing yet. I'll give you a call."

"Promise?" I plead, hoping he hears clearly the realization that once this moment has passed, it can never be recaptured. "I really want to be there when Don gets word. I'm just fifteen minutes down the freeway over the bridge. I'm waiting for your call."

By four fifteen in the afternoon, I'm jumpy. There's been no call. Without waiting another minute for the phone to ring, I get in my car, drive to the prison, park, and take a seat on the bench just outside the East Gate. Whatever happens, I'll have a better chance of being there if and when the fax comes, if I'm sitting here.

At four fifty, I use my cell phone to call Sam. "I'm here. Outside the East Gate."

"Come on down," he says. "I'm in the warden's office."

Did the fax arrive? Does he know? The guard at the gate waves me in and I all but run down the frontage road, turn up the sloping cement walkway to the front door of the warden's office, pull open the outer glass doors, and enter the inner door. The only sounds are the staticky prison walkie-talkie and the tick-tock of the clock's swinging pendulum on the wall. I walk toward Sam, who is sitting alone at the secretary's desk closest to the warden's inner office. Lying on the desk facedown in front of him are some papers.

"How you doing?" Sam asks, looking up at my face, a half-melting Popsicle in his hand. "Do you want to know, or do you want to be surprised?"

I stare at Sam, speechless.

"Do you want to know?" he repeats. "Or do you want to be surprised?"

I don't know what to say.

"Do you want to know?" he repeats, this time more serious. "Or do you want to be surprised?"

"Oh my God," I say, looking down at the papers in front of him.

"Uh-hum," he says, a soft confirmation, sucking on the Popsicle.

"Did it just come?" I fumble with my recording machine, turning it on.

"About an hour ago," Sam says into the microphone, "we received the notification from the warden in regards to Mr. Cronk's Board of Parole Hearing in which the board granted him parole. The governor has, um, reversed the board's decision." He hesitates for one, two seconds. We look at each other. "And at this time, we'll be going inside and delivering the news to Mr. Cronk."

"Can I see what the letter looks like when they reverse?" I ask. "I've seen a 'decline to review.'"

Sam hands me the multiple-page letter from the governor. It's on Schwarzenegger's official letterhead but is signed by his legal affairs secretary, Louis Mauro. I quickly skim and there, halfway down the page, in the second paragraph, "After considering the same factors considered by the Board, the Governor has invoked his authority to *reverse* the Board's decision to grant parole in your case." The word "reverse" is even underlined.

I hand the letter back to Sam. He rolls it up into a tube.

"God. I—I don't know. My face is not a good face," I mumble to him as we walk out of the warden's office and head for the sally port. "I don't lie well. . . . "

"I know," Sam says. "That's why I was saying, 'You want to know or you . . . want to be surprised?'"

ten

REVERSALS

APRIL 2008

It's just after five p.m. by the time we enter North Block. The eight hundred–plus inmates are still locked up for the afternoon count. If we hurry, Sam can deliver the news before the tiers open for dinner.

Stepping over the portal and into the massive cell block, it seems quieter than I remember. I walk next to Sam, the sound of his hard-soled shoes hitting the pavement, heel-toe, heel-toe, like percussion, carrying us down the west end of the first tier, then up the metal stairs, second tier, third tier.

Sam remembers my recorder. "We're walking down to 371, which is Mr. Cronk's cell," he says, his quick footsteps echoing as they slap against the cement of the third tier. As we pass by the cell doors to our right, faces pressed against the mesh covering the doors flash by like houses from a moving train. Maybe if they can get a quick glimpse of the paper, they'll be able to tell. If Sam is carrying a single sheet of paper, it's good news. It only takes one page for the governor to let a man go. It takes two or more to explain why he's reversing the board's recommendation. It may be the first time Sam is delivering the news, but he knows. If he rolls the papers up, no one can split-second tell how many pieces of paper are in his hand.

"Hello?" I hear a voice call out, strained.

"Mr. Cronk?"

"Yes." Like all the other cells, it's hard to see through the thick black mesh to the inside. Standing next to Sam, looking in, I can just make out the shadow of Don's body as he climbs down from his bunk and places his hands on the steel mesh covering the bars.

"How are you?" Sam asks, his voice moderate, calm.

"I don't know," Don responds, his voice anxious—weak from months and, now, hours of waiting. "I've been sick to my stomach all day."

"Well, here's the word," says Sam, his voice dropping with "word." He unrolls the multiple sheets of paper and slowly, carefully slides them one at a time through a narrow crack at the top of the cell door.

"Here's the word," Don repeats in his cage as he reaches up to grab the sheets of paper. "Well, I can tell because it's too thick." He holds the paper up to the little bit of natural light passing into the cell to read the governor's word. "Yep. Yep. He took it away. I knew it would be after it didn't come early. Yeah. What can you do? But I thank you for coming by."

Sam is careful not to say anything that would give the news away. It's up to Don to share the news with those in earshot when he's ready.

It's quiet as Don turns the papers over in his hands. "Nancy, how are you?"

"All right. How are you?"

"I'm disappointed. Very disappointed. But what are you gonna do, you know?"

"Want me to leave you alone?" I ask.

"Well," Don says, "maybe. Maybe. Just because, it's just been . . . If I had found out early this morning, it would have been . . . But we've been all but throwing up all day and the later it got, the worse I knew the news was, so. Maybe after the weekend's over, something."

Sam and I stand stone-still outside the cell as we watch Don try to read over the papers in his hands. But the papers keep rolling up in his shaking hands.

"So," Don continues, "I'll have to sit down and read this and study it and figure it out. Thank you for not letting me hang all weekend and pine about it. I don't get it but I can't give up. I have to go on and just do the best I can. Try again next year."

Sam leans close to the cell door and murmurs, "I gave Pastor Curry a call, and he's on his way in."

"That's not necessary," Don says, his voice breaking. "I just want to be left alone."

"He wanted to be here," Sam says.

"I really just want to be left alone. Sit with it and pray with it for a while. I'm thinking of Kathleen. I'm just heartbroken for her. Heart-broken. But we'll get through it. We'll make it. Yeah. I'd like to read this and read the lies and start working, get it to my attorneys and get that process going. Thank you. Thank you. I'm sorry I'm not more together."

"I'll see you next week," I say.

"I'm sorry," Don calls back. "I'm sorry it's denied. It really doesn't make much sense."

Listening to his words, I remember what he told me months ago, about inmates who don't make it—about minds that give up after ten, fifteen, twenty years. He's been in here for twenty-seven.

As Sam and I back away from Don's door, Pastor Curry approaches from the end of the tier, his steps quick, anxious. "I just got the call. Guess I'm too late. I wanted to get here before he got word."

"What's this like for somebody? For Don to receive this news?" I ask Curry.

"It's devastating. It's totally devastating," Curry says, keeping his eye on Don's cell door. "It's almost like dying. That's all I can say."

With that, the large black minister steps past us, approaches Don's cell door, and places both hands, palms outstretched, high up on the mesh. What can he say to comfort him? As he murmurs, he leans in, his nose touching the black steel of the door.

Just as the silence settles in, there's a loud *thunk.* An officer at the end of North Block's third tier has pulled the steel bar blocking all of the doors. It's time for dinner. One by one, the cell doors stringing along the tier swing open. Out of the sealed holes of their cells, men step out, blinking their eyes to adjust to the light. Moving in single file, all in the same blue, they shuffle past us toward steps that will take them down to the bottom of the block and out to the cafeteria.

Sam and I move all the way back against the railing. I can't help but stare as the men pass by. They have gray hair and gray beards. Their eyes are sunken, their faces emotionless. Some look up, catch a glimpse of Sam and me, and then just as quickly drop their eyes back down, nodding a slight greeting.

"Do you think Don will go to dinner?" I ask Sam. "Should we wait a minute before leaving?"

Sam looks over. "Here he comes."

Just as the last of the men on the tier pass by, Don steps out of his cell and files into the slow, shuffling line. I don't know whether to look at him, try to make eye contact, or look away out of compassion. No time to decide. In a matter of seconds, he is right in front of us. He looks altered. The self-confident posture of the past few months has evaporated. His shoulders are curved forward, his eyes dull, his face shiny and pale.

I'm sick to my stomach. It may have been the closest Don Cronk will ever get to being free.

Sam and I turn and make our way back out of North Block to the sally port. As we pass officers standing outside Four Post, the guard station halfway between the chapel and North Block, Sam gives subtle signs. The officers register, lower their heads, even shake them slightly, and go back inside their shack. Standing outside the warden's office, I ask him, "Now that you've delivered your first fax, what was it like?"

"Well, now that my first was a reversal, I'm bad luck. The guys will think I deliver reversals."

"But you thought Don was going home, too," I say in a not-so-professional voice. "You said so."

"Is that thing on?" Sam asks, staring at my hot microphone. "I'll talk if you turn it off."

I reach down. Sam watches as I slide the red button. I lift my recorder to show him the light is dark. He takes a deep breath. For the next hour, Sam and I talk off the record, a reporter and a prison lieutenant hashing it out, trying to make sense of what just happened. It wasn't what either of us expected. Maybe we both bought into Don's confidence and began to believe he was the one, one of the 15 percent of the 4 percent of the 7,000 lifers who went before the board that year and whom the governor was going to set free.

Now Don isn't going home to Kathleen. He isn't going to do the things he saw on television. The telephone ring in the middle of the night wasn't a sign that God was watching over him. It was just another nightmare.

"It's huge," Eddie Ramirez says, sitting at his dining room table when I go to him to process the news. "I remember the first time I was given a date. I had been in prison for twenty years and had gone before the board eight times. Governor Davis was in office, and he wasn't letting anyone go home."

"Even with a date, I wasn't excited," Eddie says, "because there was the potential to have it taken. I'd seen it done time and time again. I see how it destroys people when they get so excited. They're writing home. They're sending their things. Their families are on cloud nine. The kids and their wife are coming and then all of a sudden they get that letter from the governor slid in the cell door.

"It's like swimming to the surface," he says. "Have you ever been on the bottom of a pool, and you need air?"

I remember the last time I went too deep in a river.

"Well, doing a life sentence is like you've been living on the bottom of the ocean. It's cold. There's no air, no light. You've been holding your breath for so long, you've almost gotten used to it. Then, when you're found suitable, it's like for the first time you can see a glimmer of light way up on the surface of the water. So you start swimming to the surface toward that light. You can't go to the right or the left. The only way is to swim up.

"You see the glitter of the surface. You're almost there. Your lungs start to ache for air; the light gets brighter. You swim harder, with all your strength. You can't wait to take that first breath, but you don't know if you're going to make it in time.

"Then just as you're about to break through the surface, to get air, you feel a big hand on the top of your head and it pushes you back to the bottom of the dark pool. The bottom of the pool. You are out of air. That's what the 150 days are like when you are reversed by the governor."

The momentum for Proposition 89 all began back in 1983 with a man named William Archie Fain—although, strictly speaking, it could be traced all the way back to 1967, the year Fain shot and killed a teenage boy and raped his two female companions. The court found him guilty of first-degree murder, rape, and other crimes and sentenced him to death, a capital sentence that was ultimately thrown out by the courts. There was a retrial and the jury returned a verdict with a sentence of seven years to life.

In 1976, a decade after he went to prison, the California Parole Board (then called the Board of Prison Terms) found Fain suitable for parole, but after public outcry, the board found an error in Fain's release date and reset it for 1983.

Then, in 1982, after he had served fifteen years there was another public outcry about his impending release the following year, and the board took away his parole date. His attorney, Robert Bell, challenged that rescission, and a superior court judge agreed with Fain's attorney and reinstated Fain's parole date for April 26, 1983.

The state appealed that superior court decision to the state court of appeal, and in January 1983, the state court of appeal agreed with the superior court judge and remanded the case back to the board for further review stating in *In re William Archie Fain on Habeas Corpus* (1983) 139 Cal. App. 3d 306, "It is within the power of the people, acting in accordance with the Constitution, to define offenses, establish sanctions, and fix the procedure by which determinations of guilt and punishment are to be made. It would offend our most basic concepts of justice, however, if the decision of guilt or innocence of the accused, or the length of his sentence, were allowed to depend upon public reaction in a particular case. As the trial court put it, 'Unlike the Roman circus, where the roar of the crowd would determine the life or death of the gladiator, our community cannot survive without rules, and whether the object of the justice system is the best of us or the worst, those rules must apply fairly to all.'"

In February 1983, two months before he was to be released from prison, the parole board conducted another review and found that, aside from public outcry, there was no basis for keeping Fain in prison.

But just twenty-one days before he was to be set free, Governor George Deukmejian issued an executive order suspending Fain's release date and ordering the board to keep Fain in custody while he made a gubernatorial decision about Fain's "suitability for parole." But the state court of appeal again stepped in and said the governor had gone beyond his powers and he did not have the authority to take a parole date away. In a majority opinion, Justice P. J. Kline wrote in *In re William Archie Fain on Habeas Corpus*

(1983) 145 Cal. App. 3d 540, "Since there is no statutory authority for the Governor to grant or withhold a parole release date, neither is there any such inherent authority for him to rescind such a date. . . . Accordingly, an executive order suspending a prisoner's parole release date was in excess of the Governor's jurisdictional authority."

On September 30, 1983, the state supreme court denied a rehearing and Fain was released from prison, never to return again.

But the stage was set. Governor Deukmejian then sought the authority to reverse parole that the California state Constitution and the state penal code had denied him.

Among the few publicly opposing the amendment was Father Paul Comiskey, a Roman Catholic priest and general counsel for the Prisoners' Rights Union, the American Civil Liberties Union, and the California Probation, Parole, and Correctional Association. Comiskey remembers, "I heard this thing was going to be on the ballot, and the secretary of state was looking for people to submit arguments. I signed up. I was very aware of the big fight that had happened about prisoners being granted parole, and I knew for a governor, there was no upside to letting a prisoner out."

Now semiretired and living on a lush farm east of Sacramento, Comiskey says that in 1988 he was concerned passage of Prop 89 would "politicize decisions about whether to grant or deny parole. I could just see what was going to happen: that they were going to appoint a very conservative parole board, and even if [a lifer] got a date, if it turned out to be unpopular, the governor would reverse it."

At the time, Comiskey argued that even if Prop 89 passed, it wouldn't have changed what happened with Fain. "The convict's release date had been set by the parole board years before Deukmejian became involved in the controversy, and Proposition 89 would have given the governor only thirty days to reverse the decision from the day the release date was set." In other words, Deukmejian wasn't there when the board made its decision, so the thirty days the governor had to reverse the board had long since passed. With or without Proposition 89, Fain would have paroled.

Nonetheless, Prop 89 did not encounter much opposition. Government officials blithely shot down Comiskey's and other critics' concerns. Robert Patterson, executive director of the Board of Prison Terms, is reported by the *Los Angeles Times* as saying prior to the election, "The board feels that the governor has a right to review the board's work, and I think the board feels the governor will approve of the actions taken by the board. I don't think he'll ever have to use this law."

Patterson was wrong, as the inmates on the North Block and in prisons throughout the state know all too well. "In the prison system right now," Comiskey says, "there are a lot of people who have no hope of getting out."

In fact, twenty-two years after the passage of Proposition 89, a person serving a life sentence with the possibility of parole in California has a greater chance of dying in prison than of ever getting out of prison on parole. According to a June 2011 document issued by the California Department of Corrections and Rehabilitation, from January 1, 2000, to May 31, 2011, 674 prisoners serving sentences of life with the possibility of parole for first- or second-degree murder were released from prison on parole. Over the same eleven years, 775 died in prison, waiting to be paroled.

I ask Bill Sessa, press spokesperson for the California Department of Corrections and Rehabilitation, to estimate the average sentence for a lifer in California prisons. He says, "Nancy, the average sentence for a prisoner serving a life sentence with the possibility of parole in California is death."

Thinking he must have misheard my question, I ask again: "What's the average time they will serve?"

"Death," Sessa says over the phone. "So few are getting out, most lifers will die in prison before they get out on parole."

Joan Petersilia, professor of law at Stanford University and a national expert on parole, adds, "It seems to me that if we were never going to let people out on parole, we should have never sentenced them to life with the possibility of parole. Our system in California is,

I feel, almost illegal. The truth is, in reality, they never get out. That's not truth in sentencing! I think it is about retribution through a back-end process. These parole board members keep revisiting the sentence. That is not their job."

Vanessa Nelson, a reform activist who campaigns with the Life Support Alliance, agrees: reversing a parole date of a rehabilitated lifer given the possibility of parole in his sentence is an act of retribution, not justice. "Grief and bitterness and vengeance can eat you alive, and it's eating our society alive right now, financially and in every other way. . . . We can't let this continue. Even if we could afford to do it fiscally, which we can't, we cannot as a society continue to do this."

She brings up an element to this debate that few in California or the nation consider: longer sentences, unfairly difficult paroles, and burgeoning prisons aren't just a moral stain on our landscape; they're a financial catastrophe. Thanks in part to longer sentences and reactionary laws, there has been a 500 percent increase in the US prison population in the past thirty years. In fact, the United States, with less than 5 percent of the world's population, has imprisoned nearly a quarter of all the prisoners in the world.

Today more than 2.4 million people in America are living in prison. One out of every eleven of these people is a lifer like Don. Each one costs state and federal governments between $30,000 and $100,000 every year in living, health care, and legal expenses, and the prisoners themselves cannot contribute to the national economy in any meaningful way. In 2010, Professor Bruce Western of Harvard University and Professor Becky Pettit of the University of Washington reported that incarceration reduces former inmates' earnings by 40 percent and limits their future economic mobility. Add that to their finding that one in every 28 children in America has a parent behind bars, up from one in 125 just twenty-five years ago, and the long-term, generational consequences of incarceration become apparent.

In 1977, the average California lifer sentenced to first-degree murder with the possibility of parole served 10.5 years, and 89.9 people per 100,000 were in prison. By 2011, the average lifer with the same sentence served 31 years, and 436 per 100,000 were in prison. Despite the staggering financial implications of these figures, some might look at these statistics with relief; a locked-up murderer can't commit more crimes, can he? At least lifers are safe away from the rest of the population. But the numbers tell a different story.

In fact people who once committed murder aren't committing murder again when they get out. They have had to demonstrate rehabilitation to extremely thorough and skeptical parole boards. And once released, according to state and federal statistics, they are the former prisoners least likely to ever commit another crime. Prison officials in San Quentin know who they'll see again, and it's not people like Don—it's people who committed less serious crimes like car theft, robbery, or rape, who aren't required to participate in any counseling or job training to get out of prison.

And that's the problem. California may seem like a dangerous place to live, but not because people who commit murder may have a slim chance of ever getting back out into society. It's the 120,000 prisoners serving *determinate* sentences who are released from the state's prisons each year with little to no rehabilitation and $200 in their pockets who are creating a public safety concern.

In 2009 alone, 18,594 parolees who were released from prison on a *determinate sentence* were returned to prison for committing a new felony—146 went back to prison for murder. That's twelve a month.

Of the 1,000 prisoners paroled by the State of California in the past twenty-one years who had served a sentence of *life with the possibility of parole* for murder, not one has committed murder again. Zero.

A few days after Don hears his news, once he's had a chance to regroup, I meet with him again. As Sam escorts me through the courtyard, I notice the red and yellow roses are in bloom . . . but where are the baby mallards? The last time I was inside, there were a dozen ducklings in the courtyard—adorable little puffs of yellow floating around after their parents. Birdman, as much a fixture of the courtyard as the fountain itself, had dug the babies their own little pool of water when the fountain was drained for maintenance.

Spying Birdman again, I ask, "So, what happened to the baby mallards?"

He looks up from his work tilling the dirt under a rosebush. His face, already longer and more riveted than most, is drawn. "See that hole in the wall up there?" he says, pointing to a milk carton–size opening under an eave. "Well, that's where the raccoons get in. I came out one morning this week, and twelve little hearts were left on the top of the fountain wall.

"I kept telling the guards to seal up that hole so the raccoons couldn't get in, but they wouldn't. Now they're all gone." He sighs, turning away. I watch as he lifts the hoe and goes back to loosening the dirt around the bush.

Sam is thrown. "I don't know what happened," he says, heading for the chapel. I follow, trying to imagine twelve little duck hearts on the low wall.

When we arrive, Don looks up from his desk and smiles wanly. He says now that Governor Schwarzenegger has reversed his parole, closing off one road, he is going to do whatever it takes to legally get out of prison. He has another option: appeal to the courts for parole. "I could have gone to the courts before and fought the board's denials, but now that I have been found suitable, I have a much better case going to the courts," he says, squaring his shoulders in determination. "The first step is to file a writ of habeas corpus in the state superior court."

In other words, Don must write to the Sacramento County Superior Court arguing that the governor reversed his parole without meeting the legal standard of having "some evidence" that if Don was released from prison on parole, he would be a threat to public safety. "My thinking is this," Don says. "A fellow gets found suitable, the governor says no. Then in a year's time you go back before the board again and sometimes they find you suitable, but many times they don't. I've seen multiyear denials after a suitability. So you run the risk of smearing the record. The record I'm taking to the court, that just happened, is the parole board finding me suitable, and the governor's letter. That's what you argue in court. If I exhaust all my remedies in court, then I will have to go back before the board, and I will. But right now, legally, I don't know if that's the right thing to do.

"It's difficult, but I'm learning something about human nature and myself. Survival kicks in, and we are resilient. Somehow I've now resigned myself. I just do it. I have lost some energy and some enthusiasm, but hopefully that will come back as well once I get my legal battle under way."

As I say my good-bye to Don that afternoon, I hope for his sake that his determination and hope are not just an act. Ever since Birdman told me about the ducks, I haven't been able to shake the idea that I'm watching a tragedy unfold. Things don't look so rosy anymore.

eleven

JESSE'S STORY

Hair Trigger

MAY–JULY 2008

Sam has alerted me. There is another lifer inside his 150 days. So I'm back inside San Quentin on a bright sunny Saturday morning in May, this time ostensibly to report on Native American spiritual practices inside the prison. A few weeks before, a group of imprisoned Indians invited me to observe one of their weekly sweats inside their reservation. I had no idea. Back in 1978, the US Supreme Court issued a ruling that religious protections extended to imprisoned Indians. Since then reservations, like the fenced-in park down on San Quentin's lower yard, have been created inside prisons, not always with the full backing of prison administrators.

Sam says out of respect for the reservation and the Indians, officers don't usually go inside the fenced-in area. "You'll have to go in without me," Sam says. "I'll wait for you on the other side of the fence. It's chain-link, so I can see everything going on. You'll be okay." I've heard that before.

An hour and a half after wiggling through the gap in the fence and watching in near silence as a dozen Indians strip down to their briefs and enter the searing heat of a wool-blanketed sweat lodge, Sam walks up to the fence. "Jesse is here, if you want to take a break."

Wiggling back out of the hole in the fence, a little disoriented from the heat of the lodge, I approach Sam and an inmate I've never met before: a lifer who is nearing the end of his own 150-day wait to hear from the governor about his parole.

Sitting on one of the too-small metal stools attached to the center post of a table at the edge of a dirt track, Jesse gets up to shake my hand. He's a black guy with a brilliantly disarming smile, kind eyes, and a light laugh. "Hi. I'm Jesse Lorenzo Reed."

I introduce myself and with limited time, get right to the point. I'd like to interview him about his crime, his time in prison, and his recent parole board suitability.

"Sure," he responds, followed by another warm laugh. "If Sam says you're okay, you're okay with me. What do you want to know?"

"Tell me about your time in San Quentin. When were you first incarcerated?"

"I first got incarcerated in 1985. I committed the crime in November of '84, and I landed here in San Quentin in June of '85. I stayed here until January 2 of '90. I transferred to Solano and came back here again June 5 of '95, and I've been here at San Quentin ever since."

"So '85 to '90, '95 to '08—you've been back about thirteen years?"

"That's right, thirteen years since I came back. A total twenty-three years incarcerated."

"Funny how time flies when you're having fun. . . . "

"Yeah," he says, this time with a laugh that's big, warm, and deep. "It's been a riot. It's definitely been a riot. It's had its ups and downs. San Quentin, though, if I were to choose a place to do time, it would be here. Still the heartache of being locked up, locked away from family and people who care about you. Waking up every day behind these walls, however, what makes this a place to do time, if you have to do time, is the fact that you have all the programs you have here and the people you get to meet. It's not like any other institution you can go to within the system, so that makes it okay."

"Where did you grow up?"

"I was born in Texarkana, Arkansas, in 1959. I was there until around the age of nine or ten, when I came to California with my grandmother. She had moved to California, but she would come back to visit, and I loved my grandmother and, for country kids, California was the place to be. Everybody wanted to come to Hollywood, so my grandmother brought my brother and myself with her."

"How many children in your family?"

"Okay, let's see. At that time there were four of us. There are nine now. My father died in 2001, so my mom and dad were together forty-some-odd years. I'm the oldest. I stayed with my grandmother a couple of years until my mother and father came. We resided in San Francisco, until we moved to Oakland, and I stayed there until I came to this place. Coming to California was a lot different than Texarkana. There we had our own gardens and pigs and chickens.

"Coming out here, you didn't have the big yard like we had in Arkansas. Everything was closed in, a lot less freedom. Living with my grandmother was a little easier." He laughs again. "It was a *lot* easier. My grandmother didn't discipline us as much as my mother and father. My mother and father believed in the 'spare the rod and spoil the child' kind of thing. My grandmother, she gave us money and we could go buy what we wanted. It was really fun hanging out with her. As far as I'm concerned, she was the best. She's passed and gone a few years ago, but Annie Paxton was my girl. She was really, wow. She was eighty-six when she died."

"What was your life like before your crime? You were how old when it happened?"

"Twenty-three, twenty-four. It was a struggle." Mentally doing the math, I realize the man sitting in front of me has spent half of his life in prison.

"It was bad," he says. "I had taken some bad turns in life. When I left high school, I had these great aspirations of being a professional football player. I was a pretty talented young man. I went to Laney College in Oakland after graduating from high school. Junior college. I wanted to go to a major university, but my grades wasn't up to par. Then, when I got there I didn't really want to go to school and do the work I should have been doing. I just wanted to play ball. I ended up leaving school, which I know was one of the biggest mistakes I made in my life, because after that was when my life started changing and spiraling downhill. I had a lot of little jobs that didn't amount to anything, and as a result I got into selling drugs and doing stuff that people who are misguided do. I thought it was a quicker way to make ends meet instead of . . . I seen my father working and he was a construction worker, a finisher. The hard work, 'I don't have to do it like that. I can make money over here. It'll be a little easier.'"

"Do you remember one particular 'uh-oh' moment?" I ask, holding my microphone steady.

"Not so much one particular moment as it was just knowing my life wasn't right. I wasn't raised like that, but I think I got to a place where I gave up on life. I felt like I was a slow student in school, and so it was a little struggle for me. At the time I just accepted that I was slow and this is one of the main reasons I left Laney College and didn't do the work I should have been doing. My pride wouldn't allow me to ask for a tutor or ask for help, so it was easier for me just to quit and walk away and accept less in life. I got to a point where I was really looking for help, a better way, and went to sign up for the Marines, to go into service. I did that, but I didn't pass the written test. The math portion. I don't tell a lot of people that. I really haven't told people that. I did it three times. They only allow you to take it three times. After the third time, when I didn't pass, it was, 'What's the use?'

"I gave up and decided to stay here in this world of selling drugs, you know what I mean? Bottom life. I didn't have any aspirations of working anymore. I just gave up. Things happened pretty quickly in the down-spiral thing. Hit rock bottom. Ended up going out one night to do a robbery and ended up shooting a man and killed him. That was the most horrible moment in my life.

"I think the sad part was that when I got arrested for this crime, it was sort of like a relief. It's over. I didn't like the way I was living at all. It was like a huge weight on my shoulders, and when that happened that night, I was lying in the county jail, and it was almost like a relief. I could get cleaned up, clean myself up. Get out of the trouble I was in."

Sitting in the sun out on the edge of San Quentin's yard, with prisoners walking by, slowing to catch a snippet of whatever Jesse is saying, I ask him to tell me more about the murder.

"Yeah," he says, his voice surprised by how much he has already said, "might as well. I was doing a lot of drugs, smoking cocaine and snorting heroin, and drinking a lot. I started using my product, the stuff I was selling. Ran out of money one night and decided to go do a robbery. Saw this guy who was soliciting a prostitute in West Oakland, what they used to call Ghost Town. I decided that we rob him. He looked like an easy target. You know, uh, someone that wasn't going to put up a fight. And everything went bad. Everything went bad. I had a .22 revolver that I, uh, had that evening—"

The sound of an officer on an intercom breaks in: "Attention on the yard . . . attention on the yard." We're sitting on stools with Sam, so without skipping a beat, Jesse continues.

"I had a .22 revolver that I had gotten from a friend and unbeknownst to me, the gun was faulty. When I pulled the gun on him, I didn't know if you cocked, pulled the hammer back on the gun, that with the littlest movement it would fire."

"Was he in a car?"

"He was sitting in a truck on the curb. There was a prostitute with him."

"Were they having sex?"

"I don't think they had started."

"I opened the car door and pointed the gun at him and cocked the hammer back on the gun to scare him, you know, and in the process of him reaching, trying to give me the money, the gun went off and, um . . . I just took off and ran. My brother was with me. I have a brother that's locked up as well. He's in Solano. We just ran. We just ran. We just ran.

"A week later I was arrested for the crime. I didn't know that the guy had died. My sister was reading the newspaper and she seen that some guy had gotten shot."

"You told your sister what happened?"

"She read the newspaper every day and she seen it. When she told me, I just laid on the floor in the living room the whole day and didn't come out. It was sickening, that I had taken somebody's life. It was a bad time. It was a really bad time."

By now Jesse's voice has slowly dropped lower and lower, like it is being pulled down to the ground.

"It's something I've had to live with and I'll have to live with the rest of my life, whether I'm in prison or out. I don't really like talking about it because of the memories it brings up and the person I was at that time. It's just a dark place in my life. One of the biggest regrets, my father died and I didn't get a chance to show him, that I could be the son that he raised me to be." His voice splinters like wood. "And, um, my prayer today is that I can show my mom and make her proud of me. That's what I live for now. That's my motivation to become better." He clears his throat, his voice gaining strength.

"I was determined not to leave prison the way I came in. One of the first things we did, my brother and I, when we came to San Quentin, was we learned how to program computers. And I got into data processing in '85 and I finished that course in '88 as a Computer Programmer I. At that time, I realized that I wasn't slow," he says, drawing the last word out, then snapping it closed. "I could learn and do anything I wanted to do if I applied myself. There were a lot of nights I had to stay up writing codes and programs. It was hard, but I was able to do it. That let me know, hey, you're not slow. You just have to apply yourself more."

In 1993 Patten University, a local Christian college, opened an extension program inside San Quentin offering college-level courses to inmates. In 1998, Jesse signed up. "I went back and got my associate of arts degree. I plan on getting my BA [bachelor's degree]."

He says he isn't married and doesn't have any children. "So if you get out, you'll go home and live with your mom?" I ask.

"She has her fingers crossed. This is my second round before the governor. I was found suitable for parole for the first time last year, and the governor took my date. She was crushed by that. The whole family, they had their hopes up, and that kind of crushed them. I think one of the hardest parts of this waiting period is the family." Jesse has to raise his voice to be heard over the officer's voice blaring over the loudspeakers on the yard. "Because while I'm here and I hear the stories and see the stories of men being found suitable and then the governor taking their dates, I know there's a possibility he can take mine. But my family, they don't understand that. Their question is always, 'Why? Why? Did you do something that caused that?' And I'm like, 'No. No, I didn't.'"

"Are you counting the days?"

"I don't count the days. I don't really want to count them. It seems it slows the time down, and you get too anxious. I thought I'd just let it happen this time. It's toward the end of June, but the exact date I'm not really sure of, whether it's the 23rd."

"I wonder if your mom is counting the days."

"I'm not sure."

"Would it be all right if I visited your mom?"

"Well, sure. Let me give her a call so she knows you're coming."

A couple weeks later, I pull up in front of Lois Parks house. When I called, she said she babysits her grandchildren, but if I came around two in the afternoon after her soaps were over, we could talk.

The worn two-story house sits on a residential street in the old part of Emeryville, the one part of the East Bay town that hasn't been revitalized into short stretches of live-work-spend lofts. A long, white, old-model Cadillac is parked in the driveway. Climbing up the two flights of stairs to the front door, I can see through the black mesh–covered security door that the inner door is open. I knock, ring the bell. "Hello? Hello?" I don't know if anyone can hear me over the seductive voices of the soap opera stars blaring on the TV. A minute passes, then Jesse's mom opens the door with Jesse's same wide, warm smile. "Hi!" she says, pushing the security screen door open and welcoming me into her home.

As I step inside the dim living room, a couple of toddlers walk up; another infant is crying. "How many grandchildren do you *have?*" I ask.

"Eighteen. He's the one I keep every day," she says, pointing to the toddler attached to her leg. "But I take care of these two on odd days. I have them from seven in the morning until eight at night. Full-time child-rearing."

I take a seat on the long cream-colored leather couch pushed up against the far wall and wait. She is moving through the living room to the dining room and into the kitchen. A few minutes pass. A couple of good-looking teenage boys appear at the top of some stairs that lead to rooms down on the first floor, take one look at me, grab something to eat, and head back down the stairs. Lois calls to them, asking if they've finished their work, then takes a seat on the couch next to me.

"So, how long have you lived here?" I ask, studying her face with its strong, carved features.

"I've been a proud homeowner for more than thirty years," she says, looking around the room. "We used to live a few blocks away. I was pregnant with DeAngela and needed to take a walk. And as I passed this house—it was just a small one-story then—I saw a for-sale sign out front. It had fruit trees and a white picket fence. I wrote the name of the real estate agent on a piece of brown paper bag. When I got home I called him. He was so nice. We couldn't really afford it, but he said he liked us and offered to make up the difference in the down payment. Said we could pay him back over time. And we bought it."

"So Jesse grew up here in this house?" I ask.

"We moved here when Jesse was going to middle school."

"What was Jesse like as a young boy?"

"Jesse was easygoing. Really nice. Always helpful, just good. He was one of my best sons. That's why it was so hurtful when all this situation came into play and this happened. I couldn't believe it. He was a hard worker and he was a chef cook at the Social Security building in Richmond. He did really good."

"Could you see it coming?"

"He should have stayed in college. His girlfriends pulled him away. We were always into church, as we've always been. His dad was a bishop in the church, an overseer. Jesse sang in the choir with his siblings. He still sings. I don't know if you've heard him sing, but he has a beautiful voice. He knew as a little boy that he was supposed to be a minister. But something happened and that didn't.

"Inside the prison walls he went to theological seminary and graduated from Patten, and he has been preaching inside the chapel of San Quentin. Worked with the Scared Straight program. Still doing what he was supposed to do but on the other side: singing, preaching, teaching. And so, I think that's good. You can knock a person over, but you can't lock their mind."

"What was he like when he first went into San Quentin?"

"A wreck. We were all a wreck. Jesse was—what's the word—crushed. Sorry. Repentant. That he allowed someone to get him into drugs. That's the reason why this thing came into play. But being sorry didn't help. When we all make bad choices in our lives, because for everything we do, there are repercussions. And he's paid a bitter price for what he's done. But the family of this young man [the victim] has really spoke up for him for the last ten years and has sent certified letters and everything saying that they believe he has done his time and he should have a second chance for freedom. In fact, the niece of the man Jesse shot lives two blocks away. She's a schoolteacher and she sent a letter last year for Jesse. So the whole family collectively is saying, together, 'It's time now.' Even though the parole board has said, 'Yes, he's coming home,' gave him a date. But our governor, Mr. Schwarzenegger, said no. If the Bates family can say, 'We forgive him, you should forgive him.' If his family can say it and they're the ones hurt the most, why is our system keep holding him in? I don't understand that. It's time. Who's playing God? Is the governor God? God is a god of second chances."

"Do you know the day he's going to get word this time around?"

"No. He doesn't want us to know this time," Lois says softly. "Last year, when he got close to his release date we planned a big block party. We were going to make a feast. Everybody's a good cook in our family, and I'm from the South. My grandmother taught me to cook everything from scratch. I can cook and can anything. But we were just so excited, and the day he was supposed to come home, we didn't hear anything. Then that Monday, the call came. There was lots of tears, saying he wasn't coming home. His counselor had went home early, and they didn't give him the message until Monday morning. His aunt cried for days."

A thin, wiry middle-aged man with a taut, childlike face walks into the living room. "My son Jayvonce," Lois announces. Before he turns and walks down the stairs to the bedrooms below, I can tell Jayvonce is drunk, or high on something, if not both.

"And so we were really crushed," Lois continues. "Jesse said one of the young men came and prayed with him. He said he had to regroup and that he was going to be okay. We believe because faith is the substance of things hoped for and the evidence of things not seen."

"After you got off the phone with Jesse, what was that like for you?"

"You have to give them a lift up. You have to encourage them, and that's what I did."

Lois's daughter DeAngela walks in carrying an infant. "That's my new great-grandbaby!" Lois says. "My grandson's baby. He's five weeks. I'm also raising two grandsons that my husband and I adopted before he passed away seven years ago. They're my grandsons and I'm their mom also. I'm busy. Very, very busy. I just made sixty-five, and I'm busy in the church, and I'm busy at home. I have a full life."

"What's it like waiting the 150 days again?" I ask. "He's been found suitable again by the Board of Parole Hearings. You're just a couple of weeks away from getting word."

"We're still going to have a block party," Lois says, her children nodding, moving around the room, anxious, like they can't sit still. "We're going to get a permit, and we're going to cook everything imaginable. His sister is going to come from Texas."

"Are you more cautious?" I ask. "Or are you letting yourself feel the anticipation?"

"Anticipation is great, but I'm not cautious in my faith," Lois says, her voice gaining the momentum of a preacher. "It's solid. Solid. How can you keep someone that's never been in trouble and that made a mistake, and there are people who have gone to prison and have willfully killed people, more than one person, and they are out and they are free? Our justice system is not what it should be. I've known people whose sons have killed people and they got big lawyers and those people did hardly any time at all. And this was an accident. Someone gave them a hairpin trigger, and if you shake it hard, it goes off. What they didn't expect to happen, happened. We can't bring their young son back and we couldn't retrieve our son."

DeAngela has been sitting in a chair, listening. "I was about six when he went to jail. I'm thirty now. It's been a long time. All the excitement and anticipation of him coming home and then the big letdown. Now with him preparing to come home again, it's like fear as well as excitement because you don't know whether it's actually going to happen this time or they're just pulling your leg again and it's not really going to happen."

I wonder. If she was six when Jesse was arrested, does she know him at all?

"I talk to him on the phone," DeAngela says, "but our relationship isn't what it should be. I've visited, but I haven't visited a lot since I've been an adult. I have a child and I have to keep up. I help my mom a lot. I'm looking forward to getting to know him better, to have that big brother that I didn't have growing up."

DeAngela looks like it has been hard. The seventh-born, she grew up always knowing her two eldest brothers were in prison. "It's not just the person paying for the crime. It's their family. It's their friends. It's everybody they came in contact with. Everybody that loves them. The thought of him being subject to prison every day, it's hard. It's a mental thing. It messes with your mind, but at the same time, it makes you appreciate your freedom and keep it."

After nearly an hour, Jayvonce returns, muddles around, moving this, touching that. Taking a seat on the couch next to me, he smiles, the thick smell of alcohol seeping from his pores. Now forty, he was an impressionable teen when his two oldest brothers went to prison. "I'm the oldest in their absence."

"So you've had to raise everybody?" I ask.

"Yes, and it's been a tremendous responsibility. After Jesse and Gregory's arrest, everything basically fell upon me to be the brother, the male matriarch of the family. It did devastate me because I needed them." His words slur, and the vowels run together. "I needed their support and it wasn't there. Then I lost my dad. I'm just glad I'm strong enough."

Looking around the room at the babies needing attention, the house creaking under the weight of providing transitional shelter to all branches of a wildly extended family, the outward signs of drug and alcohol addiction, I wonder: Does Jesse know?

"It was heartbreaking," Lois says. "Many, many sleepless nights. I want to run to him and hug him and love him and let him know how much I appreciate him. I just want to say, 'Welcome home, son.'"

Before Jesse gets word on his 150th day, I make one more trip back inside San Quentin to see his world, his job as a janitor in the old prison hospital, and his home, the cell he shares with Bobby Brown, one of the first inmates I met in the little room.

Walking up the tier with me and Sam, Jesse says he used to be on the first tier, but last July he moved to the upper tier. "It doesn't make much difference. All the cells are pretty much the same size: small. Too small for two individuals to be in." Opening his cell door, Jesse says he has the lower bunk: "The upper is too much climbing." One thing he misses about living on the first tier, though: guards keep the doors unlocked most of the day. On the upper tiers, they have to come up to "pull the bar" every time they open or close the cell doors.

"They used to give inmates keys so they could lock their cell doors, but that, like conjugal visits, was back in the old days," he says.

"Did you ever have a conjugal visit?"

"Yes, I did."

"Do you have kids?" I ask, surprised at a possibility I hadn't considered.

"No. No. I don't have any kids. I was married for a little while, and we would go on family visits, conjugal visits. It was really nice to be away from all the madness that goes on in here. Get away for a few days and just be. They were little apartments and to be with family and eat good food. Just enjoy each other's company for a couple of days. In 1996 they took family visits from us, so we haven't been able to enjoy that. But hey, I'm about to go home on a family visit."

Just before we walk back downstairs, I ask Jesse how it feels to be less than two weeks away from his second fax from the governor.

"It's a little, um . . . Still, I'm joyful. At the same time anxious. Still a little bittersweet thing, you know, until I get that final word when I can really let go and finally be happy. Until that day, it's really hard. And you got everybody asking, 'cause people have heard. 'You're gettin' close. You're gettin' close. Any word yet?' And I'm trying not to think about it. 'How many days you got left?' I'm not really counting. I don't want to count, 'cause it seems like the time slows down even more and it just drags on when you count the days.

"Butterflies. It's just, wow. It's hard to explain. It's really a form of torture. But at the same time, it's a wonderful feeling, and you wait for that opportunity and that time when you bust out in joy!"

It's time to leave. On my way out, I see Don standing outside the chapel. He raises his arm, waves. He was so close, and now, if I didn't know better, if I hadn't heard his story, looking at him I might think he's no different than the other lifers dressed in their blues and grays, standing around, doing time.

Four days later, on Tuesday morning, June 10th, 2008, the call comes from San Quentin. Jesse's parole has been reversed. He was told on Monday afternoon, the 152nd day. Like Don Cronk before him, Jesse will now have to wait six more months before he'll have a chance to go before the parole board again, with no guarantee he'll get another date.

Sam is taking some time off, so Lieutenant Rudy Luna is taking me in to meet with Jesse over at the prison hospital. A few minutes pass before we see him approach from far down the long corridor. Jesse is a big man. Now he walks slowly, his body leaning to one side. As he gets closer, I can see he doesn't look good. He tries to smile. It takes awhile to find a room in the labyrinth of halls and offices where we can talk, and we finally settle in a room up in the back on the second floor. I had no idea there were so many places to get lost in prison.

"Okay, Jesse, so not the best news."

"No," Jesse says. It hurts to hear his voice. "Not at all. It's discouraging."

"How did you find out?"

His head and body look puffy. "Sergeant brought me the fax from Sacramento about two minutes to six last night. I figured it was bad news when I heard them paging me over the loudspeaker in the building and I didn't see you or Sam Robinson, so I knew it was pretty bad. So . . . um."

"What'd it say?"

He takes breaths, pauses before speaking. "Basically that the governor reversed it and using the same issues as last year, because of the crime. Felt that the positive transformation, the things I've done while in prison, don't outweigh the crime itself. Same thing he said last year.

"While this is discouraging, my fight continues. Now I have to prepare to go back to the board again in six months, and at the same time file a writ in the courts. I have one filed in federal courts from last year so I'll be waiting on them. More than likely, I'll get relief from the courts, because the Ninth Circuit has already said the issues which the governor used to rescind my date, he's not supposed to use. He can't use the crime as 'some evidence' because it's an unchangeable factor."

"What about your family?"

His voice strains. "I was up literally all night. My mother just cried over the phone, and to me, that's the hardest part of dealing with this whole thing. While I understand the political issues here, she doesn't really understand. Her question is, 'Why? Why? Why? You've done everything you're supposed to do. What do they want from you?'

"That to me is the most hurting part of this whole issue, this whole game, so to speak. This political game we're faced with in here. I just don't see the fairness in that. I can understand myself having to go through this. But they shouldn't have to suffer like that. I just apologize to them for having to go through what they're going through because of me. I wish there was some way they didn't have to know. I could just call them one day and say, 'Hey! I'm coming home!' and they could get happy. But the parole officers have to go by when you're found suitable, and they get their hopes up.

"My position now is to continue to upgrade and take programs and if I have to go back to the board if I haven't gotten relief in the federal courts to present an even better case."

"Do you think it would make a difference if the governor met you face to face?"

"I like to think so. I think it would make a huge difference. It's not just on paper. You're not just reading a person's file, but you're getting in a personal relationship with that individual. When we as human beings sit down with one another, it's a big difference versus just reading something on a piece of paper.

"He could see me and see that I'm not the same person I was twenty-four years ago. That I have grown and I can be a productive member of society. I would like to think it would make a difference."

Jesse walks Luna and me down to the hospital entrance, a low, dark corridor connecting two cell blocks, to say good-bye. Before leaving, I turn and give Jesse a quick hug and wish him well. Suddenly the armed guards standing around watching begin to yell, "Contact! Contact!" I look at Jesse. His face is stone, frightened. I don't know what is happening. Jesse turns and quickly walks away, back through the hospital doors, past a phalanx of guards staring at him, and down the long hallway.

Turning away, Luna says, "You can't hug him! He could get in big trouble for that. He's been through a lot. They could write him up!"

"No!" I say in a panic. "I did it. He didn't."

"I'll take care of it," Luna says. "You can't have physical contact with inmates. Those guards are Ad Seg guys. They're hard core."

"Give me your word," I plead, "that he won't get written up." If Jesse does get written up for my action, he may never get another date for parole from the board again.

"You're not getting parole because you got hugged . . . ," Luna says, half a question, half laughing. "I'll take care of it."

twelve

BEAUTIFUL

AUGUST 2008

A month later, the land-line phone in my office rings. It's Lieutenant Messick. Even though he's no longer public information officer, he has followed my stymied attempts to tell the story of one lifer getting out of prison on parole. Now the prison's legal affairs coordinator, he calls with an inside scoop. "Nancy, I think I've got one for you," he says. "The California Supreme Court just issued an important ruling, and I just got word one of our lifers is going to be the first released in the state on the ruling. From what I hear, the attorney general's office isn't going to appeal a court of appeals ruling to release him to the supreme court, so he's getting out next week. Probably on Tuesday."

"What was the ruling?"

"It was a ruling in a case called *Lawrence*. You should look into it. This is big. It could change things for a lot of lifers. The inmate's name here at San Quentin is Phillip Seiler. Ask Sam about him."

Seiler. The name sounds familiar. Energetic guy, light brown hair, electric-blue eyes. Yes. He participated in a VOEG session (Victim Offender Education Group) I attended about a month ago.

The way the VOEG program works is a group of specially trained counselors and therapists works with the two sides of a crime and the devastating violence left in its wake.

On the outside they meet with survivors of crime to help them heal. On the inside they meet with the criminals who caused the pain and suffering.

Jacques Verduin, executive director of the Insight Prison Project, which sponsors the VOEG program, tells me, "What we find is that when the two ends of the violence, an offender and a victim, have been through months of individual and group counseling and deep psychological preparation, and we bring them together inside the prison to meet and talk, we have discovered that this meeting offers both sides a chance to reconcile the pain they hold in common and possibly heal. The survivor gets to tell their story, ask questions, and hopefully find some closure. The offender has the opportunity to see the pain actions like their own have caused, and if they choose to, to answer questions about their own crime and apologize.

"Victims do this for different reasons. Some of them are clear that they want to reach a state of forgiveness and put it behind them. For others it just might be, 'Hey, that was my loved one. I didn't know what the last moment was and as horrible as it may have been, I need you to tell me what that was like. If the inmate is ready, they'll tell the victim survivor. There's usually an eight- to ten-month preparation, visiting each of the parties separately and deciding if the place is reached where they can meet.

"My dad was a prisoner in WWII," Verduin continues, sitting in the office of his nonprofit, a few miles from San Quentin. "When the Berlin Wall came down, he went back to find his captors and make peace. He was in enforced labor. He used to scream in his sleep. When he went back and reconciled, he never screamed in his sleep again. It just so happens, that's our biggest program: the Victim Offender Education Group."

Verduin says it isn't always possible to have the survivor or victim meet with the person who committed the crime they experienced, and if that isn't possible, the organization tries to arrange for people to meet who have experienced similar crimes, to give the victims and offenders an opportunity to share their grief.

In July 2008, before attending a meeting of the Victim Offender Education Group, I had arranged to meet victims participating in the program on the outside. One of the victims I met, a woman whose son was murdered by his college roommate, had already met with a group of lifers in the VOEG program at San Quentin. Radha Stern said the process helped her not only heal but move beyond the pain so she could begin to live her life again. The other woman I met, Jaimee Karroll, said she had been kidnapped and sexually assaulted as a child. Now, years later, she had been through months of counseling and was preparing to go inside San Quentin to meet with lifers in the VOEG program. She invited me to join her.

The day of the session, Jaimee walked into the prison and down to the Education Center with Verduin. Fifteen inmates who had been preparing for the session were waiting for them in a meeting room. As they sat together in a circle, Verduin gave everyone a chance to introduce themselves before Jaimee began telling her story.

While she spoke, the men sitting in the circle listened quietly, intently. When Jaimee paused to catch her breath, a man with short, bristly light brown hair raised his hand. It was Phillip Seiler. He thanked her for sharing her story with them, and then, in a voice wobbling with emotion, said, "I can't help thinking what a brave and smart little nine-year-old girl." Another man in the circle asked her how she survived the crime. She took her time in answering. It seemed to me, watching from the sidelines, that they were looking back, together, to find something to ease the pain of the memory.

After finishing her story, Jaimee told the men she wanted to play a song written by Jesse Winchester called "Songbird." Pulling an acoustic guitar out of a hard case sitting near her chair, she began to strum and sing, her voice softly filling the prison room: "Poor bird who has done no harm, what harm could she do, she shall be my prisoner her life long." Some of the men began to cry. When she finished singing, Jaimee, Verduin, and the men held hands. There is nothing good about crime, but years, even decades later, after the dust has settled, there seems to be at least the hope of some kind of peace.

I call Sam Robinson on Friday morning, August 22, and leave a message. That's the way it is with prisons and media access: public information officers answer when they answer; they return your call when they return your call. Usually I try to be patient, but now I don't have time to wait. This is the moment I've been waiting for. A lifer is going to be released from a California prison on my watch. I'll try to reach Sam again Monday morning. Until then I research more deeply into *In re Lawrence* (California Supreme Court, August 21, 2008) and what could represent a seismic shift for prisoners serving life sentences with the possibility of parole for murder in the state.

Since the 1988 election, when voters gave the governor the power to reverse lifers' parole, state courts had been reluctant to overrule the governor, essentially seeing his authority to reverse a lifer's parole as the will of the voters.

It wasn't until 2000, twelve years after Proposition 89 was passed, that the courts for the first time issued a ruling gently limiting the governor's review. On April 27, 2000, the Second District Court of Appeal in Los Angeles decided in favor of a lifer in *In re Rosenkrantz*.

For more than a dozen years, attorney Keith Watley has represented prisoners serving life sentences in California. He says the district court's ruling, *In re Rosenkrantz,* "marked the first time in a very long time that a court was willing to strike down a board's decision and order relief for a lifer. The court ordered the board to go back and give Mr. Rosenkrantz a new hearing, which resulted in a grant of parole. The governor later reversed that parole grant." But Watley says the district court's 2000 decision "instantly energized lifers' efforts to secure their freedom. Thousands of lifers made their way into the courts to challenge unfair denials of parole by the board and reversals of parole by the governor."

Rosenkrantz then appealed the governor's reversal of his grant of parole by the board, and on December 16, 2002, the California Supreme Court issued a ruling limiting the scope of a lifer's relief in state courts. The court ruled that the board or governor can rely solely on the circumstances of a prisoner's crime to deny him or her parole, as long as the board or the governor can identify *some* aspects of the crime that might fit within the description in the parole regulations of an "especially heinous, atrocious, or cruel" crime.

"Since the board was already describing every crime as 'especially heinous, atrocious, or cruel,'" Watley argues, "this seemed to put a stamp of approval on that practice."

Then, on January 24, 2005, the California Supreme Court issued its most restrictive ruling on lifer parole. In *In re Dannenberg,* the court repeated what it had said in *Rosenkrantz* in 2002: that the crime alone could be an acceptable reason for the board to deny parole or for the governor to block a prisoner's release. But the new decision went another step, holding that as long as the board or the governor's decision was based on protecting public safety, then it did not matter how long the prisoner was incarcerated.

"Taken together," Watley says, "*Rosenkrantz* and *Dannenberg* touched off a battle among the state's superior courts and appellate courts. Some courts interpreted the supreme court's decisions to say that as long as the board or governor could point to *any* evidence in the record that might support a factual finding that the inmate posed a current risk to public safety, the decision not to parole had to stand. Other courts believed that such a strict view would prevent many lifers from ever being released, because parole decisions were being based on facts from the past that would never change. This later view finally prevailed and gave rise to *In re Lawrence.*

On August 21, 2008, the California Supreme Court ruled in a landmark 4–3 split decision that, by itself, the seriousness of a prisoner's crime is not enough to justify denying parole. Instead, the court said that there must be some *current evidence* to show that the prisoner remains dangerous. "In other words," Watley says, "prisoners with strong records of rehabilitation, who have demonstrated that they could safely be released, must be granted parole, even if their crimes were really bad."

By Tuesday morning, August 26, three business days after the supreme court issued its ruling in *Lawrence,* I still haven't heard from Sam. I have, however, found and contacted Phillip Seiler's attorney, Michael Satris. Satris isn't just any postconviction attorney. For more than twenty-five years he has earned a reputation for representing, oftentimes successfully, the "liberty interest" of lifers incarcerated in state prisons.

I drive north on the freeway fifteen minutes to catch him at the Marin County Juvenile Court before he heads in to try a case. I find a parking space in a crowded lot and follow anxious parents accompanied by suited attorneys to the courthouse door.

A uniformed guard puts his hands up. "Excuse me, Miss. You can't bring that recorder in here." He points to the tape deck hanging from my shoulder and the microphone I'm gripping in my hand.

"Do you know Michael Satris?" I ask, explaining that I don't want to record anything happening in the juvenile court but that I'm trying to find the attorney for an interview.

"I don't know if he's here, but you can't bring that thing in here. You'll have to wait outside."

I take a seat on a small bench outside the single-story, cement-block building and wait for Satris. Five, ten, fifteen minutes pass before my luck turns and a rugged man wearing a rumpled, dark blue tailored suit and carrying a worn leather briefcase appears on a walkway connecting the parking lot to the courthouse. "Excuse me, are you Michael Satris?"

His face brightens. "Yes, but I'm late."

"I'm Nancy Mullane," I say in a rush. "I'm working on a story for National Public Radio about the supreme court's ruling in *Lawrence.*"

He slows his beeline to the court door and turns his tanned, Marin County face toward mine. I've caught his attention. "Your secretary,

Sabine, said you might have a minute to speak with me about Phillip Seiler," I say. "I've been told he's getting released on *Lawrence.*"

He says yes, and I beg him to talk with me for a minute about the court's decision.

"What *Lawrence* was, was the executive, the governor in the state, acting unconstitutionally, as is their regular practice in these parole consideration hearings," Satris says. "In Phillip Seiler's case, he got a parole date from the parole board because it was clear in all ways that he was suitable for release and would not pose a danger. They rarely grant a parole date under those circumstances as it is. He was one of, basically, the cream of the crop.

"The governor reversed Phillip's parole, but the trial court sent it back to the governor, saying you have no basis to deny or reverse parole on these grounds. And, uh, the governor basically issued another decision where he basically reiterated what he said before: 'Solely because of the facts of the crime, I find that you would be a risk twenty years later.' The trial court again said, 'No, I told you before that you acted unconstitutionally denying him parole on the basis of the crime. I'm not going to send it back to you again, because it's clear you're unable to follow the law, or in this case at least, and so I'm going to order him released.'

"The state appealed this order, and the court of appeal stayed the trial court release order until they determined the appeal. Then the only issue was whether the state was going to seek action [appeal the state court of appeal's order to release Seiler] by the California Supreme Court. So they [the state, the prison] were continuing to hold him in custody pending that determination. And right in their ten-day period that they had to act to file in the supreme court, a decision came down from the California Supreme Court that said basically, 'The governor cannot reverse a parole grant on the facts of the crime when that's the only facts, uh, that he's relying on to conclude that the person is a danger when it was so long ago and so many things have happened,' and such reform and rehabilitation and it was showing that it was the kind of crime that was the product of stress.

"On that basis, the state gave up and realized they had no basis to seek review. The court sent a message to the governor of fundamental fairness. They said, 'Look, Governor, you can't raise the banner of public safety as a basis to deny a prisoner release on parole when he has shown through reform and rehabilitation and age and maturity that he is no longer a threat.'"

"Do you think any others will benefit from the supreme court's ruling last week in *Lawrence*?" I ask.

"Yes. There's a handful of cases where before the *Lawrence* decision, the state sought review by the supreme court, and the supreme court granted review and put the cases on hold while it decided the *Lawrence* case. Two of those cases concern my clients and they fit firmly within the guidelines of *Lawrence,* and I expect when the court acts, it will result in their release."

"So, this is a good day for lifers in California?" I ask.

"It's a good day. Phillip Seiler is getting out of prison."

I wonder how the state feels about this turn of events, so I track down Julie Garland, senior assistant attorney general in the Criminal Law Division of the California attorney general's office. She supervises the attorney general's correctional writs and appeals section and argued *Lawrence* on the governor's behalf.

Garland tells me that despite the disappointment of losing, arguing *Lawrence* before the California Supreme Court was "a great experience. It was probably one of the highlights of my legal career so far. There was a lot of expectation about it from our end, our clients, the governor, and the Board of Parole Hearings. In this case, it was a governor decision that was at issue, so I was officially just representing the governor in this case. But we knew the outcome would affect the board as well." I find it interesting that as assistant attorney general for the State of California, Garland represents both the parole board and the governor—two entities whose decisions could be at cross purposes in lifer parole decisions.

"How would the decision affect the board as well?" I ask. "The parole board's decision wasn't really at issue. It was more the governor's reversal of the board's decision that was at issue."

"Right, but we knew we were asking the court to clarify the standard of review that would apply to executive branch parole decisions," she says. "So we knew that the standard the court adopted here would be something the board would be held to as well."

"So what was the argument for the governor? What were you arguing before the supreme court?"

"Our argument was based primarily on separation of powers. We felt that judicial review needed to respect that separation between the executive and judicial branch, and the standard of review that the court of appeal had applied in Ms. Lawrence's case did not respect that separation and really took it out of the hands of the governor and decided her suitability."

"And this goes back to 1988 and the initiative that gave the governor the authority to override any parole board decision," I say. "That's what the people of California voted for?"

"Correct," Garland says, as if to end the interview right there.

"But the courts have been increasingly split on this, whether to back the governor or not, because the board has been deciding one way and the governor reversing it. It must have been hard to argue."

"Because the board decided one way and the governor decided the other?" Garland asks. "Well, the board and the governor are two separate decision makers. The governor's decision is independent of the board's, and the supreme court in the *Rosenkrantz* case in 2002 held that it's just fine that the governor can disagree with the board, be more strict or cautious than the board, and so there are often differing opinions and they take different things into consideration."

"Since 1988 the board has been more conservative, finding fewer lifers suitable for parole," I say, trying to hold my own with this attorney, whose job it is to argue the thinnest slivers of the law. "But the governors—Wilson, Davis, and Schwarzenegger—have overturned something like 90 percent of the parole grants, or even higher. So who decides? In '88, the people of California decided we want the governor to decide in the case of murder, but then the governors started reversing so many parole decisions that it seemed like the courts have begun acting as a balance to the governor's decisions. Do you think the courts saw this opportunity in *Lawrence* as a correction?"

"It's hard for me to say. It certainly is possible," Garland says. "There have been more adverse decisions against the governor in the past couple of years than prior to that. It's a bit ironic because this governor [Schwarzenegger] has approved a much higher percentage of parole grants than probably the previous two governors combined."

"Do you feel the court made a bad decision?" I ask. "It was a 4–3 split decision. It wasn't an overwhelming ruling against your case. Are you concerned about the impact of the court's decision?"

"I'm not sure what the impact's going to be yet." Garland says. "I don't know whether we should be concerned or not. We were certainly disappointed. We feel the dissent really understood our argument and respected our argument and respected the separation of powers more than the majority did. We were certainly hoping the majority would go along with what the dissent said, but we were just one judge short of that. That's a bit tough to handle. As far as the impact, I really think we'll have to wait and see."

I nod and throw her another question. "One of the issues that was brought up in this case before the supreme court was whether or not the governor's decision to reverse the board's grant of parole was supported by "some evidence" the inmate remained a current threat to public safety. That he or she, whoever is serving as governor, can't just say that the original crime, however long ago it was, is enough justification for denying or reversing a parole decision. Now the governor needs to include some evidence of the current state of the prisoner's status. Is that the crux of the decision?"

"What the court focused on was that the governor's findings need to relate to the *potential* dangerousness of that inmate if he or she were released tomorrow. And that's what the governor does already!

He looks at the whole inmate: his crime, his in-prison conduct, pre-prison conduct, attitude, demeanor, parole plans. The whole picture. What I think the change is: now the court can look at that big picture and come up with potentially a different conclusion about whether that means the inmate will be a danger.

"The courts have always had the power to overturn a decision if they felt it violated due process. What the court changed to some extent, although the majority said it didn't change *Rosenkrantz,* was that what they're looking for as far as the 'some evidence' is not the objective sort of factual accuracy of the decision, it's more of a subjective conclusion the governor made and whether the evidence supports that subjective conclusion. So it's possible the court's subjective conclusion about it will be different than the governor's. Before, courts really weren't authorized to second-guess the governor's conclusion. The way I read the decision, there'll be more."

"Do you think this will in any way make the public in the state less safe?"

"I hope not," Garland says, her voice dropping. "I really don't know how to answer that."

Garland's feelings about the ruling may be mixed, but for thousands of lifers locked up in California prisons—and men like Messick, who've watched their struggles for decades—*In re Lawrence* seems to signal an end to the practice of governors reversing nearly everyone's parole dates. Twenty years after the voters of California gave the governor the authority to single-handedly take a lifer's parole date, the state supreme court has checked that power. And for Phillip Seiler, the ruling hasn't come a minute too soon.

thirteen

PHILLIP'S STORY

Crazy Hot Day

AUGUST 2008

The day Phillip Seiler gets out of prison, he doesn't have time to shave in his cell. After twenty years and thirty-four days, he has run out of time. Far below on the first tier, a guard has yelled up into the cell block, "Seiler! Roll it up!" That's prison lingo for "You're going home."

Phillip's cellie, the man with whom he has shared a thirty-six-square-foot cell, helps him carry the first of a half dozen cardboard banker's boxes down the twisting stairs that bookend the tiers to the bottom of the cavernous cell block. As they pile the tattered boxes on a metal dolly, each step Phillip takes is one step closer to his last in San Quentin.

If it was another day, the lifers of North Block would be standing outside their cells, patting him on the back, even following him out in a pack. But a few days before, Sam Robinson says, a prisoner got beaten up pretty badly. As a result, all the white prisoners have been put on racial lockdown and have to stay locked up in their double-bunked cells twenty-three hours a day until things calm down. A day, a month. Longer. That's the way it is.

Heading for the one open steel door at the south end of the cell block, Phillip glances over at the bank of old phone booths lining the wall. For most of his adult life, they have been his link to the world outside the walls. Now he won't have to wait his turn to make collect calls to his mom, his girlfriends, or his sons. He'll get a cell phone—a contraption that was bigger than a brick the last time he breathed free air.

Just before Phillip steps out of North Block, an officer standing at the far end of the tier bellows out, his voice bouncing and echoing its way down the cavernous walls. "Behave yourself," he says.

Phillip looks back down the long tier, smiles, and is gone.

Sam and I meet Phillip at R&R, Reception and Release. He's waiting for his parole officer to come pick him up. (Not all prisoners being released from California prisons have to wait for a parole officer to escort them out the prison gates to their first moments of freedom. Only men convicted of murder must do so.)

As we walk up to the front door of the mobile home–style R&R office, a bus full of new prisoners wearing bright orange jumpsuits has just arrived. Handcuffed, disheveled, the men tumble out of the bus and into a line where they blink in the sun as they survey their new world. The cycle begins anew.

Just inside the back door we see Phillip, standing at a small sink, shaving with a twinkle in his bright blue eyes. "How ya doing, man?" Sam says with a half chuckle.

"Rollin', man, rollin'," says Phillip, a contagious smile across his face. "Just shavin' and gettin' ready to go see my family and friends. They're all waiting for me at home. Got a little party for me."

He turns the tap, slaps his face with warm water, and lathers up. Carefully pulling a disposable razor over the stubble, feeling the results with his free hand, he looks out at the ever-present gaggle of wild geese scattered across the prison's yard. He stops shaving and smiles: not a little smile, but a massive, blinding grin. Then he lets out a laugh, his shoulders and his whole body shaking with an irrepressible anticipation. Watching, it's hard to measure what this moment means to this man. It's the golden ring. The lottery. It's winning something more precious than money. It's a second chance back out in a society that locked him away twenty years before.

From the other end of the trailer, an officer calls out, "Hey, Phillip, are you really getting out of here?"

"That's right," he yells back, turning to the window and laughing again, the sound echoing through the long trailer. Even for the guards, this isn't just another day inside R&R. Phillip pulls a paper towel out of the dispenser on the wall and wipes his face and chin dry. Turning to me, he asks, "Do I have any blood or shaving cream on me?"

"No. You did a good job."

Before walking back down the hallway, Phillip grabs another towel and carefully wipes around the sink area, making sure to leave it as clean as he found it. Opening the trash can, he pauses. There's no trash bag in it. He puts the wet paper towel back on the counter, reaches inside the short double doors of the cabinet beneath the sink, finds a trash bag, shakes it open, pushes it down into the can, drops the wet paper towel in, and closes the lid. Satisfied, he trips down the long hall.

"Have you said good-bye?" I ask.

"Oh yeah. Everybody's been saying good-bye. Lot of my volunteer friends have been coming by."

"How did you actually find out?" asks Sam.

"I found out the day before yesterday. My counselor came up with a piece of paper. It was just a small little fax. It was from the Board of Prison Terms to the warden, I think. It was, like, one line. I can't remember exactly what it said. The board was saying to release me. I couldn't believe it. My cellie said, 'Man, you're going home. You're going home.' I thought, 'Nah. They're going to appeal it. This is nothing.'

"I'm ready. I got tons of support out there. Family, friends, cars, jobs, places to stay. I'm fortunate. A lot of guys don't have that. But I spent these last twenty years keeping close connections and helping out in any way I can. I'm really fortunate that I got a lot of good people. A lot of people I knew before prison and a lot of people I met *in* prison. I'll be calling all of them."

Stepping back into the guards' office, Phillip takes a chair opposite the door. Placing his hands firmly in his lap, he is ready to go.

Phillip says he knows from observing the few lifers who have left San Quentin over the past twenty years that he has anywhere from a few minutes to a few hours to wait for his parole officer to come to drive him home. Until he sees the parole officer's car, he says, it will be difficult to believe it's really happening—there have been so many false stops and starts over the years. But if all goes as planned, he will go with the officer to a parole office, hear the conditions of his parole, and then drive with the officer to his parents' place, where he'll live for now.

"Then what?"

He takes a deep breath. "Well, my girlfriend is going to be there. She's waiting for me. So, that's all I'll say." A little mischief escapes from the corner of his smile. "Then just connecting with family and taking it easy. I don't drink. I don't use drugs. I don't get into drama. I've got tons of support out there. They [the state] made a good choice. And they'll know that next month and next year, and ten years from now they'll know that.

"I'm going to go out there and be a good citizen and work with at-risk youth. I've been doing that for fifteen years in here; I'm not stopping now. There are youth agencies that want to hire me right off the bat, plus a plumbing company I used to work for twenty-five years ago. He's hung with me all this time, and he says I've got a job as soon as I get out. But he already knows. I'm not showing up for two months. I'm giving myself two months to reconnect with family and friends." Then he repeats, "As soon as I get home, there's going to be a party."

A young officer sitting at a desk against the far wall turns. "How are you going to celebrate your first weekend out?"

"I'm going to Cal Expo!" Phillip says, sounding a lot like a teenager planning his summer vacation. "I always went to the state fair when I was a kid, and that's what I'm gonna do. Can't wait. It's been a long time. Hang out for one, two hours."

The guard leans back in his beat-up swivel chair. "The Sacramento fair? There's nothing but trouble there now. I ain't been to the fair in years. Too much trouble."

"Is that right?" Phillip asks, his voice dropping. "Cops are probably all over the place?"

"They need to be all over," the officer shoots back.

"I'll stand by them," Phillip says with a nervous laugh. "Okay, here's one over here, there's one over there. I'll make my way through the fair like that."

"On opening night, there was gunfire and all that," the young officer says.

"Maybe I won't go to the fair," Phillip concedes. "That'd be just my luck. I get out of here and I die the next day getting shot. Man."

The officer smiles back. "Days are cool. Just don't go at night."

"I want to live a long time," Phillip says. "I want prison to become a smaller and smaller and smaller part of my life. I was twenty-seven when I came to prison."

An officer standing against the doorjamb is looking hard at Phillip. "How long you got?"

"Twenty years and change," Phillip answers, straightening up in his chair.

"Twenty years," the guard repeats, reaching his hand out to Phillip.

"Yep," Phillip continues. "I did a little over twenty in here and now I want to do another forty or fifty so it will just be a piece of my life and not all bad. I've had some wonderful times in prison. I've met some beautiful people. Had some great experiences. I've been through some drama. Some tough times and some scary times, but I've also had a lot of good time in here thanks not only to the guys but the volunteers and free people that come in here and give us their time, from their hearts. Came in to help us and help us with our programs." Phillip's voice cracks. The air in the room is electrified.

Collecting himself, Phillip asks one of the officers to use the office phone to call his mom. "She wants to know whether it's really happening or not. She wants to know if I'm really getting out today."

"Sure," the officer says, motioning to a phone sitting on a desk in the far corner of the room. Phillip walks over and dials. *Beep, beep, beep.* A misdial. The officer helps him get an outside line. Standing with the phone in his hand, the room grows quiet.

"Ma. Yeah, it's me. . . . I'm in R&R. . . . Yeah, it's really happening. . . . I'm just waiting for the parole officer to come and get me. I don't know, I think he's driving me to the PO office in Sacramento, then home. . . . Maybe a couple of hours. . . . I'm fine. Really. Are you okay? . . . Who's there? . . . Wow. . . . I know. . . . Sure. Hey, sis. Yeah, I know. Hey, would you mind if a reporter comes home with me? . . . Yeah, she's all right. . . . Okay." He looks over at me, smiles, and gives me a thumbs-up.

After he hangs up, I ask if we can talk. "Sure," he replies. "What do you want to know?"

Even though I have spent hours with Phillip in the VOEG program, I have never had an opportunity to talk to him privately.

I lean in close and lift my microphone. Amid all the celebration and good wishes, there's a reason Phillip is here. He killed someone. Now he's so close to getting out, I almost hesitate. He's paid his debt to society, lived almost all of his adult life in a prison cell, volunteered in prison self-help programs, worked as a clerk, taken classes. He's done his time. Is it fair now, in front of these officers, to ask him to talk about the murder that got him locked up in the first place?

I push on. "I've never heard about your crime. What happened twenty years ago? What did you do?"

He takes a mountainous breath and pulls his chair forward, closer across the tile floor. The room is pin-drop silent. A guard on the far side of the room moves a piece of paper, an attempt to cover up what everyone else knows: they are all waiting to hear the story.

"I was a good provider," Phillip begins, leaning into my microphone. "I worked hard, made good money. Took care of my family. So in that respect, I was really responsible. But when it came to emotional stuff, when it came to interacting with my wife, in a sharing from something deep inside me, I never made it to that point. I just kept everything to myself. Smashed everything down, for all my life, whatever it was, ever since I was a kid. And that's a big reason I ended up shooting Charlie. That's where it all exploded: on Charlie."

Phillip stops, his voice dropping as though it's weighed down by rocks. He takes a breath, looks up, continues. "About two years before all this happened, my ex-wife now, my wife then, had got back on meth. She didn't like it. We didn't like it. She just got hooked. I set up appointments for her to go to drug counseling, and I'd come home from work to pick her up to go, and she'd be gone. The deepest talk we ever had was we thought, 'What if we move out of town and you won't be around it?' I quit my job. Got another job in Roseville, and she quit cold turkey. Great job. We was doing fine for a couple of years.

"We moved back to Sacramento because there was a big job in carpentry. Didn't seem to be a problem. Not even a year after that, she hooked back up with the same [drug] house, the same people. The difference was that the first time, she was going and doing the drugs and coming home. This time Charlie came in the picture, so she was going and doing drugs with another guy."

For months, Phillip says, he suspected his wife was having an affair with Charlie Horner, a thirty-four-year-old local drug dealer and gang leader. "None of this is an excuse for what I did. I don't blame it on Becky or Charlie or the circumstances. There was a lot of nonviolent things I could have did. We could have moved. I could have divorced her. I could have got some help for me and talked about my issues, dealt with my own stuff. They only knew each other for a couple of months. She was coming and going. She'd come home for a few days and then go over to the house he was staying at. Back and forth, few days here and there.

"Then one day Charlie threatened me with a gun. Told me don't interfere with their relationship: him and my wife's relationship or him or one of his boys would take care of me."

Phillip says he tried to put it out of his mind, but in a moment that changed everything, he did what a man with two children at home never should have done. "That was where I made the biggest mistake I ever made in my life. I had a couple of guns, a couple of rifles. Me and my buddies used to go target shooting, never hunting." He clears his throat. "And so, after he threatened me, instead of calling the cops and saying, 'This guy threatened me; he's a scary guy. What do I do?' I put my gun in my car. That was the beginning of the end.

"Who knows. Maybe if I'd called the cops, they'd have felt the desperation in my voice and maybe hooked me up to a psych. I mean, I was lucky. I was never molested as a child. I was never beaten. I went through some childhood drama. I grew up in tough neighborhoods. The only white kid and new schools all the time, and things like that, 'cause we moved a few times. Been through a lot, never knew my dad, but I never shared none of that with nobody."

Suddenly a phone rings in the guards' office. It sounds like a shot. Everyone jumps a little, startled. A guard picks up the phone and quickly gets rid of the call. With all the guards' eyes back down on paperwork, Phillip resumes his story.

"July 20, 1988, three days after Charlie threatened me, started out like most summer days. My wife dropped our two little boys, Phillip Jr. and Anthony, over at her mom's house so she could hang out with Charlie."

That was the day the wheels came off. Midday at his construction job, Phillip says, he was laid off. He desperately needed the job and the money that came with it. Worried about where the next paycheck would come from, he got in his van and drove home.

"When I came home, Charlie and Becky was driving away. They was trying to get one of my cars. They called it her car, but it wasn't her car; she didn't have a license. I had four cars. Of course, in California marriage law everything is half-and-half, but she didn't have a license and didn't normally drive around. As far as the court was concerned, it was her car, and they was going to get her car. Charlie had tried to hot-wire it, and they was leaving and that's when it just—*whooo.*" His voice sounds like the rush of a backdraft. Now the pattern of turning away from what was happening right under his nose, the drugs and the lies, was broken.

Watching them get in the car and pull away, Phillip did what he knew he shouldn't do. He made a split-second decision that led to another split-second decision. He jumped in his car and chased after them. "I just went berserk. I started following them around the neighborhood. I was trying to show them how serious the situation was. I was trying to chase them out of the neighborhood, and once we hit the main street, I was just going to turn around."

Phillip stops and looks up, his eyes pleading. He knows what's coming next. He takes a breath. It was so long ago and today is his day of freedom. After a short inner conversation with himself, he keeps going. He has lived with this moment for twenty years, played it over in his mind from every angle, color, sound. Telling everyone in the room exactly what happened won't add to or diminish the pain. He has accepted responsibility for the life he took, and today's telling won't change anything.

"This is where I really lost it. I wasn't thinking. I just lost it. That's no excuse, but that's what happened. We was coming up to stops, and the driver wasn't stopping. They were just slowing down and going. And then the last stop, they stopped real abruptly, and I was right behind 'em. And so I bumped the back of the car. I didn't slam into it or anything, but I was too close, and I bumped the back of the car. And then, um, they pulled over and I pulled over. I reached behind the seat and grabbed my shotgun. Becky had told me he always carried a gun with him, so I was thinking Charlie had his gun. But for some reason he didn't have it with him that day.

"We all got out and exchanged a few words. I had the gun pointed right at him: sawed-off twelve-gauge shotgun. Charlie said, 'She's not yours. She's mine.' When he said 'mine,' he was right there in my face. And, uh, I shot him. Shot him in the chest. Shot him in the chest and he was probably dead before he hit the ground. Hit him right in the heart."

The gun blast filled the summer air with heat. Horner went down. It was done. Phillip lowered the gun and turned away. "I jumped in my van. Went to my mother-in-law's, where my two boys were, two and eight years old. And I just, I called the cops and turned myself in, told them where I was and went to sit on the couch with my boys and cried." Phillip's voice cracks. Caught without air, he sobs. "I just held onto them, told them Daddy did a terrible thing and he was going away for a long time and I was sorry. And then the cops came. And I went."

Within minutes Phillip was arrested, taken to Sacramento County Jail, and booked on murder charges. A year later, just before jury selection in his first-degree murder trial was to begin, Phillip says, his lawyer, Jan Karowsky, encouraged him to take a plea bargain of second-degree murder. "He said it was the best he could do. If I went to trial, there was a good possibility I would be found guilty of first-degree murder and sentenced to twenty-five years to life or worse."

Phillip pleaded guilty to second-degree murder and was sentenced to fifteen years to life with possibility of parole, with two additional years' enhancement for using the gun. That's when Phillip Jay Seiler's life as a convicted murderer began. His name was replaced by a CDC number. To other lifers, Phillip Seiler became simply "PJ." Based on PJ's calculations, he wouldn't be eligible for parole for ten years. In his mind, he settled on doing fifteen before he would even begin hoping for freedom. By then his oldest son, his namesake, would be twenty-three, his youngest seventeen.

"It's been twenty years," he says. "I'm going to be there for my boys. I'll help them out of their mess. They're in a big mess. Phillip Jr. is twenty-nine. Anthony is twenty-three. Both of them in prison." Phillip struggles to keep talking, to hold back the gulps. "I'm going to do my best if they want to. They have to want to. I can't make them. If they want to go to drug rehab and go to anger management, I've got all the connections in the world and they're all right there, people I've met right here," he cries out, realizing his two worlds are going to come together. "And if they're willing, I'm going to do the best I can to help them get back on track. Because if they're not willing, I have to back off. I can't," he continues, realizing what he's saying, "be around drugs or drama. Nothing like that. Because I'll be on parole and they'd return me to prison if I was caught around drugs. I'll have to stand aside and let them know I'm there when they're ready. I can't even be around somebody that's on drugs. So, I've done a lot of work around that"—his voice recovers— "around being prepared to tell 'em I can't go to their house if they've got drugs there. And I can't have them come to my house if they're under the influence of drugs, or drinking. I've already told them and I've wrote them a lot. But most of the mail never gets to them because they're in a prison and they stop it [the mail]. But they know that it's 'cold turkey' time and I'm there for them 100 percent. I've got some good psychologist friends that I've met here and they've offered to sit down with us three to go through a healing process because"—his voice breaks again—"their dad left them at two and eight years old and killed a man. And they're hurtin' and I want to heal with them." He's crying openly now.

An officer reaches for a box of tissues and hands it to Phillip. Like a runner on a last lap, he breathes out and in, in short, strong bursts of air.

"What are you most looking forward to?" I ask, trying to cheer him up. "On the outside?'

"Camping. Me and my boys used to go to Yosemite all the time, camping, picnics, swimming. That seems like the most fun. Out in the wilderness. Good family, good friends, having a good time. Yosemite is top of the list for us three."

Even so, it's clear it's going to be awhile before Phillip and the young sons he left behind are free, all at the same time.

It has now been more than an hour since Phillip finished shaving the stubble off his deeply dimpled chin. He looks around. "Where is that parole officer?" His wide blue eyes begin to turn from raw anticipation to veiled fear. He has never been this close to getting out before, but that doesn't mean he's out.

"Don't worry," Sam says. "I'm sure he's on his way. It's only eleven-thirty. It takes a good hour or more to drive from Sacramento."

"Yeah, sure. I know," Phillip says, looking at his watch, then out the office door at the dozens of new arrivals in bright orange jumpsuits locked up in large cages waiting to be processed. It's been a long twenty-year journey from the day he wore one of those jumpsuits.

"While we wait, tell me: How did you get to where you are today?"

"San Quentin has more programs than all the other prisons," Phillip says. "There's nothing at the other prisons. You just sit in your cell, walk around the yard, and do time. I didn't graduate from high school, so when I got to the county jail in 1988, I began taking classes and got my high school diploma. Then I kept going and once I got here, there were programs."

He enrolled in Patten University, an inside-prison satellite branch of a local Christian institution offering college-level courses to inmates. He joined IMPACT (Incarcerated Men Putting Away Childish Things) and Squires, a national organization that brings troubled teens into prisons to hear from the other end of the road they are traveling on. Phillip says if he couldn't be there for his own locked-up sons, he would be there for the boys he could reach.

By 1998, after serving five years at San Quentin and a total of ten years behind bars, Phillip became eligible to appear before the California Board of Parole Hearings, for what's known as the initial hearing. The commissioners gave him a two-year denial, meaning he would have to wait two years before going before the parole board again.

Over the next two years he joined IPP, the Insight Prison Project. He attended counseling sessions with a group of men dedicated to turning their lives around by taking a head-on look at the psychological walls and emotional problems that led them to their acts of violence and the impact their crime had on the victims.

In 2000, Phillip says, the Board of Parole Hearings was so backlogged, he had to wait not two but three years to go before the board again. Again the commissioners found him unsuitable for parole and gave him another two-year denial.

Then, in 2003, after presenting his case to the Board of Parole Hearings for a third time, the commissioners determined Phillip was no longer a threat to society and found him suitable for parole. One of the commissioners, Carole Daily, was on the board that had denied him parole back in 2001. This time she said he was ready to go home. "The board doesn't go from a two-year denial to a date," Phillip remembers Daily saying at the hearing, "but you've made such a change you are ready to be released."

But like Don Cronk and Jesse Reed, before being released on parole, Phillip had to wait 150 days for the governor of California to decide whether to reverse his date. Governor Gray Davis was in office. As Phillip's file made its way through the 120 days of review inside the Board of Parole Hearings, he watched the calendar, hoping his file would be one of the first to reach the governor's desk just as Arnold Schwarzenegger took the chair.

But in a simple twist of criminal fate, in his last week in office, Governor Davis took Phillip's date and sent a fax to the warden of San Quentin announcing he was reversing Phillip's parole. Devastated, Phillip knew how much the decision would hurt family and friends who were waiting for him on the outside. He would have to wait two more years to go before the Board of Parole Hearings again.

One month after Phillip's parole date was reversed by Governor Davis, his eldest son, Phillip Jr., was arrested, beginning the first of many prison terms to come. Within a few years, Phillip's second son, Anthony, would also be arrested on drug and violence charges and sent to prison.

Inside San Quentin's North Block another lifer and jailhouse lawyer, Sterling Scott, convinced Phillip not to give up. Now that Phillip had been found suitable by the board, Scott said he would help him fight for parole in the courts, free of charge. Later, when Scott won his own appeal and was released from San Quentin on parole, he continued to help Phillip with his appeals from outside, sending documents back and forth, inside to out, out to in, through legal mail.

With Scott's help, Phillip filed his first writ of habeas corpus with the Marin County Superior Court, suing Governor Davis for reversing his parole date. In his filing Phillip argued, "The Governor overstepped his bounds by reversing my parole date without probable cause."

The Marin County Superior Court reviewed his writ, found the governor did not have cause to reverse, and ordered the state attorney general's office, representing the governor, to show cause for the governor's reversal.

The attorney general representing the governor appealed the ruling to the state court of appeal, which agreed with the superior court, that the governor did not have cause.

The attorney general appealed the state court of appeal decision to the California Supreme Court. The California Supreme Court ruled Governor Davis did have cause for reversal.

Phillip then appealed the California Supreme Court's decision to the US District Court for the Northern District of California, which upheld the California Supreme Court decision that the governor did, based on Phillip's original crime, have cause for reversal.

In a writ Phillip wrote by himself, he appealed the US district court's decision to the Ninth Circuit Court of Appeals.

Then, in 2005, two years into his court battle, Phillip was again scheduled to go before the Board of Parole Hearings. Hours into the hearing—after he spoke with the commissioners about the crime, his prison record, his work in programs, his remorse and reformation—the three commissioners again found Phillip suitable for release.

Again, five months later, on the last possible day he could issue his decision, Governor Schwarzenegger sent a fax to the warden of San Quentin announcing he was reversing Phillip's parole date.

This time Phillip's response to the reversal was radically different. Instead of falling into weeks of despair, Phillip responded to the governor's multiple-page fax by filing another writ of habeas corpus, this time in Sacramento County Superior Court, which had previously denied his writ.

The Sacramento County Superior Court denied his appeal. So Phillip appealed the superior court's denial to the California Court of Appeal, which remanded his writ back to the superior court, asking the judge to reevaluate her decision.

A year later, in 2006, with both cases working their way through state and federal courts, Phillip appeared before the Board of Parole Hearings again, for the fifth time in eight years. By then Phillip had amassed more than four hundred "chronos," chronological reports documenting good behavior, in his file. And yet the two commissioners on the parole board gave him a two-year denial.

"After doing nothing wrong and only good stuff, I was denied," Phillip says, shaking his head, eyes wide.

This time Phillip filed a writ of habeas corpus with the Sacramento County Superior Court suing the Board of Parole Hearings for denying him parole. In December 2006, a judge in the Sacramento County Superior Court said she wanted to see Phillip in her courtroom. At the end of the hearing, she ordered the California Department of Corrections and Rehabilitation to release him.

Surprisingly, freedom for Phillip would remain out of reach. Governor Schwarzenegger refused to release him. Phillip attempted to appeal the governor's refusal to the California Court of Appeal, but the judges on the court of appeal told him to go back to the superior court and file a new writ.

The Sacramento County Superior Court judge again ordered Phillip released from prison, and again Governor Schwarzenegger refused to release him. The battle was still going on when, on August

21, 2008, the California Supreme Court issued its ruling *In re Lawrence*.

"And that's why I'm getting out today," Phillip says, sitting inside San Quentin's R&R, waiting for his parole officer to arrive. The guards, who have been listening quietly to his story, shift in their chairs. As if someone hit the play button on a paused movie, the guards go back to work, pretending they weren't listening. Now that he's told his story to the men, who for the past twenty years have held the keys to his life, Phillip looks relieved. He has accepted what he did, paid the price, and cleared the table.

Phillip gets up and walks out the front door to join the few lifers allowed out of their cells standing vigil, waiting for the parole officer's car. Then, a little after noon, a dark blue sedan appears at the far corner of San Quentin's lower yard. Someone calls out, "He's here." Phillip turns and stares at the approaching car. It has that official state vehicle look.

"Yep, that's him," Phillip says, half under his breath. "I hope he's cool." Guards and inmates alike turn to follow the car as it inches its way slowly, deliberately past the guard tower and along the forty-foot wall. I take a quick look at Phillip's face. He looks anxious. What will his parole officer look like? Will he be a fair man, or will he make his first thirst-quenching moments of freedom a living nightmare, handcuffing him in the car and treating him like an unreformed prisoner?

The inmates and officers standing with Phillip on the ramp watch as the car door opens. Wearing a loose-fitting, short-sleeved casual shirt, slacks, and aviator sunglasses, the officer, a tall, brawny man, gold badge clipped to his front pocket, gets out and walks up the ramp toward Phillip. Phillip steps forward, smiles, and holds out his hand.

"CDC number?" says the officer, humorless.

While Phillip recites his number, the officer looks down at a number printed on a form in his hand.

"Okay, let's get you signed out," the parole officer says, pulling open the door to the R&R office. "You got any boxes?"

"About eight," Phillip says, following him inside the modular double-wide.

"We don't have room for eight," the parole officer says, looking at Phillip with a "What were you thinking?" face. "We can take a few; you'll have to get the rest mailed to you later."

Boxes, number, a parole officer with a little attitude. Now that it's really happening, Phillip allows himself to change out of his pale blue button-down shirt with its drooping pocket and repaired buttonholes and into the civilian clothes his family bought and sent to him inside. Holding a brand-new light gray Gap T-shirt and a fresh pair of jeans, Phillip steps into the bathroom at the back of the R&R trailer.

Actually leaving will still take a little while longer. Turns out, the parole officer who has come to collect Phillip was once a corrections officer at San Quentin, and now that he's back, he wants to check in with the men on duty, getting the latest news on changes at the prison and the gossip firsthand.

At about one in the afternoon, the door to R&R swings open wide. Phillip's parole officer emerges, catches Phillip's eye, and says, "Let's go." Lifers standing around help Phillip push the dolly stacked with his boxes to the open trunk. After some shifting and shoving, the officer announces half the boxes will have to be left behind. A woman who works as a volunteer at the prison walks over to Phillip and hands him an envelope. He carefully pulls it open. Inside is a good-luck card covered with hand-scrawled messages from the volunteers he's known and worked with and is now leaving behind. No longer a lifer, now in the care of the Parole Division of the CDCR, Phillip gives the slight, gray-haired volunteer a kiss and a hug.

Turning, he walks to the back door of the four-door sedan, takes a quick last look at the men, prisoners and officers standing side-by-side on the ramp, and with a bounce, jumps into the backseat.

Just like that, the dark car backs up, swings out, and begins making the long, slow drive around the yard, past the baseball backstop and the education building and through the farthest gate. As they watch the car disappear, there is grief among the band of brothers left behind. Phillip is gone. Like mourners leaving a burial, they turn, look back, and then walk away. It's over. Guards go back to their desks. Lifers head back to their cells, their heads low. They all know that unless they too get out on parole, they will never see their friend again.

fourteen

SIDEWALKS

AUGUST 2008

A hundred miles away in Sacramento, the scene is set for Phillip's long-awaited homecoming. Using directions Phillip gave me from memory while we were still inside the guards' office, I drive away from the cool ocean breezes of the Bay Area and head for the hot central valley and Phillip's family home. If I overshoot the freeway speed limit and test the ticket gods for the next seventy-five miles, I just might make it there before Phillip.

It works. Phillip and his parole officer have to make a prerelease stop at the North Sacramento parole office to check him in and go over his parole conditions before he is officially released. That gives me about an hour's lead: just enough time to meet the folks and friends waiting for him to walk through the front door.

Skirting south around the center of the capital, and pulling off the freeway, I drive down a long artery past a sprawling high school, a church, and a corner market. Hanging right, and then making a quick left, I slow to check the house numbers and park directly across the street from his family's single-story manicured tract house. One of the large, leafy plane trees lining the comfortable middle-class street blocks the late August sun, and for just a moment, I stop and take a breath of the stiflingly hot air surrounding me. It's midday quiet. People are at work. Except for a car every now and then, no one seems to be around.

I recheck the address against the notes scribbled on the notebook in front of me. That's the one. It doesn't stand out. It looks just like all the other houses on the block, only today this one is different. I pull my body, drenched in sweat, out of the car, grab my equipment, and cross the narrow street. Yanking open a waist-high latched gate and stepping up to a screen door, past a row of flowering rosebushes, I stop. Are they expecting me? Will they let me in? I knock and wait. All I can do is try.

The inside door opens slightly, then more. A composed woman of about thirty, with short hair, a kind mouth, and intelligent eyes, looks out. "Hello?"

I introduce myself as a reporter, trying not to say the wrong thing. "Oh, I'm Phillip's sister, JJ," the woman says, pushing the screen door open. "Why don't you come in? It's so hot out there."

As I step by JJ, I can see her face is flushed. I could have been Phillip, but I wasn't. Disappointed but gracious, she closes the inner front door behind me. The change from bright sunshine outside to living room inside is dramatic. Heavy curtains are drawn across the front picture window, making the living/dining room cool and dark. It takes me half a minute to adjust to the pairs of eyes staring back at me from around the room.

Phillip's mom, a squat, overweight woman with wavy white hair, is sitting in a padded rocking chair midway between the door and the dining room table to the back. "Oh, you must be hot," she says in a strained, excited, but weary voice. "Would you like a glass of water?"

Now standing in the middle of the room, encircled by people sitting in chairs, on a couch, and on the carpeted floor, I stumble a bit. The heat has made me dizzy. Gently they pepper me with questions: Who am I? Why am I here? How do I know Phillip? Now that he's getting out, they want to do everything they can that they haven't been able to do for twenty years: protect him. Some are willing to accept me as one more part of their reunion celebration. Others, staring at the microphone in my hand, aren't so sure.

Phillip's mother breaks the uncounted tie by asking if I'd like to see the dining room table. It's set up for Phillip's homecoming party.

"Yes, I'd love to see it," I say, moving toward the even darker dining room. A cake decorated with balloons and flowers is in the middle of the table, surrounded by potato salad and chips. She says they've been cleaning the house for days. They want it to be perfect when Phillip walks in the door. She wants to give him the best of what he's been missing all these years. Her voice stumbles. "Until he walks through the door, I won't believe it."

Phillip's stepfather, a man he calls Pops, keeps watch at the window, pulling the heavy curtains to the side just enough to see the street out front. He is so excited he can hardly sit.

Phillip's girlfriend, a volunteer he met inside San Quentin, is sitting in the middle of the sofa, glowing. A perky, bright, professional woman with short brown hair and blue eyes, she says they've got plans. She's rented a room at a nearby hotel for when the little celebration at the house is over. No, she says, they don't have plans to get married. Not yet. "Phillip," she says, "is going to stay single for a year. That's clear."

Waiting patiently over to the back of the room is Jan Karowsky, the lawyer who represented Phillip a little over twenty years ago when he first went to court for the murder. He says Phillip never denied the crime and never shied from doing time, and he has always respected him for that: "I wouldn't miss this day for the world."

There are others, including people who knew Phillip in high school. Turns out, he kept in touch with his old friends through long letters and shorter phone calls. It was all in preparation for today, the day he would have a chance to start his life anew.

Everyone settles back into an almost-silent waiting. They don't know how long it will be, but together in this cool, darkened living room, it doesn't seem to matter. They've been through board denials, governor reversals, and court rulings. Today is different. Today he's coming home.

Suddenly the front door swings open. Phillip appears, the bright, blinding sun shining behind him. "I'm home!" he calls out in an almost unrecognizable cry. His mom, already standing, rushes to hug him, their first embrace in years without the eyes of guards watching.

"Oh, Phillip," his mom cries, grabbing him by the waist.

Stunned, the others stand and watch, giving mother and son the first few beats of happiness. Phillip melts into her arms and drops his face into the deep of her neck. "It's over," he says in a muffled whisper. "They didn't appeal. It's all over." She begins to sob, which is the cue for everyone to move in.

"Pops!" Phillip calls out. Then his sister and his girlfriend—he takes one in each arm.

There are tears and hugs, broken by choking laughter. Lifting his head from the arms and faces circling him, Phillip takes his first good look around. "Man," he says.

Stepping up behind Phillip like a bad epilogue is his parole officer, white-brimmed baseball cap shadowing his eyes. He introduces himself to Phillip's parents. Pops takes him on a tour of the small house, into the little hall that connects the living room to the bathroom and the two bedrooms. "This will be Phillip's bedroom," we can all hear Pops tell the officer.

The parole officer: "Are these the only windows?"

Pops: "Yes. And this is the bathroom."

The parole officer: "Are these all of the medicines you will keep in this cabinet?"

Mom has stayed behind in the living room. She looks worried. "Phillip, is everything okay?"

Phillip nods. "Everything's going to be okay. He just has to check things out."

Seeing an officer walk into and through their private, curtained-off world seems to shock Mom and Pops, who strike me as somewhat hermetic. In the small bathroom, the officer picks up each round orange vial and reads the contents. Next it's a check of the exits. "Show me all the windows and doors," the parole officer orders. "I'll be stopping by every now and then, to see how things are going."

Pops looks nervous. "What time do you think you'll be coming by? We like to go to sleep at about ten."

No give in his voice, the officer shoots back, "I won't be calling first." He pulls the lip of his cap down and heads for the front door. Phillip and Pops follow the officer out to the sidewalk. A quick goodbye and the last vestige of prison pulls away. Phillip watches the officer drive around the corner and out of sight. Now it's real. He's standing on the sidewalk, free. There's no one to tell him what to do, where to go, or how to do it.

Shooting his arms in the air, a release of twenty years of tightness, Phillip opens his chest and takes a breath. He looks around. It's hot. "Wow. Sidewalks," Phillip says, his voice tripping like a child's. "I forgot about sidewalks. They're so cool. You can just walk down sidewalks in front of people's houses and it's okay. I used to ride my bike around, and I forgot about sidewalks. They don't have sidewalks in prison." Then he turns back toward the house and his family waiting inside and takes a leaping skip from the sidewalk to his parents' front door.

Back inside, this time without the parole officer, everyone cheers. Someone pours apple juice into tall plastic flutes. "Does everyone have a glass?" his mom calls out in a voice tight with relieved anxiety, like tears hanging at the lip of a waterfall of pain. She lifts her arm, glass held high. All around the circle, glasses clink with a train-track percussion of plastic repetition. "To Phillip." Tears choke the air. "To Phillip. To Phillip. To Phillip." For the first time in so many years, there is a real reason to celebrate and be happy.

Phillip goes shopping for new clothes—khaki shorts and cotton button-down shirts in anything but blue—and on Saturday morning, just four days after he walked out of San Quentin, we walk through the turnstile at Cal Expo, the California state fair. People are everywhere. Parents push kids in strollers, squirmy prepubescent groups run this way and that, self-conscious gaggles of teen girls strut the walkways, passing within a few feet of pants-slung-low tough looking wannabes. I point to one group of bad-looking boys and ask Phillip if they're trouble. Phillip takes a quick glance. "Nope," he says. A human Geiger counter after years in prison surrounded by serious criminals, he can identify people who are real trouble in the real world.

"What about them?" I ask, pointing to another menacing group of kids.

"They're just having a good time. Won't hurt a flea. If they were trouble, I could tell. Believe me."

"But how?"

"I just know. The way they walk, hold their bodies, their mouths, their eyes. It's obvious who's trouble and who isn't."

Phillip wants to remember the fair the way it was when he was a kid. He's giddy with excitement and wants to jump on a ride, but vetoes the massive, colorful roller coasters. "No way. I didn't spend twenty years in prison to get out and die my first Saturday on a roller coaster that breaks."

In the end, we share a water log ride down a thirty-foot shoot, screaming and laughing all the way down. Before he leaves, there is one ride Phillip says he has to take. It's a forty-foot drop on a bright yellow water slide into a pool of water. Wearing swimming trunks he brought along for just this moment, Phillip runs over to the base of the spiral stairs and climbs to the top. Standing on the platform, high above the trees and the pool of water far below, he doesn't hesitate. Holding onto the bar at the top of the slide, he pushes off. Crossing his arms tight to his chest, feet crossed at the ankle, he shoots straight down, water shooting in all directions. "That was awesome! I'm going up again!" he shouts. He rides the big yellow slide again and again, playing with the thrill.

fifteen

SHIFTING FORTUNES

APRIL 2009

Four months later, on November 11, 2008, the winds of liberty shift for Don Cronk.

With his writ challenging the governor's reversal of his parole moving forward in the Sacramento County Superior Court, Don goes back to the board for another parole hearing. This time he asks for a postponement, concerned that if the board doesn't find him suitable, the decision could hurt his chances in court.

Just as his judicial appeal is gaining traction, Thanksgiving and Christmas put the world and the court in full holiday swirl with delays, postponements, extensions. But then, on January 31 of the new year, Don receives a summons to court.

He's terrified. Prisoners who need to go to court in Sacramento usually get transferred to a county jail there for the duration of the hearing, and San Quentin usually moves new prisoners into their cells while they're gone. So they lose their cell and their cellie, and no one on the outside can understand how traumatic that is. "Our cell is our only safe place in prison, and it's hard to find a man you can live with and go through all the things you have to go through," he tells me several weeks later. "And then you lose your property. And your cellie is going through all the changes, too. And I'm not a young man anymore. Going to court meant I was going to the war zones, back to the county jail, and I didn't know what was going to happen there. If I had to defend myself in some ruckus, I could lose my whole thing," meaning his appeal and his chance for release.

He goes anyway. "I walk into the courtroom in handcuffs and wearing prison clothes—an orange jumpsuit. I sat down with my court-appointed attorney, Joseph B. de Illy. After I sat down, they took the handcuffs off. The deputy attorney general lady was at a table to our left." Don pauses, looking me in the face. "And then the judge [Emily Vasquez] walks in. Everyone rises. She sits down and says, 'We're here for the matter of habeas corpus, Donald Cronk.' And she tells my attorney, 'Present your case.' He did, and he spoke eloquently for about twenty, twenty-five minutes. He had everything laid out perfectly. The judge was listening attentively and writing notes; of course, they have a stenographer writing, too.

"He gets all finished and the judge looks over at the deputy attorney general and says, 'Okay, so I reiterate my original question to you. Where is the evidence that this man needs further incarceration? Why are we here?' The deputy attorney general, Heather Heckler, had stacks of paper, and it looked like she was going to present who-knows-what. That I was the Son of Sam, that I'm probably the Zodiac Killer. It looked like she was armed for battle. And the deputy attorney general stopped and looked at the judge and she said, 'Your Honor, we don't have any evidence and the governor doesn't have any evidence. The state doesn't have any evidence against this man.' And the judge said, 'Well, why are we here, then?' And Heckler said, 'Because we disagree with *Lawrence*.' And the judge said, 'You're here because you disagree with current law.' And Heckler said yes. The judge said, 'I'll issue my ruling in two, three weeks.' The judge knew I was having surgery for my neck and ordered the sheriff's deputies to get me back to San Quentin in time for my operation. Then she said, 'That concludes this hearing.' It was over. My attorney and the deputy attorney general picked up their papers and the sheriff's deputies led me back to the van.

"I think it could go either way. I think there's a good chance she'll order me released. Kathleen was sitting in the courtroom, and she'd brought her friend with her. In fact, when we walked into the courtroom I could see Kathleen and I mouthed, 'I love you,' and the deputy yelled, 'No talking.' Throughout the hearing I couldn't turn around or anything."

Judge Vasquez's promise of "two or three weeks" stretched to nine. And then—one day in the first week in April, just like that—she ordered Don free.

The only problem was, no one told Don.

By the time I return to San Quentin on Friday, April 10, Don is giddy. "I found out Tuesday afternoon, April 7th," Don says, "almost a year to the day after the governor took my parole date. I called Kathleen like I normally do at two o'clock on the prison pay phone. We're just talking away for a couple of minutes and she says, 'How does it feel to be a free man?' I said, 'What?' She thought I had already gotten the legal mail.

"About an hour later, at lockup for count time, I was lying on my rack, and they called my name over the loudspeaker to report to the desk. I got dressed and went down, and I was expecting to see administration, the warden's people, standing there; Messick. Nobody's there. I thought, 'Oh, he just brought the paperwork over and threw it on the desk and didn't want to see me.' I get to the desk, and the officer tells me to call this number. I do and it's my counselor. He goes, 'I have a fax here from the attorney general. Apparently they don't want to mess with you anymore and to begin parole immediately.'

"The officer told me, 'Hopefully you can go Thursday!'" Don is beaming like a lightbulb. "It didn't happen on Thursday. Today's Friday. Maybe my parole officer will come and get me tomorrow."

"How are you doing?" I ask, studying the lines in his face, the dark shadows around his eyes.

"I have not slept. It's been off and on, twenty-minute catnaps. I've given everything I own away." He laughs. "I have three boxes, but it's just books. Books that I've used, audiobooks, counseling books, everything I've learned and studied with, I'm taking those home. Other than that, I'm not taking anything. I've given away watches, CD players, televisions. I want nothing from here. The only things I'm taking are the things that made me a better person. I'm going home! Can you believe it? I'm really going home? And I have no idea what to expect."

It's late afternoon outside the San Quentin Protestant chapel. As Don, Sam Robinson, and I stand together talking, other lifers mill about, staring at Don as though they're looking at a ghost. "I've heard from lifers who have gotten out, they'll call in and the pastor will put them on the speakerphone, and they'll say, 'When you get home, you're not going to be able to sleep. For a week or so, you're gonna look like crap and feel like crap. Just let it happen. Then one night, you're going to fall asleep and wake up, and you'll be fine.'"

"You'll be out by Easter," I say, suddenly realizing.

"The stone is being rolled away!" Don laughs. "I'm coming out. They're gonna look in my cell and my body isn't going to be there. Praise God for that."

"When's the last supper?"

"Tonight," Don says. "Tonight's the last supper. One more plate of gruel, and no more. Last Sunday Kathleen was here in the visiting room before the judge had ruled, and she said, 'If the judge rules and the attorney general doesn't appeal, what would you like for your first dinner?'

"I want two thick, juicy pork chops," Don says, licking his lips. "I have not had pork in thirty years. I got to have some pork."

Leaving San Quentin that Friday afternoon, I drive straight to Kathleen's house. Standing at her door, she is glowing with a bubbly sort of charm. "Isn't it wonderful? Don is coming home!"

Leading me into the kitchen, she points to a mound of fresh fruit on a plate in the middle of the table. "As I was putting the fruit on the thing, I was thinking, 'Well, there's fresh fruit he has not seen, and if he has seen it, there's been brown spots on it. Now he can just take as much as he wants, eat what he wants.' And I was buying yogurt, and I was putting it in here," Kathleen says, yanking the refrigerator door open. "He's going to open this and go . . . " A look of shock crosses her face as we both look into the deep refrigerator stuffed with fresh this and that. "Do you know what I'm saying?"

"Where are the pork chops?"

Kathleen smiles, reaches in, and pulls out not one but two plastic-wrapped packages of fresh pork, each about three-quarters of an inch thick. "Look how thick they are!" Then she pulls out two plump sausages. "He's from Wisconsin, and he's always talking about Johnsonville Brats. He says they're the best, and I saw them and I went, 'Oh, I have to get those.' I don't even know what I paid for them.

"I'm starting to drool at the thought of eating all of this. I made homemade soup last night, and I made a meatloaf so we can make a sandwich tomorrow when he comes home. I want to give him some homemade stuff. Anybody can get a turkey sandwich, but this has got to be homemade. Then we'll make pork chops and homemade applesauce. I didn't buy stuffing. Somebody told me to buy stuffing. I don't eat stuffing, so I don't know anything about that. I'm going to make Swiss chard the way my mom used to make it, with garlic and olive oil, the Italian way. Later on he can tell me if he doesn't like something." She turns to me, a look of concern on her face. "He'll like it, right? For Easter—he's not a big ham eater, so I bought a beef roast. My mom was an excellent cook; that's why I am following in her footsteps. She cooks it in the oven with pieces of onion and you melt a whole cube of butter over it and I'm telling you, it is to die for. And this is crucial. And I'm only telling you this secret. When you take it out, you slice it in the pan. So all those juices mix with the butter."

"When do you think he'll be home?" I ask.

"I don't know, but I'm done," Kathleen says, brushing her hands together. "The house is clean. The groceries are bought. I'm going to change the sheets on the bed, take a shower, wash my hair, get dressed. I have breakfast if he comes. I have lunch if he comes. I have dinner if he comes. I'm covered."

Motioning for me to take a seat at the kitchen table, Kathleen confides, "Now, I'll tell you the serious thing about this," she says. "It is truly, truly overwhelming. Yesterday I went through this big depressing thing. It was dreary and rainy. I just started thinking, this is too much. It's too big for me to handle. After fifteen years of knowing him and wanting him to come home, it's come down to that, and for some reason, you just go, 'Oh my God, I can't do this.' You just get a fear for a minute.

"Don and I have never, ever hidden anything from each other, so I told him that this morning when he called and he was silent. I thought, 'Oh no. What's he thinking?' And he said he had the same feeling. For one split minute he said he thought and almost said, 'This is too much. Just leave me here and let the world pass me by.' You do. It's just overwhelming. It's not like we really want that, but you're thinking, can I really, really, really do this? Can I have him come here and work him into the world and my family and my friends? If you think about the big picture, it's overwhelming. But if you think about day by day, by day by day . . . Okay. Breakfast? I'm good. Lunch? I'm good. Dinner? I'm good. But if you think about, well, there's the family vacation at Lake Tahoe coming up this summer. Is he going to be able to go to it? Is he going to be accepted? Then it gets overwhelming. You can't do that. You have to take every day one day at a time. Last week I had two people who knew nothing about Don say that every single person that has ever committed a murder should be in prison forever. For life. They should lock 'em up and throw away the key. Two people in one week said that to me."

"Maybe when they meet Don, they'll feel differently." I say.

"That's what I'm hoping for. That's what I'm betting on, because he is so squeaky clean. But some people are never going to change. And when I talked to him this morning, all that fear went away. But I do get a fear when I talk to people, and some people are so opinionated. It's that way with everything."

"When's the wedding?"

"One day at a time, lady!" Kathleen giggles. "He has to court me. And I have to make sure my dog, PJ, likes him. That's a deal breaker. If my dog doesn't like him, he's out."

"What is the plan for his release?"

"Well, he got word on Tuesday, and now it's Friday. I thought he might be home by today, but I'm thinking tomorrow at the latest. I just want him home for Easter. It is truly his favorite holiday—ten times more than Christmas. Being a Christian, Easter is what it's all about."

Today, just like it was a year ago, when she thought Don was getting out, her house is decorated like an Easter wonderland. Small ceramic bunnies are arranged in small herds around bowls and baskets filled with colorful jelly beans. Everything in Kathleen's world is exactly right, and now, the moment she has been waiting fifteen years for, has finally arrived.

Friday night comes and goes. By Saturday morning, Don has moved his three packed boxes over to the chapel and is sitting, waiting for the call from R&R telling him his parole officer has come to pick him up. The day passes with no call and no parole officer. By Sunday morning, there's still no word.

Kathleen calls. I can hear the desperation in her voice. "Don is pacing the floor, waiting for the call. We don't understand. Why is this taking so long? He has to come home. Yesterday [Saturday] I went in to see him in the visiting room. He said he hadn't heard anything. He was supposed to go home Thursday, then Friday, then Saturday. Now we don't know what to think."

By Sunday afternoon Kathleen has reached the end of her own breaking point. Then she remembers. When the Board of Parole Hearings sent the man who would become Don's parole officer to check over her house to see if it was acceptable for Don's parole plans, the officer handed her a business card. She still has it somewhere. Digging around in her papers, she pulls it out. What's the risk? She dials the office number and gets an answering machine. Looking at the card, Kathleen sees a cell number. What is there to lose? She dials the number. A man answers, the sound of birds squawking in the background.

"Is this Gordon Hodgeson?" Kathleen asks.

"Yes," Officer Hodgeson answers. "Who's this?"

When she explains the reason for her call, he's stern but sorry. "'I'm on a fishing boat miles out in the ocean,'" Kathleen recounts the officer saying over the phone. "He said there was no way he could get back in time to pick him up today, and he would look for the order when he got back to his office tomorrow. There's no way I can let Don know! I just want to tell him it's going to be all right. He was supposed to get out before Easter, and now he won't be getting out until the day after Easter. Of course it's wonderful he's getting out, but these past five days, not knowing what's happening, and no one telling us—it's not right."

Is this really how the system works? Apparently the parole system hasn't caught up to the changing numbers of lifers paroling out of the state's prisons. I can't imagine what Don's going through, waiting for someone to come and let him go.

Monday morning, I drive to Kathleen's house, walk up to the screen door, and knock. "Kathleen? Don?" I call out, hopeful. The inside door is open.

"Nancy?" Kathleen calls back. "Is that you?" Her voice is strained, tired as she makes her way from the back of the house to the screen door, pushing it open. "He's not here yet. I'm waiting. He called and said he thinks it's happening because his counselor said to go to R&R. But I haven't heard anything more. So, just waiting."

I've spent enough stressful time with Kathleen to know she is a pretty cool person, not one to get easily rattled. But this not knowing, when she thought she knew after years of having nothing but hope, has worn her down to her last nerve. "I'm just drained," she says. "But I know it's been worse for Don. I'm hoping he'll be here any minute."

I'm a reporter. I like being where things are happening, the moment they happen. But looking at Kathleen's face, my human instinct tells me to back away. When Don walks up, I can tell they're going to need all the space and privacy they can find. Some things need to be done alone.

"I'm going to go," I tell Kathleen. "If you want to give me a call when Don gets home, that would be wonderful. I'll wait to hear from you."

"Okay," she says. "I hope he gets here soon."

Walking back down the wide stairs leading to her front door, I am hoping the parole officer's car pulls up—right now. No, it's not to be. Instead I get in my car and head for a nearby coffee shop. Trying not to watch the time, an hour later, I figure he must be home by now. I won't interrupt, I reason. I'll just drive by, to see if the officer's car is there.

Turning onto Kathleen's narrow, winding, tree-lined street, I slow as I approach her house. There, sitting high up on her front porch's half wall, are Don's three boxes. He's home.

—

I wait two weeks before dialing. "Kathleen?"

"Hi, Nancy!" Her voice rises like a happy balloon floating up into a blue sky. "He's here! Let me get him for you. . . . "

"I know I said I'd wait for you to call, but . . . "

"Nancy?" Don's voice is warm. "Hi! I'm here! It's better than I ever expected." For the next few minutes he practically sings into the phone. "Kathleen's house is so beautiful. I knew it would be, and the deck outside . . . "

Two days later I head back to Kathleen's place to hear it all in person. As I pull up in front of the apricot-colored bungalow, there he is, standing at the top of the steps, holding a cup of coffee. I flash back to the day more than a year and a half ago, when the board first found him suitable.

"I'm free!" he says, opening his arms wide to give me a hug. I take a good look at his face. "Can you believe it? I'm still in shock!" How long does it take for an imprisoned man to look free? His skin has color; the muscles around his eyes are tired but relaxed.

"Fresh air and sun," Don says. "I had a sadness over me for a long time, and it left. I feel fifty pounds lighter. Real food. Healthy food. Air. I even have battle scars from working on the rosebushes." He looks over his shoulder at Kathleen's now-pruned bushes. "I'm just overwhelmed."

I follow him up the steps. Up on the porch, he pauses before passing through the open screen door. "See that?" Don says, looking over at the porch swing. "I sit there late at night and watch the moon in the sky. It's beautiful, the air, and the sky and the moon and the stars. I just love that swing."

"Do you want to sit outside?" I ask.

"No. I'm freezing," Don says. "That's one of the things I've noticed. I'm cold all the time. I got the gas fireplace going, and that helps." Stepping through the front door and standing in the middle of his new living room, he grins. "This is my new world!" He turns and walks through the archway that leads into the narrow hallway filled with the framed photos of Kathleen's family, and turns right (away from Kathleen's bedroom) and into the sunny room at the opposite end of the hall. "This is my room," he says, turning and opening his arms like wings. "This is my den, my study. I have a computer. I have an iPod. I have a fax machine. I have a cell phone. I have some clothing. We're getting some more. There's the television and my books are up here on a small shelf, because I love books. I love to learn. I love to study. One of the hindrances in the cell was they always had to be in boxes because you have a little space with two men. If I wanted to do a reference, it wasn't worth pulling out four boxes and digging around. I always said, I want a room where I can put my books up and I can get on a computer, and it's just so phenomenal for me. I just love this little room. Of course, I will replace those little tinny computer speakers with some Bose."

I look at his bed in the corner. "A twin?" I ask. How thoughtful. He will have a room of his own.

"Kathleen's bedroom is down at the end of the hall," Don says.

"You have separate bedrooms?"

"Yeah. It's really good that way. When I wake in the middle of the night, I can turn on the light and read or take a walk. We have visiting privileges. And look, I have these pillows, a down comforter, clean clothes, fresh air. It's been a little chilly for me, but I can open the windows right above my head. I keep them open a crack all night long and I can feel the fresh air over my face. It is heaven. Inside you can't get fresh air unless someone opens the windows on the wall, but with the mesh on the gates, it doesn't filter through. It's always stuffy. I really like my bed; it's at least a foot and a half wider and a good foot longer.

"But my favorite place, my absolute favorite place, is the front porch from six o'clock on. The sun sets to the west, and the sun comes over and radiates and warms the tiles, and Kathleen has this beautiful swing. Almost every night, about six thirty, seven, I go out with PJ the dog, and Kathleen comes after she does the dishes. And I'll sit until ten o'clock. One night Kathleen asked me, 'Why do you like it out here so much?' I said, 'I'm looking at the stars. I'm watching a plane fly by. There's trees and birds and bats and night creatures. I haven't been outside at night after eight thirty for more than half my life.'

"The first day, the parole officer dropped me off; he helped carry a box up the steps. Kathleen was standing on the porch and I was so overwhelmed and exhausted. I just sat down and I looked out and I saw the view, and I said, 'This isn't real.'" Don's voice cracks. He begins to weep. "This isn't going to be permanent, is it? I'm just visiting. I'm going to have to go back."

We are standing in the hallway. I wait for the emotion to settle.

"This is Eden to me. Yesterday, all by myself, I walked to Fairfax," about a mile through leafy neighborhood streets. "Enjoyed the little town, the little stores. Culture shock. The hippie stuff. Had a hamburger at M&G's—junk food. I loved it. I walked back and I saw my turn here and I thought, 'I'm going to walk to San Anselmo.' I called Kathleen and asked how far it was. She said it wasn't too far. So I walked about five miles and loved every step of it. I must have had a silly grin on my face.

"Some guys who parole say, 'People are kind of rude. They don't get close.' So I was expecting that. That's not really what I found. Maybe the average person doesn't want to say hi on the street. But I vowed that I don't care if anyone's rude. I'm going to be a nice guy and I'm loving it. 'Hey, neighbor, how are ya?'

"I'm loving life. I was so overwhelmed by joy, liberated. I felt free. I wanted to do something nice for Kathleen, so I went into Longs drugstore and I found the most awesome card. And right next door was Safeway and I bought her an orchid. And I went into Subway, which is a sandwich shop, and bought a water and a cookie." He laughs. "And I sat on the bench, drinking my water and writing in my card and it was the most awesome thing. Every day is an adventure."

I propose an adventure of our own: a little trip west to an out-of-the-way restaurant for lunch.

Looking at the menu, Don is a bit flummoxed. It's been twenty-eight years since he has held a menu in his hands, a list of things to choose from. There are breakfast pancakes and egg dishes, lunch sandwiches, and burgers with topping choices, as well as all sorts of ingredients to add to anything.

"I'll have whatever you're having," Don says. The panicked look on his face is one I will come to know often when I go out to eat with paroled lifers: even simple choices are overwhelming after decades of life without choice.

We each have a sandwich, french fries, and a milk shake. It's a lunch anyone could love, and Don is like a sensory sponge: the people, sights, tastes.

"They lied," Don says as we drive through forests and look out over the mounds of green hills to the ocean beyond.

"What?"

"When we're inside, people on television say the world outside is polluted and dirty," he says, his eyes fixed on the expanse before us. "That there's nothing beautiful left. They lied."

By late June, lifer paroles are happening like dominoes. Two months after Don has gone home, ten months after Phillip, Jesse Reed's parole is also granted by a superior court judge, who cites the *Lawrence* ruling.

It takes days for the ruling to become official inside San Quentin. "It was Friday afternoon," Jesse says, "around twelve. I was on the upper yard just outside North Block when an officer came up and said, 'Someone called from Sacramento and said to cancel your board hearing on Tuesday.'

"So I'm thinking it could be and it could not be. Maybe they gonna let me go home eventually, 'cause they say I'm not going to the board. I'd already received my papers a week earlier from Judge Larry Goodman of the Alameda County Superior Court saying I'd won my appeal challenging the governor for taking my parole. I was just waiting to see if the state was going to appeal it. So I'm sitting there thinking eventually I might be going home."

Jesse knew better than to call his mom. "I didn't want to get anybody's hopes up, you know what I mean? To be let down. Disappointment after disappointment, your family takes it so hard."

For Jesse, that meant getting through a weekend, and the one thing he didn't want to do was sit around and think about it. He'd rather be busy taking care of business. For years he had worked as a janitor inside the prison hospital, mopping the floors, emptying the wastebaskets, and cleaning the bathrooms.

On Friday afternoon Jesse figured he would get busy stripping and waxing the prison hospital's floors. By Saturday morning there was still no official word. "So I'm in there pushing the mop full of wax in my little blue smock. All the hospital workers have to wear these little blue smocks to identify they are inmates working in the infirmary. I've been sweating 'cause it's hot in there. It's June! So I'm working in this little heat box in there, sweating like a madman, and I take off my smock and I've got my T-shirt on. I'm standing in the hallway, waiting for the wax to dry, and Officer O'Malley, a woman officer, comes by. She works in A section. She starts giving me the business, getting on me 'cause I'm standing in the hallway without my smock on. I'm like, 'O'Malley, you know I'm working.' She's very serious, saying, 'You know better. I'm going to write you up.' And she complains to the officer in charge of my area that I'm trying to impress women around here." It's true: Jesse's biceps are quite impressive. "Like I'm trying to score. So I'm stressing now. A write-up on my last weekend in prison? I couldn't believe it. I was going to lose my freedom because I was waxing the floors without my smock on? But my officer knows I'm stripping and waxing the floors and he tells me not to worry about it. That it's going to be all right."

Later that night Jesse is in his cell and he hears his name over the intercom: "Inmate Reed, report to the officer desk."

"So I go to the officer desk and the officer says to call the infirmary. I call the infirmary and Officer Perez says, 'Reed, can you come back and get Mr. B's ID card? I can't find him.' So I went over and picked up Mr. B's ID and came back and gave it to Mr. B.

"By now," Jesse says, "it was eight and the officer in North Block said I could have a phone slot. I was just getting ready to call my aunt when an officer got on the intercom and said, 'Reed. Reed. Inmate 370, report back to the infirmary immediately.'"

"I hung the phone up and headed back to the infirmary. On my way over there, I see Sam [Robinson] walking away from the infirmary. He usually brings the official word if someone is going home. I said, 'Hey, you heard anything yet?' Sam said, 'No, haven't heard anything yet.' So I said, 'Okay, man. Let me know, man! You know?'

"I get there to the hospital and all these officers are standing there at the front door. One of them, Officer Martinez, says, 'Reed, go in the cage [a small holding cell], right here. Go in there and have a seat for a minute. Someone wants to see you.' I'm like, 'Cool.' I'm not trippin'. I go in there. I don't know what this is about. Then, when I go in the cage, the officer closes it and locks it. Then he's like, 'We ought to strip his ass out.'"

"What does that mean?" I ask.

"Strip-search me. You know, make you take all your clothes off and strip-search you when you're in trouble. And I'm like, 'Strip me out? For what? What are you talking about stripping me out for?' Now I'm starting to trip. I'm sitting there and I'm sitting there and nobody is saying anything. They're out there talking. I'm just sitting in the cage. Ten minutes go by. Nothing. Fifteen to twenty minutes more go by. An officer from B section comes over with some papers in his hand. I see some 115s. Now I'm like, 'Whoa—115s are disciplinary write-ups. O'Malley wrote me up?' The officer comes in and says, 'What's your name?' I say, 'Reed.' 'What cell are you in?' I say, 'North Block 370 low.' He says, 'Yeah, you the one.' I see these 115s. What the hell?

"I see Sam walking up. He looks at me and he starts smiling and he reaches out his hand and everybody busts out laughing. Right? I'm like at the lowest low right now and all of a sudden, it's like, 'Congratulations.' Oh my God. Sam says, 'Congratulations. You goin' home.' And he gave me my paperwork. That was such an experience.

It was funny. It was exciting. Then all the officers congratulated me. Officer Martinez said, 'Congratulations, Reed. You made it.' I said, 'Thank you. Thank you so much.' So it was official and they said I was gonna be out no later than Tuesday."

Jesse says he was afraid to laugh or cry. "If I didn't have a strong heart, it could have did it right there. My feelings were mixed. I went from a real low sad to an extreme excitement, extreme joy. I went from the lowest low to the highest high, all in a matter of seconds.

"It was an honor they cared enough about me to play a trick on me like that. I'm sure they don't do that with everybody. I did work in the hospital. All those officers knew me. They didn't all like me. Officer Martinez didn't like anybody in blue. It was a nice surprise. As stressful as it was, when it was all played out and said and done, it was okay. It was a nice go-away."

I'm not so convinced this was good-natured kidding around. Jesse was on the edge, concerned he was being written up, getting a 115. It's a good thing he didn't have a heart condition.

Back in North Block, Jesse finally got a chance to call his family. "I called my aunt 'cause my mom couldn't accept collect calls anymore, and she started screaming. She dropped the phone. My uncle picked it up and said, 'What's going on?' And I told him and said, 'Can you call my mom on a three-way so I can tell her?' So he called, and my mom was crying and praying. It was something."

Early the following morning, Jesse joined the usual procession of lifers making their way to the prison's Protestant chapel for Sunday services. There would be Christian rock music and singing, born-again preaching and praying.

Midway through the packed service, Pastor Curry asked for Jesse to join him up on the low stage in front of the congregation: "Our brother Jesse is going home."

Like a gray cloud overhead bursting open above the room, men sitting elbow to elbow, thigh to thigh on the long golden oak pews jumped to their feet, their arms and faces raised to the ceiling, everyone shouting a chorus of "Hallelujah" and "Bless me, Jesus! God is good."

By the time Jesse reached the stage, he was surrounded by a couple dozen other men in blue, their hands touching his shoulders and lowered head. Standing tall over the circle of men, Pastor Curry held his hands outstretched for all to see and presented Jesse with a ministry license for his years of Christian study and service. "Yes," Pastor Curry said, beaming. "God helps those who help themselves. Jesse Reed is proof God has not forsaken you."

On Monday Jesse's counselor called him to her office and handed him the official parole paperwork for his signature. As he signed, she said, "We're gonna try and have you out of here Tuesday. No later than Wednesday."

Monday passed, then Tuesday. On Wednesday, someone else in the prison administration made his way to Jesse to tell him they were going to try to have him out of there by Thursday.

Late Wednesday afternoon, a fellow lifer named Stone told Jesse, "I seen your paperwork, and you're going home tomorrow."

On Thursday morning, Jesse got up early so he would have enough time to go to the chapel and say good-bye to his mentor. Pastor Curry handed him a Bible. "While I was in there talking to him, they called the chapel and said, 'Have Reed report to R&R immediately.'"

With just minutes left of his twenty-four years, eight months in prison, Jesse returned to his cell to grab his property. "I took some legal papers, letters, pictures, stuff like that. Sweatpants and one pair of jeans I wanted to wear out. That was it. Two boxes. I gave the combination of the lock on my cell door to my friend Demetrius 'Flip' Daniels and said distribute it all, my TV and radio. I made sure he gave my typewriter, a 500 series Brother word processor, to Noel. He helped me with my legal work."

With his papers signed and his few belongings passed out, Jesse headed down to R&R to meet his parole officer, the man who would escort him to the other side.

—

After twenty-four years in prison and two parole dates snatched away by the governor, Jesse's freedom is his mother's. While Jesse is being processed out of San Quentin, twenty miles away, across the bay, Lois Parks sits in a folding chair on her small front porch, waiting, watching. When the spirit moves her, she sings words of praise to her Lord, thanking him for taking care of her son, her eyes wet with tears, her hands open.

All morning long, people who have heard through the vast neighborhood's grapevine that Jesse Reed is coming home turn at the corner, past the small market stocked with candy and cheap beer, and drive past her house, yelling from the car windows, "Is he home yet?"

"Praise the Lord," Lois yells back. "Not yet, but my baby's coming home today!" However long it takes for Jesse to step out of a car and onto the sidewalk in front of her house, Lois Parks isn't leaving the front porch.

Jesse's Aunt Theresa, his mother's sister, knows her nephew. She knows how much it will mean to him, after wearing prison blues for so long, to have nice clothes to wear stepping out onto the sidewalk. Days earlier, she went shopping and picked out a buttercream-colored linen suit and a pair of chestnut-brown shoes and dropped them off at the nearby parole office.

When the state car bearing her son finally turns the corner, Lois can no longer sit still. Standing on her porch, she sings louder and louder, her years of pain filling the air. Her firstborn son, the mirror of her smile, is returning to her. Now the broken family she has barely held together all these years can finally begin to heal.

Sitting inside the parole officer's car, looking out at the family home he left nearly twenty-five years before, Jesse knows how hard it will be to reenter this world. But for now, in this one suspended moment, everything is good. He has returned home to his mother a free man.

He pushes the button on the automatic seat belt. As it slides off his chest, he pulls the lever opening the car door and steps out, putting one foot onto old territory.

Lois rushes as fast as her arthritic, swollen legs can carry her down the stairs toward him. Before he can even step through the gate, she is holding him in her arms. They stand together and cry.

Word flies: Jesse is back. From inside the battered white house, the security screen door swings open and slams shut for one relative after the other. "Jesse! Jesse!" His youngest brother, Jayvonce, rushes up to him, his breath thick with the smell of alcohol, his words sped up by too much cocaine. Jesse smiles and hugs his little brother, though his expression betrays a hint of his fear about sharing a house with someone embroiled in all the old trouble.

Lawanda, Jesse's eldest sister, who has come all the way from Texas for his homecoming, calls out, "Hallelujah! Thank you, Jesus." Like a gospel singer, she raises her arms over her head, palms to the sky, and sings, certain her thick, passionate voice is being heard by God himself: "Oh, happy day. Oh, happy day. When Jesus walked, he washed my sins away. Oh, happy day."

Family and friends jump in on the chorus: "Oh, it's a happy day . . . when I get to heaven."

One of Jesse's eighteen nieces and nephews stands to the side, silent, watching. "I've never seen him before," says Darnell, a good-looking ninth grader at the local public high school, "just pictures. I know he's my uncle. He looks happy to be home."

Within minutes, word has spread. Cars are parading, headlight to bumper, up and down the street, horns honking, deep bass pounding hip-hop from their speakers. As each driver reaches Jesse, who by now is holding court, alternately standing and sitting in a lawn chair positioned in the middle of the sidewalk, the drivers throw open their car doors, jump out, and bounce over to give the big man a hefty shoulder-led hug and "brutha" handshake. Others approach on foot over cracked sidewalks and quicken their pace as they get close, pushing their way in to give Jesse a hug.

Deep in celebration, Lois begins to sing her favorite gospel song: "'Wonderful. My God is so wonderful. He is my shepherd. He's been a mighty good guide. Whatever I need, my God will supply. My God is so wonderful.' . . . I love that song. Now he's here embarking on a new life. Tonight he'll be home in his own room with DirectTV, music, and a queen bed that's bigger than his 'room' was!"

Neighbors pull back their curtains. It's a big day at the Parks house. Do they know? If they did, would it matter? Jayvonce ushers a middle-aged white woman through the crowd and up to Jesse. "Jess, this is our neighbor, Gina. She helps Mom a lot. She's been there. She's on board."

"Nice to meet you," Gina says. "Welcome home."

"I'm back now," Jesse says.

Jesse and I take a little walk around the block. Strolling down the sidewalk, past the turn-of-the-twentieth-century single-family homes, Jesse realizes again he is really free. "Wow," he says, laughing. "It's amazing. So many people are coming to say hi." Looking around, he says so much has changed. "I don't remember those stairs, and all these trees. Wow!"

"What," I ask, "does freedom look like?"

"That's a heavy question right there." Jesse stops. "Right now for me freedom is a little bittersweet. It's looking bright. I know there's a lot for me to do. A lot I have to do. There's a lot expected of me. It's a great joy."

A short black woman rushes up to Jesse. "Hi, brother-in-law," she says. "You don't know me but I want to give you a hug." Reaching up, she puts her arms around his shoulders, embracing him. "Welcome to the world!" Then moving on down the sidewalk to his family house, she turns back. "You look just like your mama." Jesse laughs.

"Jesse," I say as we make our way back down the sidewalk, "I've only known you inside San Quentin, clean and sober. Your family is so happy to see you, but many of them have been drinking, and Jayvonce looks tweaked. Is this going to be hard for you?"

"It's okay. I can handle it," he says, all joy evaporating from his face. "Now our mission is to get my brother Gregory home." He's nervous.

Two weeks later, on the Fourth of July, Jesse's extended family of blood relatives and friends holds an Independence Day picnic at a small urban park at the end of the street. Jesse sits down at a small table, much like the one where I first interviewed him on the San Quentin yard, only this time he's facing his Uncle Carl in a long-delayed game of dominoes. As they shift and slide the rectangular pieces around the surface of the table, the men and boys of the family stand close behind, watching.

"It's amazing how the children have latched onto him. They follow him around," Lois says. "I love getting up every morning and making him breakfast. We just sit and talk. Just talk. I'm so happy. It's better than birthday, Christmas, and New Year's all together."

A thirty-something man wearing a track suit and holding the hand of a young girl, presumably his daughter, walks through the middle of the small park, stops, and approaches Jesse. "My name is Terrance. Is this a family event, birthday party?"

"I'm Jesse. It's a family, friend, welcome home, er . . . getting out party," Jesse says, holding out his hand to the man.

"My name is Terrance McDonald. I go to this park every week and I never saw this. I'm glad you're living it up."

"The world gonna know in a minute," Jesse says under his breath. "I been gone for twenty-five years."

"I did ten, homie, at seventeen," Terrance says. "I got out when I was twenty-seven. Now I'm thirty-four. So I feel you, man. I got my shit together. I bring my daughter here. Wow. Good for you, Jesse. Wow. How long you been out?"

"This is my third week," Jesse says.

"Have you adapted?" Terrance asks. "When I got out—the freeway, McDonald's, the lights. They have no fucking clue what you been through. Ten. Trust me."

"Ten. He understands," Jesse says, turning to me.

"Where your head at, Jesse?" Terrance asks. "I met a lot of old fools inside who weren't ready to get out."

"What makes me different," Jesse says, "is my faith base is God. I believe it's because of God I'm standing here today. In the crisis in my life, I had hope. A lot of men inside don't have hope. The faith in God, where they're willing to depend on something or someone greater than who they are. They're caught up with what they can do for themselves. What they don't understand is they can't help themselves and they're trying with everything they have in them. They're learning law. They haven't understood it's greater than what you can do or some lawyer can do or the governor can do. Men having their dates taken."

"OG, OG," Terrance says, using a prisoner's term of endearment, short for "old gangster." "I've seen some go before the board after being caught with weed after being down twenty-seven years. But prison is something you have to outgrow. It's a mentality."

"Maturing and becoming a man," Jesse says. "We know weed is illegal, so when you take that chance, then you got to know you playing with your freedom!"

"I been down with a lot of lifers," Terrance says, "and the board plays with their freedom. I've witnessed it."

"They played games with mine," Jesse says. "I had two dates, and the governor took both of them."

"God, Jesse. God, man," Terrance says, looking genuinely thrilled for Jesse. "I'm so happy for you. But when I got out after doing ten, I had no help. The same program we had in the penitentiary that kept you out of trouble is the same program we need out here, man. I'm really rooting for you. Man, twenty-five years? That's a long time. You look good. But I talk to a lot of youngsters, and they doin' twenty-five years on the installment plan, and they don't really get it." He's talking about the lost men who go to jail over and over, serving determinate sentences.

"No," Jesse says, "they don't get it."

"The best thing you can do, Jesse—I'm gonna swear to God, besides the rhetoric—is be an example. Shine. You ain't got to do nothing else, man. Just execute. They gonna realize: Jesse knows."

"That's the same way I lived my life in there," Jesse says. "It's the same thing out here. Sometimes the best teacher we can be is to live our life. Better than any book."

"What have you learned, supremely?" Terrance asks Jesse, looking for insight from someone who has been down and gotten up. "If you was to sum it up, condense it in a few words? 'Cause when I was seventeen, I shot somebody. Jesse, to this day, I still can't figure out what someone could have told me to prevent me from doing what I done. When I go back to seventeen, it's just darkness. I wonder if I had met a Jesse or a Barack Obama, would it have altered the course my life was taking?"

"That's something right there," Jesse says, "you'll never know. Time has passed. We don't know. There's a possibility you wouldn't have went that way if someone said something to you, but there's also the possibility that you would have stayed on the same course. But time has passed and once this day is over with, it's gone."

"But we have hindsight," Terrance says.

"Only thing we can do is disseminate information. It's up to the individual to choose," Jesse says.

"You right, OG," Terrance says. "I'm too optimistic. You can look at a seventeen-year-old street punk, and you can look at his action, OG, and you can paint his profile with precision. It's nothing new. With our insight, don't you think it's incumbent on us to craft a way to sort of bridge some kind of line of communication with these wayward knuckleheads? They dangerous out there. You see them with clarity. You see right through them, OG. There's nothing they can tell you. So you're more like a therapist, an expert in the life they live. I would love to get involved with someone like you and other people because there's a wealth of insight and wisdom. God damn. These dudes really think it's a joke. They don't understand what twenty years is. I heard it, OG. I didn't listen to it."

"They don't," Jesse says. "Until you decide you want to change, there's nothing. We can put the information out there, but whether you choose to hear it or not is another story. Only thing I can do is put it out there, tell my story, share with you what is happening to me."

Jesse then tells Terrance about a program he watched on television about elephants in a nature preserve in Africa. In this particular preserve, all the male adult elephants had been taken away. As a result, the juvenile elephants were rampaging, killing rhinoceroses, threatening farmers. A couple of them were so dangerous park rangers had to kill them. The juvenile elephants had no bull elephants there to teach them how to behave.

"In society today," Jesse says, "grown men are being locked away. Young men on the outside really have no direction. They're growing up in the streets. They've taken away after-school programs. So, now young men don't have anything to do but hang out on the corners and pick up habits from drug dealers, pimps, hustlers. These are the role models they see in the ghetto: all the negative things. These young men don't know how to be men. Those of us who have learned how to be men are afraid to go back in the jungle and say, 'Hey, look. There's a better way.'"

"Why are you afraid?" I ask.

"We're afraid of what they'll do!" Jesse says. "When they put the bull elephants back in the refuge, the young male elephants challenged them. But the bull elephants didn't back down. This is the thing that's missing today. We are the bull elephants, and we cannot back down."

"I've been staying the hell away from them," says Terrance.

"You got to speak out," Jesse says. "We don't have to go challenge what they doing, threatening them. Talking, what we're doing right now: dialoguing."

"What is it like being the bull coming home?" I ask him as Terrance walks away.

"I'm not a savior, but I can do my part to try and effect change as best I possibly can," Jesse says. "I plan to live my life in that spirit: trying to effect change however I can. I don't know what each day will bring, but I think I'm equipped with the tools to deal with it. It's the programming, it's the counseling, it's the life experience in a nutshell. The growth process is not unlike growing up from a child to an adult. It was a long process. It's continuous."

With that, Jesse's mother, Lois, calls everyone together in a wide circle, reaching out to hold the hands of the first few to join her, everyone connected through fingers and palms. Uncle Carl speaks up: "Hats off."

The men in the circle, young and old, reach up to pull off their baseball caps. Before they all bow their heads, Jesse looks around the circle. "You guys don't know how much of a blessing this is for me today. It's been a long time. It's been thirty years since I did something like this. I've been gone for twenty-five, and it was at least five before that. So I'm just grateful and I thank you all for coming out and being a part of today."

Then, as if on cue, they bow their heads, and Jesse continues, his voice dropping into a serious register. "Gracious Lord, help me, Father, God of heaven and earth. Holy is your name, Lord God. We want to thank you, Father God, for this time you've allowed us to be assembled here, family and friends. Father, if we can come together and enjoy this day you have made, Father God. It's been a long time coming. We are mindful my brother Greg is on his way as well and we're going to do this again at his homecoming. We thank you for this day, for all that showed up today. We thank you for the food, the laughs, the joy, the wind, the breeze. We thank you for the sun that shines today. We just thank you for all you are doing in our lives. Lord God, I just ask that you would bless every one individual here today, that you would bless their families and their children. Father, we honor you today for your awesome display of power. The mere fact that I'm standing here today, I know it was all orchestrated by you and without you it would never have happened. As I embark upon this new life, this second opportunity at life, I thank you today and I know that everything will work out all right. In Jesus's name, everybody say it, 'Amen.'"

"Everything going to be cold as long as you praying," says DeAngela, Jesse's sister, with a laugh.

sixteen

ONE SCREW-UP

2009

Whether they're crossing a street at the crosswalk or staying just under the speed limit on the freeway, lifers on parole exist knowing their beautiful freedom is spider-thread tenuous.

Now that Phillip, Don, and Jesse have joined Eddie and Richie out among the free, it's blue skies and sunshine, pork chops and long walks. At least that's how it looks to me, from the outskirts looking in. That's only because I can't see the long-term forecast. Out on their horizon, just beyond the puffy white clouds of freedom, a big, black storm cloud hangs.

Before a freed lifer puts his first step onto the sidewalk, their parole agent drives them straight from the prison gates to the agent's home base, usually an office in a nondescript business park in the county where the lifer originally committed the murder. There, one-on-one, staring the lifer in the face, the agent spells out the terms of his parole. If he violates just one term, however technical or trivial, he could be sent back to prison.

Parole, which for a lifer typically lasts five years, is a promise not to screw up—not even a little. Some parole agents are strict, others more lenient. Either way, the rules are black and white, right and wrong. A map is pulled out. A circle with a fifty-mile radius from their residence, marking the limits of their parole, is drawn. "That," the agent says, "is the limit of your freedom. Anything outside the line means you have to file a special request for a pass. You need to give me at least three weeks to get the six signatures required for a pass. Got it? Parolees are not to drink alcohol or use drugs. If you get called in for a random drug test, you could be asked [i.e., required] to unzip in front of me and pee publicly. No weapons, not a single one. No contact with law enforcement; that's a parole violation. Show up for your weekly parole check-ins on time in my office. I'll be visiting your residence whenever I feel like it. If it's after ten p.m., you better be there."

Once the inmate and parole agent have gone through the rules, it's time to go home.

The first few weeks after men like Phillip, Don, Jesse, Richie, Eddie, and Bryan get out, everything is surreal, vibrant, new. Moving from their cells to bedrooms with pillows and bathrooms with doors is like being born again. After decades of institutional monotony, their senses are alert, absorbent.

For days, weeks, and even months after they get out, the simple act of walking down a sidewalk is a social challenge. They watch free people to see how they do it. In prison there were clear rules about eye contact and body language. Now they have to learn the unspoken codes of the never-incarcerated, the vast human community of people who have never been locked up, have no concern for those who are, and become alert and afraid if and when they discover someone near them has been.

In the middle of the night they wake soaked in sweat, terrified their freedom is just a dream. In the morning, when they open their eyes, they realize everything they want to do takes more money than they have. The $200 in gate money they receive from the state upon their release evaporates in the first few days. There are bus tickets and food, clothes, shaving cream, movies, snacks. Worst of all, they have no money to spend on the people they love, the people who for years have cared for them. It's not easy, but it doesn't matter, they say, as long as they are free.

A few months after our trip to the fair, Phillip calls. "You'll never guess what I'm doing!" he says, out of breath.

"Not a chance," I say.

"I'm riding my bike! I can talk to you on my cell phone while I'm riding my bike! I ride it everywhere all day long. I just left the library downtown and now I'm headed for the river. I'll stop and take a swim."

"So, what's it like, being on the outside?"

"It's great. To help me get oriented, I'm keeping to my old prison schedule. Each morning I get up at five thirty and tiptoe to the backyard. When I get outside in the fresh morning air, I stand beneath the big cedar tree and take deep breaths. That tree was just about my height when I went in, and now it's—what?—thirty feet tall! That's when I do slow-motion yoga. I did it every morning inside Q."

"Q?" I ask.

"You know, San Quentin," Phillip says, without saying more. I get it. Using the letter will make it easier to talk about the past and present without alerting anyone listening in that we're talking about prison.

Over the next six months Phillip and I talk on the phone fairly often. He's getting tired of having so much time on his hands and says he's ready to talk to his old boss about getting his old plumbing job back.

Then things take a surprising turn. Eight months after Phillip was paroled, he calls me. His voice is altered, worn down. "I had to move out of my mom's house," he says. "It's been really hard. I don't know what happened. I didn't have anywhere to go. Fortunately, my boss is building some apartments, and he said I can stay in one of them while they finish."

"Your old boss? So you're working for him again?"

"Yes. I had seen him when I first got out. You know I was with him way back when he had just started his plumbing business. There were just a couple of us then. Over the years we've kept in contact and he's a really good guy. So, I went and had a meeting with him and he offered me a full-time job, just like he promised all those years. So, I've been back at work for about a month."

"But what happened? I thought things were going so well with your mom and Pops?"

Phillip's voice cracks. He sounds like he's on the edge of crying. "I don't know. All of a sudden everything just fell apart. I knew Mom was getting anxious. She was saying something about my bike. I asked them if we could sit and talk about my being there, to be sure we kept the lines of communication open. Mom said, 'No. Everything's fine.' But then one day when I came home from work, Mom said, 'You have to leave.' I said, 'Okay. But is there some way we can talk about this? I don't really have anywhere to go. Can I just have a little time to arrange for a place to stay?' And she said, 'No, you have to leave now.' She said she was going to call my parole officer and tell them to come and get me if I didn't leave. 'You need to go. Now!' I panicked. I didn't know what to do."

"Did something happen leading up to this?" I ask, trying to get my bearings.

"No. It came out of nowhere. I knew having me around was difficult for them. They don't go out and they don't have visitors. They're pretty isolated. But I thought we could talk about it. I was so afraid she was going to call my PO. I don't know what she would tell him. I didn't do anything. But I was so scared. I didn't know what she would do."

"So," I ask, concerned, "when did all this happen?"

"Just about two weeks ago."

"What did you do?"

"Well, I didn't really know anyone that well yet. I called my sister but she lives in the city [San Francisco] and I have to stay in Sacramento for my parole."

"Did she have any idea what this was all about?"

"It was sort of strange," Phillip says, his voice hollow, confused. "She didn't say much. I called an old friend from back in high school, and we met at a bar. I told her what happened and she offered to let me stay the night at her place. The next day I went into work, and my boss saw something was wrong. He asked me to come in his office to talk. I told him what happened, and he said, 'We'll figure this out. Don't worry. I'm sure it will all blow over. In the meantime, I have these apartments I'm renovating. You can stay there as long as you need.' I don't know what I'd have done if he hadn't come to my rescue. It's really devastating. Thank God I have had all the training inside Q for this kind of crisis. I knew I had to keep breathing, and just give it some time."

"I'm coming up," I say.

"Okay. Don't go to my mom's house," he says. "I'll give you directions to my new place."

A few days later I drive to North Sacramento, an area of the city that's slowly transitioning—gentrifying, some might say—from gangs to Generation X first-time homebuyers. An early summer has grabbed hold and it's hot. Peeling myself out of the car, I cross a business intersection and see a man working in a small garden. From the back it doesn't look like Phillip. This man's body is softer, more relaxed. But as he turns, I recognize his face.

"Phillip!" I call out. He looks good. He's all filled out. His face is golden brown; his eyes are a clearer, brighter blue than I remember.

Reaching out to give me a hug, he laughs. "Hey, Nancy. Good to see you." He holds out a bunch of wild roses. "They had thorns all over them, so I plucked them off. So, how you been? Good seein' ya."

"So this is your new neighborhood?"

"Yeah, for now," he says, looking around. "Did you want to step inside for a minute? We can go to a park after. It's too nice to be stuck inside."

The small apartment building, located at the tip of a five-stop traffic signal, is being renovated by his boss into a half dozen apartments with historic brick walls, iron frame windows, and plastered arches. It's the nicest building on the block. "There's six units in here," he says, pulling out a set of keys and unlocking the common front door at the sidewalk level. "Downstairs on this level is businesses. He's renovating the whole thing. It was trashed. They're not even rented out yet." Up the stairs to the second floor, Phillip walks ahead to the end of the hall and opens the door. "As you can see, I don't have a whole lot of stuff in here 'cause they're still doing some things. . . . "

It's a small, nearly bare studio apartment with a full redbrick wall, a big casement window at the back, and brand-new appliances in the kitchen. A paisley cotton tablecloth covers a fold-up card table, the only piece of furniture in the living/dining room. A white cotton futon mattress is rolled up tight and shoved in the closet. "I just pull it out at night," Phillip says, "and put it away in the morning. I don't like it cluttered. I like it open. And I don't want to bring a lot of furniture; they're still painting and there's a couple of electrical things they have to do. I don't need a lot. When they're done, I will bring a bed in here.

"Hey, you must be hot after the long drive," he says. "Do you want a drink of water?"

"Yes, love one."

Reaching into the bare cupboard, Phillip pulls out a sixteen-ounce lime-green plastic cup. "All I have left is this San Quentin tumbler."

"Why did you keep it?"

"It's a good tumbler! I used to drink tea in it all the time." He points to a small white plastic fan sitting on the open counter. "That fan right there is from San Quentin. I just pulled it out. Kind of dirty. Got to dust it off. And . . . one of my coolest new things I got from my boss is a laptop he sold to me for $250. It's Wi-Fi hooked up and I can go online. It sat on a desk for three years. They used it for business but were going to sell it on eBay for $450. He knew I needed one and sold it to me, right then. So," Phillip says, pointing to the dusty old fan, "that's the old, and this is the new! Quite a contrast."

"So your boss is letting you live here for free?"

"Yes. Absolutely free. And when he rents out the five and I'm in the sixth one, he'll drop it to half price if I want to manage the building. He's renting these for $750 apiece. Some of them are one-bedrooms. Or I may just move out. I really want a house with a yard and a garage and in a better area 'cause this isn't the greatest of areas."

"So have you spoken to your mom yet? Is that sorted out?"

"No," he says, the wound still fresh. "I tried to call and she won't take my calls. I even sent her a letter apologizing for anything I may have done to upset her. But she hasn't responded. I really don't know what to do. My sister says to give her some time. But it has been a shock. It's hard. I don't want to keep calling."

I wonder how being locked up in prison for a quarter of a century, half of his adult life, is affecting his ability to understand and cope with changing relationships—the problem that led to his crime and incarceration in the first place.

Changing the subject, Phillip points to some photos lying on the counter. "Look what I got today in the mail!"

I pick up the half dozen five-by-seven photos. Phillip is standing before a group of teens. They're listening, watching him.

"I went with this woman who works for victims services. We went to the California Youth Authority Fire Camp to talk to these youngsters who are getting out in a month or so. Seventeen to twenty-three years old. They're trying to do the right thing. So I talked to them of course about my crime, the time I did and blah blah blah, but also how I made my adjustment. How I prepared before I got out, to get out, and how I dealt with my issues, my stuff. I told them whatever it is, everybody has had issues as a child, all kinds of different things. Talk about it. Deal with it. Get through that. So when you get mad at somebody it's not that junk that's coming up with your anger. Deal with that stuff so you can deal with things easier and more confident. Bunch of stuff like that. She took pictures, and this is it. About thirty kids."

This isn't the first time Phillip has tried to counsel teens. Inside San Quentin, he was a member of Squires, a group of lifers who met with teens who had already been convicted of breaking the law. By telling their stories, the lifers tried to help the wannabe gangsters turn their lives around before it was too late. "Is this the first time you've talked to kids on the outside?"

"Oh no. I've been doing a lot of this," Phillip says, holding up one photo in particular. "Here I'm doing a one-on-one with one of the guys that's getting ready to get out. I just got these in the mail. Yeah. Things are good. Things are going well. Yeah . . . "

For years Phillip has helped other men's sons. Now that he's out I wonder how he will ever make it right with his own. "How's your relationship with your sons?"

"Other than writing," Phillip says, "we still don't have one, because they're still both locked up. My younger son, Anthony, he got three and a half years for some violent drug-related crimes. He was actually going to get out five months ago, but they charged him with another crime that he committed before he went to prison that caught up to him. Somebody told. I don't know exactly what happened. But when he was supposed to get out, instead of getting out, they took him back to Butte County and he had to go to court on this other crime. They found him guilty for that and sent him right back to prison. He never got out. He went from prison to county jail and back to prison."

"How long does he have left to serve?"

"He's got about three years left," Phillip says.

"Does that mean you can't go see him?"

"Not while he was in the Butte County Jail." He shakes his head.

"You're not allowed to?" I ask, to be clear. "Because of your parole?"

"You have to get a lot of approvals, and I tried and tried and tried to see both my boys," Phillip says, "and it just didn't happen."

"Where's your older boy, Phillip Jr.?"

"He's in Jamestown, at the fire camp," he says. "He's getting out this month."

"Will you get together?"

"Hopefully."

We take a picnic to Capitol Park and sit on a blanket under some of the towering redwood trees surrounding the massive white capitol building and the offices of Governor Arnold Schwarzenegger.

"Do you ever think about San Quentin?" I ask.

"At random times during the day or evening I think, 'What would I be doing in San Quentin right now in that small little place and what *am* I doing? I'm sitting at the river or I'm hanging out, talking to a friend.' What would I be doing right now at six o'clock at San Quentin? I'd probably be getting ready to go to one of my evening programs. Let's see. Today is Wednesday, so I'd be going to REACH, the literacy program a teacher and I started ten years ago, where any prisoner on the line [the mainline population in the prison], if they want to learn how to read, or write a letter to their family, or need to up their math skills. Whatever it was they wanted to learn, we matched them up with inmate tutors we had trained. Which is cool."

A state capitol security guard passes by. Phillip watches, an almost knee-jerk quick check to be sure he isn't breaking any rules.

"That was your universe," I offer. "It's not like you want to go back, but that was your home."

"Fortunately, I've been able to see most of the free people: volunteers, teachers, people that I worked for and worked with inside San Quentin. I've seen a lot of them. They've come and visited me, or I've gone to the Bay Area and visited them. So I'm able to continue on with a lot of those friendships but the guys that are in there, I can't go in and see them."

"Can you write?"

"You can write a little bit and you can send your hi's to them and they can send their hi's to you through friends, but that was my life for all these years, and now I'm cut away from that. I climbed up to the top of Mount Tam the other day with my sister and some friends. From up at the top, San Quentin is a speck. I thought to myself, 'Geez, I lived in that little tiny piece of property for fifteen years. That little tiny area, that little tiny yard, those little buildings.' That was it. That little speck for fifteen years. And then all the other little specks, the other prisons I lived in for all those years.

"Some of the people I was with went down, but I stayed up there at the tip-top for at least another hour thinking, 'Wow, I'm really up here from the outside looking in.' Finally. It was a good feeling. It still is. For so many years I stared up from the San Quentin yard to Mount Tam. Now I'm looking down."

Suddenly Phillip stops talking and grabs his jacket, which is lying nearby. "I have to check my phone. It might be my parole agent." There's a touch of frantic in his voice. "It's been vibrating and I didn't hear it until now."

Looking at the open face of the cell phone, he breathes a sigh of relief. "No. It's okay."

It looked as though Don had the sweetest landing of all. Unlike most lifers who parole back to the county of their conviction, Don paroled to the upscale neighborhood of his fiancée, Kathleen, where the sun is always shining and real estate is only for those with the deepest of pockets. For Don, it all looked perfect. There was no history, no past. Even his own family, his brother and two sisters, were far away, living where they all grew up, in Wisconsin.

Which is why I was surprised when I heard there was trouble. "Not with Kathleen," Sam Robinson says, "but it's bad. I always thought if one guy was going to come back, it would be Don."

"What happened?" I ask, trying to push Sam to tell me what happened to make him such a critic of Don Cronk. "I have to know."

It's late May 2009. Don has been out for only about six weeks, and I've returned to San Quentin to witness another lifer's parole hearing. While we are standing around in the hall outside the hearing room, waiting for the commissioners to announce they've come to a decision, Sam drops the bomb.

"I can't say anything more. You'll have to talk to Don about it. I can tell you the local police, prison officers, and his parole agent were all in on it."

My hands turn cold and sweaty. "You're just fooling with me. Nothing really happened," I say. "Right?"

"No, it really happened," Sam says, looking at Officer James Gary for support. "Didn't Don Cronk almost come back in?"

"Yep. That was something," Officer Gary says. "Have you heard anything more about that?"

Sam looks at me as if he now has confirmation that life prisoners will always be unreliably dangerous.

"Well, I'm going to be seeing Don later tonight," I say. "We're supposed to have dinner together. I'll ask him what happened."

"Yeah," Sam says. "Then you'll be calling me next week, saying, 'I've been played.'"

"But how can you be so sure your story is right?" I ask the prison's public information officer. "Have you spoken to Don?"

"It's a murderer's word against a doctor's word," Sam says. "What's the question?"

The minute I get back inside my car, I reach for my cell phone and give Don a call. My husband and twenty-five-year-old daughter have heard so much about Don, they want to meet him. Now that he and Kathleen are coming to my house for dinner, Sam's troubling announcement has left me nervous, on edge.

Hearing Don's voice, I feel a little less panicky. I ask how everything is.

"Things are okay," Don says, "but I've been shaken. Something really terrible happened. I can't talk about it now, but I'll tell you all about it when I see you."

I can't imagine what has happened. Sam's assurance that it was "so bad" and "so close to Don coming back in" that I begin to wonder. Had I overlooked some critical gap in Don's rehabilitation? Was I making a mistake introducing Don to my daughter?

I set the dining room table with candles, linen, and peonies. I decide to wait for him to bring it up. In the flow between the salad and main course, while my daughter, Nayeli, clears the plates and my husband, Max, returns to the kitchen to pull the braised osso buco from the oven, Don takes a deep breath and begins, "Well, we have had a terrifying experience."

Kathleen is sitting next to him. I look at her. She looks back at me and shakes her head. Before saying another word, Don reaches down and lifts the cuff of his pants. There's a thick black band about three inches wide encircling his ankle. In the middle of the band is a black box.

I look up at Don, dumbfounded. "What is that?"

"That's an electronic bracelet," he says, his voice breaking.

Kathleen's face slowly shifts from pain to anger. "Can you believe this?" she asks.

"What happened?"

"You aren't going to believe it," Kathleen says. "It's insane."

"Okay. I want to hear everything from the beginning," I demand. "Let's wait until Nayeli and Max are back. I know they will want to hear this as well." Actually I'm thinking I need them to hear whatever this is, so I can grill them about it later, for their take. My husband is a senior investigator for the San Francisco Office of Citizen Complaints and is responsible for investigating complaints about police misconduct. He's pretty perceptive.

"Okay," Don says when everyone has their dinner in front of them. "This is what happened."

It was early in the evening, about a week ago, a little over a month after Don had been released from San Quentin. He and Kathleen still hadn't made it to the top of Mount Tam to take the hike they had always dreamed about taking together. So after a trip to the farmers' market, she suggested they drive up a winding road near her house to a spot where they could at least look out on the mountain. As they got near the top, they saw an "enormous" estate, one that seemed to take over the top of the hill with an olive orchard and a vineyard.

"It was like an Italian villa," Kathleen says. "I've been up that road many times. I grew up there. This is my neighborhood. This was the first time I ever saw that. There was a big wall going all the way around. It must be the biggest property in all of San Anselmo. You can't avoid it. So we stopped the car for a minute to look at it before we kept going on to the place a little further down the road where the lookout is."

"So we sat there for, oh, I don't know, about twenty minutes," Don says, "to watch the sun set. It was real nice. And then we turned around, and we were coming back down the road. Kathleen is driving, the windows are down. I'm in the passenger seat looking out the window at the big house, and a man standing on the deck calls out to us, 'Hey, are you guys all right?' I called back to him to say we were just sightseeing. That's when I realized I recognized the man. It was the doctor who did the surgery on my neck just a few months ago. It was such a surprise. I mean, what are the chances?"

"Who's this doctor?" I ask.

"The California Department of Corrections had hired this local, private doctor to perform my neck surgery. I told Kathleen to stop the car. I got out and waved to him, saying, 'Hi, Doctor.' He was really nice to me when I was having my surgery, so I thought I'd just say hi and tell him thanks for doing such a good job. But he turned and sort of quickly went inside the doors. I thought that was strange. We both did. But I figured he must have been busy or something. So I got back in the car, and we continued our way down the road."

"I was driving, 'cause Don doesn't have a license," Kathleen says. "So we get home and go to bed. We had no idea."

"When we woke up, that's when things all fell apart," Don says. "Pastor Curry called from San Quentin and said he heard a disturbing rumor that I was coming back. I said, 'What?!' Curry went on to tell me that he heard I had confronted this doctor, demanded drugs, and the doctor had called San Quentin and the sheriff and other law enforcement saying he felt threatened now that I knew where he lived. When I got off the phone with Curry, I called my parole agent. He said he hadn't heard a thing. A half hour later, my parole agent called back and said I should report to his office. He said they had received some sort of a complaint the night before, and that's all he knew. We got in the car and Kathleen took me to his office."

When Don got to his parole agent's office in Santa Rosa, about a half hour north on the freeway, he says, recounting the moment his freedom hung in the balance, his parole agent was waiting.

"He took me in his office and said, 'Okay, I'm going to give you a chance to tell me your side of what happened; then I'll decide what to do next. You're only out now because I vouched for you 'cause I haven't seen any risky nonsense.'

"But before I could tell him my side, I had to ask what I was being accused of. He asked me, 'Were you up on a road above San Anselmo last night?' I remembered the drive Kathleen and I took, but what would that have to do with any of this? 'Yes,' I told him, sick to my stomach, like I was going to throw up, 'Kathleen and I took a drive.' Then he said, 'Did you stop your car? Did you see anyone you knew?' I had to think back, and I remembered seeing my doctor out on the porch. 'Yes, I thought I saw the doctor who operated on me a couple of months back. I wanted to say hi, but he went back in his house. I just waved.'

"My agent was staring me in the eye. 'What happened then?' I said, 'Nothing. I thought it was really interesting I would see him out of the blue like that, but figured he had something else to do or didn't recognize me. So Kathleen and I drove on down the hill. We had some dinner and went to bed.' He said, 'Is that your story? Did anything else happen? Did you get out of your car? Did you approach the doctor's house?' 'No,' I said. 'We just went home.'"

The whole time Don is telling us his story, Kathleen is staring at Don, listening, nodding. Every few minutes she breaks in with "That's right" or "I couldn't believe it." For eleven years Don had to sit in front of commissioners on the parole board and represent his rehabilitation all by himself. Now he and Kathleen are together, and you don't mess around with a good Italian Catholic girl who gives up sweets for Lent. It just would never occur to her to lie, or even think someone wouldn't believe her.

When Don finished telling the officer his version of what happened the night before, he says his agent sat back in his chair, took a deep breath, and began telling Don the other side. "He said, 'The prison started getting calls from a doctor about eight p.m. The doctor said a just-paroled murderer was outside his house, banging on his windows and doors, yelling, "Give me drugs. Give me drugs." He said he was afraid for his life. We got the call this morning. My boss wanted to recommit you, send you back—now. I told him I'd been observing you for a month and I hadn't seen any irrational or dangerous behavior. I asked him to give me a chance to talk to you, find out your side of the story. So, I'm going to have to take this to my boss, but I'm sure he's not going to approve anything less than six months of nighttime curfew. You'll have to be in your house from ten at night until six in the morning, and you'll have to be on an electronic monitor. That means you'll have to wear a bracelet. That's if he agrees.'"

I get down to look at the bracelet a little closer. The wide black band is harder than it looks and there's a squat black box that sticks out about an inch and a half from his leg. On the side of the box is a little light. Apparently the box can tell when Don is within range of the homing device that has been set up inside their house. If he goes outside the range between ten p.m. and six a.m., an alarm goes off at the parole office. If that happens, an agent calls the home number. If Don doesn't answer, or if there's any sign the box has been tampered with, it can trigger an immediate cause for taking Don "back in" to San Quentin.

"How do you take a shower?" I ask.

"I have to leave it on all the time, even when I'm in the shower," he says. "And because it's hard, it rubs on my ankle and leaves a burn."

I wonder what really happened that night. Beneath his calm voice and wire-rimmed spectacles, Don can sometimes be inscrutable . . . but I trust Kathleen completely. Then again, why would that doctor make this up? It all seems so strange.

After Don and Kathleen leave, I quiz my husband about what he thought of their story. "I thought their story was plausible," he says. "They were just out looking at the sights in her hometown and inadvertently stumbled across the doctor's place. Don had no idea there'd be any adverse reaction from the doctor if he said hi." Ultimately my husband is baffled. It makes no sense to him why the doctor would go off and make up a story like that.

The worst part, the part Don doesn't want to talk about, is the humiliation. He was out. Free. Society had found him worthy of its conditional trust. Yes, he had to report to his parole agent every week and take a pee test, but as long as he showed up on time, tested clean, and didn't break any obvious rules, he earned the ongoing right to go where he wished within the fifty-mile radius, when he wished. Now he has to watch the clock. But if this is what it takes to stay out, it's a price worth paying.

Meanwhile, Jesse had learned the hard way he couldn't trust his troubled family with his fragile parole. As we sit together on a bench in the sun, looking out on the San Francisco Bay, Jesse tells me he's had a "close call."

It was late at night. He'd recently passed his driver's test at the local DMV, and after twenty-four years had gotten his photo driver's license reinstated. It was a big step on the path to becoming a fully functional member of society, but it was also a boon for his family, who promptly started using him as the Reed family taxi service. "I'm the only one of my brothers and sisters with access to a car," Jesse says.

It wasn't a holiday, but an all-day family get-together in the backyard, "oysters on the grill, having fun." After the party Jesse borrowed his girlfriend Lisa's red Lexus sedan to drive his younger brother Joshua and his kids home. On the way back, it felt good to be out alone on a summer night, cruising the streets he had known so well as a much younger man.

Driving down one of Oakland's doublewide boulevards, just a few blocks from his mother's house, Jesse got a call from Jayvonce, the brother who always seemed to have alcohol on his breath. "He wanted to know if I'd give him a ride to BART so he could take left-overs to his girlfriend's house. He was standing at a bus stop with my other brother, Chris."

Without much thought, Jesse made a quick U-turn, pulled along-side the bus stop, and motioned for his two brothers to jump in. One of his cousins was there, talking to a woman who could have been a prostitute. His brothers jumped in the Lexus, one landing in the back-seat, the other in the front, next to Jesse.

As he pulled away from the bus stop, an Emeryville police car pulled up behind him. "I'm not trippin'. He follows me. We're driving along, a mile or so. Maybe it was just headed in the same direction. But as soon as I made a left turn, he lit me up, turned on the siren, and over the loudspeaker said to pull over. I pulled over."

Pulling to the side of the road, Jesse felt his heart pounding in his chest. His hands seeped, wet with panic. In his head he could hear his parole agent's voice admonishing him not to break the rules, and one of the first was "No contact with the law." Now it was all too late. He had been out only a little over a month, only had forty days of free-dom, and now he was going back.

But what had he done? He was driving at the speed limit, if not slower. The car was registered and he had a valid driver's license. Was a light burned out?

As Jesse sat frozen in fear, his brothers began mouthing off, saying they were going to challenge the officers. Keeping his hands high on the steering wheel, his head straight ahead, Jesse told his brothers to be cool. It wasn't working. As a police officer approached the driver's side, Jesse rolled down his window.

"'You know that young lady back there that was at the bus stop is a known prostitute, and that's why I'm pulling you over, yaddayaddaya,' and I said, 'No, I didn't know that woman was no prostitute. I just picked up my brothers. My brother called me and said he wanted a ride to the BART station, and I was giving him a ride.' The cop didn't have an attitude at all. So I gave him my driver's license and all and he said, 'You on probation, parole, or anything?' I said, 'Yeah, I'm on parole.' He said, 'What for?' I said, '187; homicide. I just got out after twenty-five years.' He said, 'Okay.' And he went to his car and came back and said, 'Well, you know I gotta do a felony search.' I had no idea but I guess because I was on felony parole he had to search the car. I knew they could search me but didn't know anything about that."

Jesse got out of the car. After nearly twenty-five years in prison, he knew how to move without an attitude, how to do exactly as he was told. Placing his hands on the hood of his girlfriend's car and moving his feet wide, he could feel the officer checking his body for a weapon. He knew he was clean. "Hands behind your back," the officer ordered. Leaning forward, Jesse moved first his right, then his left hand around to his back, exposing himself, ready. The officer pulled a set of cold steel handcuffs out of his waistband. Flicking them open, he snapped first one, then the other tightly around Jesse's wrists.

"He said, 'I gotta do this. I'm gonna put you in the backseat of the patrol car,'" Jesse recounts, like he's watching it happen all over again in front of his eyes. "'You're not arrested. I'm just gonna search the car and because you're on parole, I gotta do it like this.' I said, 'Okay. No problem. I'm cooperating.' So he puts me in the back of the police car, and I'm watching up ahead. First they pull Jayvonce out and search him."

After determining Jayvonce was clean, the officers ordered him to sit on the ground, his back against a nearby building. Jesse took a breath. Maybe this was going to be okay.

"Then they pull Chris out. And when they pulled Chris out, they start taking stuff out of his pockets and putting it on the top of the trunk of the car. There's some drug paraphernalia, a straight shooter pipe; I guess he's smoking meth stuff. Then I see them pull out a gun! They put it on the top of the trunk with the other stuff. Now I'm freaking out! 'Oh my God. I'm going back to jail. What has this dude just done? Why did Chris do me like that?'"

Jesse watched helpless as his own private nightmare unfolded before his very eyes. The word had gone out. A parolee out from a homicide had been stopped. There was a gun. Backup was needed.

Within minutes, four more Emeryville police cars screamed to the scene, their lights flashing, sirens whooping. Jesse began to cry. The freedom he had fought so hard to earn was going to be ripped away from him by the family that said they loved him.

The officers had to make a decision. "One of the cops comes to the back window of the parole car," Jesse says. "He says, 'Don't worry. You going to be all right. You be all right. But your brother? He is going to jail. But you're going to be all right.' I'm like, 'Oh my God. Whew. What a relief.' It ended up being a BB gun. All I know is it looked like a gun, a small gun. Then the officer that initially stopped me, he came and was taking the handcuffs off and said, 'You know, be careful who you give a ride to.' I said, 'They're my brothers. I didn't think nothing of it. But you don't got to say no more. I will be careful from now on.' So, needless to say, Chris don't get in the car with me anymore. Jay, every now and then I'll take him somewhere. But I ask 'em, 'You ain't got nothing on you, do you?' I don't ask everybody, but if I think somebody's not right, yeah, I'll ask 'em. Sure will. No problem. If I get stopped, I'm going to jail? I may start literally frisking people." He laughs. "'Can you stand a body search?' You know what I mean? 'Before you get in this car? Otherwise you not getting in my car, period.'"

Before the night was over, Jesse's brother was arrested and charged with possession of a weapon. Jesse was released, his driver's license returned to his care.

"It was horrible, but I learned a lesson," Jesse says. "My family just don't get it. I'm on parole. If something happens, they get a little sentence. If I go back, I'll probably never get out again."

I wonder whether Jesse will be able to keep himself clean for very much longer living in his family home. Could anyone?

seventeen

NIMNH

(Not in My Neighborhood)

MAY 2010

It wasn't planned; it just happened. A normal bit of everyday life. Walking down the aisle of the local supermarket, Jesse ran into a familiar face. For most of his years inside San Quentin, Lieutenant John Reid had been in charge of his life, at least when he was on duty. Now here he was, just another free man shopping for his dinner.

"I looked up and there he was," Jesse says.

"We were both shopping," John Reid tells me later, "and he saw me and I looked up and we saw each other, and I said, 'When did you get out?' I shook Jesse's hand. He looked well. Been out awhile, fattened up a little. I gave him a little hug and said, 'I'm glad to see you out. If anybody deserved it, I really felt you did. I'm glad to see that. Now you got to prove for the other lifers it's worth letting them go home.' Jesse said, 'What do you mean, Reid?' I said, 'You got to walk that line, even though lifers generally don't come back, especially for stupid things. You can show the State of California and maybe even the governor's office and parole board we can take a chance on lifers. They're not coming back to prison.'"

For more than twenty-six years, until he retired in 2006, Reid says, he went to work every day with a simple philosophy: you treat them like men and give them respect, and they'll reciprocate and treat you the same. "Some of these guys don't come to the understanding that the reason they're in prison is because of their own decision-making, and if they don't come to that, then they will always be in prison and they will always have that prison mentality, that subculture existence. When they start to process the information—that 'I'm the only reason I'm here. Not because you planted the dope in my car. I'm the reason I'm here because I put myself in a situation to get busted and incarcerated'—once they come to that realization, they start looking at themselves as, 'I don't want to go that way again, so I'm going to avoid this situation and that situation.' When you see that kind of change in a man or a woman, then you'll see their chances of getting a parole date are greater. If he's doing well, he's done a considerable amount of time in prison like Jesse, those are completely different men than they were when they came to prison. Completely different guys."

The worst part of working in North Block, Reid says, was watching an inmate given a parole date by the board have that date taken 150 days later by the governor. "It was devastating, especially when you work so hard and the parole board tells you to do this and do that, all the way from A to Z, and you go and do those things and do them well. Some of them learn journeyman-level skills and some get union cards so when they get out they can find work, and then the governor says no. They would come to me and say, 'What's it worth, Reid? What's it worth?' If I thought someone was hurting, I would take time with them: 'Come in my office and let's sit and talk, 'cause I don't want you to lose hope. You cannot lose hope based on politics.' That's basically what it is. It's easy to overturn a parole board suitability. You just reverse it. 'We're only going to keep him in a little while longer. Maybe he can get another date when the next governor comes in. Let him do it.' 'Not going to happen on my watch' is a bad scenario. So I would always tell the men who had their date taken by the governor, 'You gotta stay calm and know there's politics in this life that you're living now. It's all politics. Don't lose focus. You have a goal. Don't look at it like "I'm going to be here 'til I die." That's not necessarily true.'"

Reflecting on the hundreds of lifers he left behind in North Block, Reid says a good 75 percent could go home today and they wouldn't do anything to violate public safety. "I could live next door to Jesse Reed and there's a lot of prisoners from North Block I could live next door to and feel safe. When these guys get a date, they're coming home, and home is their community, and people don't want that. People say, 'Not in my neighborhood.' But these guys grew up here. Their moms live down the street from me. Where else a guy or woman gonna go? Lifers know when they get out, if they go back, they're going to do another thirty, forty years before they see the parole board again. That keeps them in check. They know when they go out there, they really got to walk on eggshells, so to speak. Lifers don't come back."

When one of Jesse's best friends from inside San Quentin follows him out on parole, we meet up at the Ferry Building next to the San Francisco Bay, for happy-hour oysters. Sitting together at a small table, drinking lemonade and iced tea, and slipping raw oysters down our throats, we watch people pass and laugh at how normal it all seems. After twenty-three years inside prison, Demetrius Daniels is thrilled to be out, sitting in a restaurant, having dinner. "It's beautiful," he says. "Everything is beautiful."

As the sun sets, I suggest a long, slow walk along the pier in the evening half light. Jesse says they already have plans. Every other Thursday night, he says, "I go to the Healing Circle. Tonight Demetrius is going." Would I like to come along?

"What's the Healing Circle?" I ask.

"It's a way for lifers to give back by supporting the survivors of violence," Jesse says. I agree to go and follow him and Demetrius across town to the Paradise Missionary Baptist Church, a small building in one of San Francisco's poorer districts. By the time we arrive, the city's infamous summer fog is whipping around, making everything look and feel ice cold. Inside, where it's a little warmer, a dozen men and women sit scattered in the long pews, waiting for their turn to talk to everyone through a microphone being passed hand-to-hand around the sanctuary. As Jesse and Demetrius walk in, a tall black man rushes to give them a big hug and a pat on the back. Taking seats side by side in the pews, Jesse and Demetrius listen.

Across the aisle, an older man with broad, hunched shoulders slowly stands. His body is heavy. His knees and joints don't work as well as they once did. He grips the top of the pew in front of him to brace himself. In a slow, broken, barely audible voice, he tells everyone how much he misses his son's smile. He says the night his boy was shot, his family fell apart. "It's never come back together again." Before he sits back down, he reaches behind him to pass the black wand to the next living victim.

A worn, tired mother tells everyone in the room about her daughter. She was killed in a drive-by shooting. While they talk, children too young to sit still walk and skitter up and down the aisles, the roomful of grieving parents and the sisters and brothers of the dead shushing them.

There's more pain in this room than can be absorbed by all the world's kindness. But at least here, in this room of shared grief, they aren't alone.

Toward the end of the meeting, the minister who has been walking around, offering support to those who need it, accepts the microphone from the last survivor. It's silent. "Let us pray."

After "Amen," the minister looks out and calls the lifers in the chapel to the front of the congregation. Standing exposed before the wounded souls, Jesse speaks first.

He apologizes for the life he took. No, he didn't kill their brother, father, son. But tonight that's not important. Tonight he is a man who killed, apologizing to people who have lost someone. He apologizes for the days, weeks, months, and years to come when their sore eyes and broken hearts will have to live without the person they love and miss. No, they won't ever come back. But tonight a person who caused pain to others is acknowledging theirs.

"I messed up." His tenor voice fills the sanctuary. "I want to give back. This is an opportunity for me to give back. What can I do to help you stay strong? What can you do to help me stay strong? We reach out our hands together. We join hands together and we move as one together: the perpetrator and those who have been victimized. I don't have any kids. I don't know what it is to be a parent. I don't know what that is, let alone lose one. I know the hurt I've caused my mama when I did what I did and had to go away for twenty-five years and she never knew if I was going to come back home or not. So I can imagine what the people felt who I victimized knowing theirs wasn't coming back home again. But I had to do some work. I had to ask them for forgiveness. And not expecting forgiveness, I received it because I was serving God. We cannot know the future, but know that your work is not in vain."

Some nod. Others look down. This is a room filled with the forever hurting people trying to fill a raw hole left behind by a very bad day, a long time ago. Tonight is a warm balm that may help to soothe the wounds that have never and may never quite heal.

eighteen

BITTERSWEET

2009–2011

No one really goes to prison alone. An invisible rope stretches from the heart and mind of a prisoner out through the bars of his cell, up into the sky, over hills and water, dropping back down to earth far away, inside the lives of the people he left behind. As the years pass—five, ten, twenty, thirty—the fibers of that rope become frayed, and sometimes they snap.

The inmates who get out are the ones whose hearts are already on the outside. They are the ones whose friends and family held on, took phone calls they couldn't afford, hired lawyers instead of taking vacations, prayed, visited, and held their incarcerated loved ones aloft.

By the time Eddie Ramirez first met his wife, Lupe, inside San Quentin's visiting room, he had been locked up for fifteen years. She hadn't come to meet a murderer. She had come to support a friend who was visiting her husband. While giving her friend some privacy, Lupe and Eddie would talk in the visiting room about this and that. When Eddie realized they were getting close, "I told her, 'to be involved with me is to be involved with a lot of pain, and you don't need that.' I told her to walk away. 'There's too much pain.' She didn't understand. By then I had been denied by the board six times. I didn't want to put her through what more denials would mean."

Now, years later, sitting together at their dining room table, Lupe says, "I don't remember the exact time when it changed, but we became very close friends. He was someone I could share important things, confidential things with. Personal things I was going through as a single mother raising my two boys. He told me his family hadn't visited in a while and I contacted them to try and get them to come see him. I reminded them he was that nice uncle and nephew that wrote. People in his family said at one time they believed he would come home, but year after year, when he kept getting denied, they couldn't really believe it anymore. I can't pinpoint a date when it changed. It just evolved and"—Lupe breaks into a gentle smile—"he liked me."

"I felt close to her from the beginning," Eddie says. "But you probably got an indication when I kissed you on your cheek. It shocked her. I remember that day. She was leaving and I just kissed her on the cheek. I was getting ready to duck for the right cross." He laughs. "But she didn't. She just looked at me. Her eyes were wide."

"I was shocked," Lupe says. "We had been friends. We hugged. I was just being careful. In fact, I tried not to visit as often, but my girlfriend really needed me."

"After he kissed you on the cheek?" I ask.

"After I felt like I was falling in love with him," Lupe says, "I tried to keep my distance. I wasn't sure what kind of life that was going to bring me, so I would try not to visit. But my girlfriend, Ana Marie, would ask me to go with her so she could see her husband, Tony. I could never say no to her and there I would go again. Ed would tell me, 'You don't know what you're getting into.' I got scared for a while. I went home and thought about it. I got pressure from friends not to be involved with him. I had no idea."

"Before I met Lupe, I would never go to visits," Eddie says, "not even for family. Even though I wrote my family every other week, tons of letters, as the years went by, me and my family got further and further apart. Whenever they would bring up coming to visit me, I would tell them something, make an excuse why they shouldn't. For me it was better to stay distant. That was my life in there and it had nothing to do with out here. It was a life of pain."

"After we met, we went through a few board hearing denials," Lupe says. "It was awful. Everyone who knew him would speak highly of him. For him to be denied, I couldn't understand. We saw a pattern with the board and governor and realized it was going to be really hard."

A few years into their courtship, Lupe and two dozen of Eddie's family and friends pooled their money and raised $3,000 to hire Steve DeFilippis, a private attorney, to represent Eddie. As Eddie's attorney, DeFilippis challenged the parole board's denials in Marin County Superior Court. Eventually the court ordered the parole board to release Eddie, but the parole board fought back, appealing the court's ruling to the state court of appeal. "It was back and forth," Eddie says, "but it felt like for the first time, I could possibly go home."

The following year, with his appeal hanging in the courts, Eddie went to another parole hearing, and again the board denied him parole.

The next time Eddie went to the board, in 2003, for the first time, the commissioners found him suitable. "The commissioners asked me, 'We see no emotion in you. Don't you want to go home?' And I said, 'Of course I want to go home, but I know there's still a lot of red tape.' And they said, 'That's smart.' I said, 'I'm not going to set myself up to be hurt. I've had too many hurts in my family and in my life and I'm not going to set myself up for that again.' I called Lupe and left a message. I knew not to sound excited."

"We thought, 'He's coming home,'" Lupe says. "But my dad was ill, and my best friend, Ana Marie, the person who connected us in the visiting room, had died from cancer. Thinking Eddie was coming home and he would parole to Southern California, I moved to Los Angeles to live closer to my family. Then I got the phone call that Governor Gray Davis had reversed Eddie's parole date."

"We were devastated," Eddie says. "My attorney, Steve DeFilippis, would keep moving forward, holding the torch, filing appeals.

Every setback he would file in the courts. The next time I went to the board, nearly a year later, they denied me parole. Steve couldn't believe it."

"It was getting hard," Lupe says. "I had put a down payment on a home for the two of us in Los Angeles, and when he didn't get out, I backed out of the deal too late and lost my down payment of $3,000. I was thinking of coming back up north. I had gone to San Jose State [University], and I wanted to get my administration credential. That's when I told Edward I couldn't do it anymore. He called and I said, 'I can't keep this relationship up. I'm raising two sons, working full-time, going to school, and have no time to visit.' It was the hardest thing." Lupe's eyes fill with tears. "My heart was dying."

Though he loved Lupe, Eddie could not bear to keep dragging her through year after year of hope, only to have their common dream crushed at the very last minute via a fax from the governor. If he wasn't going to get out, he reasoned, at least Lupe should have a chance at a real life with someone else. "I really believed it was over," Eddie remembers, "and I vowed to myself I wouldn't have another relationship."

They didn't talk for months. Lupe says she missed Eddie and wanted him to call and write. Eddie didn't see the point. "It was like a scab. The wall was still there. It was like I was intruding in her life."

"When we talked on the phone, I had to be careful that I wasn't warm and friendly," Lupe says. "I always cried when I hung up with you. Then I realized I was going to be with Eddie whether or not he ever got out. But I never told Eddie."

"I'm in there thinking it's over," Eddie says. "I saw the chaplain and I told him I didn't think I could make it anymore. I'd lost Lupe and I'd lost my oldest sister, Patricia. After the governor took my date, she died of a drug overdose. I was at the bottom of my rope. I was on the yard and I asked God to let me die. The chaplain pulled me to him and hugged me and rubbed my head and cried. He didn't preach to me or give me scriptures of hope, he just cried. It hurt him, too. It was like he was hugging his son. Somehow things started to feel better. It felt like a boost that I could go on. Just that much. After that I wasn't depressed anymore. I was going to fight for myself."

The next time Eddie went to the board, they found him suitable for a second time.

Lupe asks if I want to hear the message Eddie left on her answering machine.

"You still have the message from 2004?" I ask.

"I will never erase it," she says, and walks over to press the play button on the machine. "Hello. This is just Eddie. I called earlier to let you know the good news: they gave me my date back. I'll try to call you tomorrow. Bye-bye."

"I said to myself," Lupe says, clicking the answering machine off, "'He still loves me.'"

One hundred fifty days later, Governor Schwarzenegger surprised everyone by signing Eddie's parole papers. In California, of the nearly 5,000 lifers scheduled for parole board hearings in 2005, Eddie Ramirez would be one of only thirty-five the governor released on parole.

"I couldn't believe it," Eddie says.

He hurried to the prison pay phone to call Lupe. A few days later, when he finally stepped out of the parole officer's car, he walked up to Lupe, put down the box he was carrying, and hugged her.

"And I gave him a big kiss. And that's how he knew, 'This is it!'" Lupe says. "It was great."

With that kiss, Eddie says, "I knew all our plans could go on. We could continue. And we've been attached ever since. That was February 24, 2005. We got married a few months later on May 14th at a friend's church." It was a small wedding, just their immediate family, his sisters, Lupe's parents, and Eddie's Aunt Eloise and Uncle Beto. Since Eddie was on parole, they couldn't really go anywhere, so they spent their honeymoon at a hotel in Redondo Beach. Someday they would take a real honeymoon in Hawaii.

For fifteen years, beginning in the early '90s, Kathleen drove the twenty minutes from her home to the east gate of San Quentin. And nearly every weekend she came, Don submitted to a full-body cavity search so he could sit the required inches from Kathleen in the visiting room. There, inside the bare-walled room with barred windows, coin-operated snack machines and ice-cold water fountains, Kathleen and Don talked about their radically different lives: one incarcerated, the other free.

That wasn't their only form of contact. In the middle of the day, before being locked up for count, Don would take his turn inside one of the phone booths down on North Block's first tier and call Kathleen collect. Restricted to fifteen-minute phone calls, Don would make all of his calls to Kathleen.

Sitting at her kitchen table or out on her private deck, the arbor overhead dripping with sweet-scented purple wisteria, Kathleen would tell Don stories about her free life and work: all about caring for her sick mother and her upcoming travel to Italy, Hawaii, Alaska—always tempering her tales in a way that wouldn't make it harder for Don to do time.

Sometimes at night, when it was his tier's turn at the pay phones, Don would call Kathleen to talk about his evening thoughts and wishes. Taking the phone into bed with her, they would talk like lovers do.

Day or night, Kathleen counted on Don to soothe her unchecked private anxieties, and in turn, she comforted him.

Somehow they knew if Don ever got out they would fit together like a pair of misplaced gloves.

So it was when Don got out of prison after serving nearly twenty-eight years for murder; no one could have imagined a sweeter place for him to land than Kathleen's world.

Still, back in April 2009, when the word was definite that Don was going to get out of prison, Kathleen says, it was scary. "I had always been able to do what I darn well pleased. Right before Don came home, I opened up my medicine cabinet," she says, over a woman-to-woman chat a few months after Don got out, "and I got my toothpaste and looked at all my stuff in there and I thought, 'Seriously, Kathleen. What is this going to be like to see a can of shaving cream and a razor? Won't it be an invasion on your things?'" Kathleen stops and looks at me.

"But oh my God! Not one of those things have become an issue. He just fits like an old shoe. He's just as neat and clean as I am." Kathleen says with a chuckle. "He even comes up with better ideas about how to do something or store something. A few days after he moved in, I looked at the can of shaving cream. It's perfect. The toothbrush isn't icky. It's perfect, too. My God, this man thinks the way I do. He's not annoying to be around or have around. And he loves everything I cook."

Kathleen is the ultimate homemaker. She loves to cook and clean. To her, holidays are one more opportunity to dress her childhood home in decorations that have been in the family for generations. And with all the generations around to keep an eye on their beloved sister, aunt, cousin, there were bound to be questions.

Where was Aunt Kathleen going every Saturday and Sunday? Did she have an unknown friend?

To quell their concerns over the years, Kathleen told her older brother (who lives next door) and most of her extended family about her "friend inside San Quentin" only on a "need to know" basis. But now that her friend was going to be living with her in the family home, she knew the questions wouldn't be so easily shrugged off. She just hoped her family members would give themselves enough time to get to know Don for the man he had become, rather than judge him for his criminal past.

The trouble with the local doctor and Don's parole agent didn't help matters. With a GPS monitoring device on his ankle, there weren't going to be any trips to the beach or the local pool, where anyone wearing full-length pants on a hot summer day might draw attention. So Don set about fixing their shared home, scraping, priming, and painting what was peeling; trimming rosebushes; and planting a vegetable garden in a small plot of land at the back of her brother's yard.

Don says he is content to sit inside the house or outside on their back deck or front porch. The silence is sweet. Leaving the house, he says, is still disorienting. "I can't seem to figure out direction," he says, living in a valley among hills, "which way is north or west." It will take time for him to get his bearings.

"Are you getting married?" I ask Don over a cup of tea in their kitchen, nearly eight months into their new life together. "Remember when you were inside, you said when you got out, you were going to get married right away. It's been nearly a year. So, when's the wedding?"

"I don't know," Don says. "When I was inside, making things official seemed important, but now that we're together on the outside, I don't feel it's really all that necessary to rush into it. We have time and things are going really well. So, we're not in a rush."

"And Kathleen?" I ask. "How does she feel about it?"

"You should ask her," Don says. "We haven't really talked about it that much, but I think she feels the same way."

A year after that conversation, Don and Kathleen—still engaged, not married—invite me and my husband over for a Saturday-night dinner to celebrate Don's second year of freedom. When we arrive, Robert, Kathleen's first cousin, is in the family kitchen cooking up an Italian storm. He's stout, middle-aged, gregarious. His fondness for her is as clear as it is for Don. For three hours we eat and drink and watch the San Francisco Giants on the flat-screen TV Don has installed on an extendable arm on the kitchen wall, so it can be pushed out of the way. All night I watch Don, Kathleen, and "Robbie" move together, laughing, jabbing each other with jokes, easy. There are a couple of references to where Don's been, and to San Quentin. I remember Kathleen's request for me not to talk about Don around her brother, but it sounds like things are all out in the open with her family now.

To be sure, a week later I ask Kathleen if it's all right if I call Robert to ask him what he thinks about her relationship with Don.

"Sure," she says. "Fine with me. Do you have his number?"

I call Robert at his office. He's general counsel for an insurance company and has spent his career defending against worker's compensation claims in Sacramento. He's not someone easily fooled.

Robert says he knew for years that Kathleen was visiting a man she knew inside San Quentin but assumed she was just doing it to be nice. "I didn't know it developed into something more than that," he says. That all changed one night early in 2009. "I was out on the deck talking to her niece, Katy, and she said, 'Don's getting out,' and blah blah blah. I said, 'Well, what's their relationship?' Katy looked at me and goes, 'You don't know?' I said, 'I know it's her friend.' She said, 'They're boyfriend and girlfriend.' I said, 'Oh, okay. Okay.' That was the first time I heard it. I didn't know at the time he had been convicted of murder, but I found out real quick."

Robert got on the Internet and Googled Don. When he found out about the crime, how there had been a bad deal, drugs, burglary, and Don ended up shooting someone, "it didn't jive. I couldn't see my cousin dating a guy who had committed a murder. The type of person who would do what he did, I couldn't put the two of them together. It didn't make sense.

"We met him almost right away, in May 2009, about a month after he got out. I go down to Kathleen's every couple of months and my brother, who passed away last July 4th, used to go there, too. It was both of our birthdays, and Don was out. We were going to meet Don.

"We were all together for the whole weekend and we spent time together. My brother and I watched them interact. We considered at one point taking him aside and saying, 'You fuck over or screw around with our cousin, and we aren't going to be two happy campers.'

"But once we met him, we realized we didn't have to do that. We could tell that he really loved Kathleen by the way he treated her. And he was not the type of guy you get concerned about. The only concern you have is how he could be so stupid when he was young and waste twenty-seven years of his life? It was sad because you could see he would have been a productive person if he hadn't gotten into the stupid shit he got into when he was a kid. In the end, we both said, 'He seems like the nicest guy in the world. If you told people his background, people probably wouldn't believe you.' 'Come on. You got to be kidding me! He couldn't do that!' That's the impression you get from Don. And he likes to eat and we're a family that likes to eat. So if you like food and you like to eat and you have an interest in food, you've got one leg up on our family."

Robert says one surprise is Don's enthusiasm. "He's so much fun to be around. He's waited all this time to live life, so he's enthusiastic about everything, whether it's fishing or cooking a pork chop. We all get jaded as we get older and Don doesn't seem to have that. He waited so long, and now he's a hog in high cotton, and he's loving it."

It's been eight months since Phillip Seiler got out of San Quentin. I've driven up to Sacramento to interview some state legislators, and we have plans to meet for lunch.

"What was the worst part of being locked up?" I ask him.

"Being away from my family. That's the worst part. Not the cells. Not the food. Not the violence. Not being told what to do 24/7," Phillip says, a haunting, empty look on his face. "It's not being with your family. Of course, losing your freedom comes a very close second. But for me, it was not being with my family for twenty years. Missing all the wonderful things, the weddings, the births, all the wonderful things and not being there through the tough times when I could have helped out in one way. Family member getting older and needing help. Kids getting older. That's the hardest part of doing time. That's what I tell the kids: It's not only [that] you come to prison and you're locked up—the danger involved. You're going to miss your family. You're going to miss your mom and your brothers and sisters and friends and going to the movies and getting in your car and going to the park. That's the biggest part for me: being so far away from my family and just having phone calls, or letters, or occasional visits that are so structured that they're really limited visits. And all the crap they have to go through when they visit because of untrained officers being rude and disrespectful. Not all of them. There's some really good staff inside CDC, but there's also very bad staff, so our people have to suffer the indignities. I know there was a lot of really bad things that happened, that my family and friends didn't want to ruin the visit by telling me what happened. For some people, over and over again, it gets so bad, they can't do it anymore."

In 2006 the Urban Institute released a report, "Understanding the Challenges of Prisoner Reentry: Research Findings from the Urban Institute's Prisoner Reentry Portfolio." It's a long title, but the information in the report makes a lot of sense. For instance, the authors report, "In recent years, research has found that strengthening the family network and maintaining supportive family contact can improve outcomes for both family members and prisoners. In fact, maintaining family connections through letters, phone calls, and personal visits has shown to reduce recidivism rates. Yet given the challenges of maintaining this contact—including visiting regulations, transportation costs to distant corrections facilities, other financial barriers, and emotional strains—more than half of incarcerated parents report never having received a personal visit from their children."

Phillip says he tells the teens he speaks to that he has been able to fit back into society because he spent twenty years laying the groundwork to come home. He kept in contact with his law-abiding family and friends. He cut off the friends who didn't follow the law. He kept in contact with his former employers, "so everybody that I know, except the people I've met since I've been out, know my whole history. They know I was in prison. They know why I was in prison. They know what I'm about, what I do, who I am, and how I am. And people that I meet find out real quickly that I was in prison for murder, because I think it's important. If I meet a woman I want to date, very early on I let that woman know who she's looking across the table at, because I think it's my responsibility. I'm not just some average Joe who is dating. I was in prison for twenty years and, yeah, I killed somebody. So I think that's important for someone you're going to spend some time with to know early on."

"Has anyone said, 'Oh, forget it'?" I ask, wondering if once they discover his past, the women don't want anything more to do with him.

"Yeah. I never heard from her again," Phillip says. "A couple, yeah. Two. But most, they'll be set back a little bit. But I say, 'Ask anything you want.' It's not like I went to prison for writing bad checks. It's a very serious thing. So I think it's important to let whoever it is, really early on, to let them know this is who I am and this is what I did and this is your chance to burn rubber. This is your chance to escape, exit stage left. It's not who I am now but it's in my past and this is something I did. So everybody I know, knows my history."

"Was it hard to be apart from women for so long?"

Phillip makes a gasping sound. "Yeah. Hard."

"So, are you dating?"

"Yep."

"Do you have a lot of girlfriends?" I ask gently. Phillip's response is laughter—a silly, upbeat, I've-got-a-secret sort of laugh.

"How many?" I ask.

"A few. I have a few. I don't keep numbers," he says, his voice soft, low, "but more than a dozen."

"More than a dozen? Are you kidding?"

"No," he says, slightly proud.

"What about your friend who was waiting for you that day you got out?" I ask.

"We're still friends," Phillip says matter-of-factly. "She's way up in Portland, so we talk on the phone all the time. Talked to her just a few days ago."

"Does she have a special place," I ask, "because she was the first one you saw when you got out?"

"All my friends have a special place for different types of reasons. But I really think if I don't have a year of playing the field, so to speak, I will regret it. There was one woman. We really hit it off and it was starting to get more serious. We had to break it off. But, yeah, it's really amazing. I think I'm getting close to wanting to settle down. I want to be in a steady relationship. I just want to keep my promise to myself."

Back in prison, Phillip says, he made a pledge to himself that if and when he ever got out, he wasn't going to get into a serious relationship for at least a year. He knew it would be healthy to have some time to be free, to figure things out.

"My year's not up yet," he says. "So, I'm going camping this weekend for the first time and she's got all this camping stuff, so it's totally cool. I'm doing what I can do, but she's doing most of it. She's camped and hiked before. Then I'm going kayaking the following week down the American River. I used to go river rafting all the time before prison. But this was just some people I met at the river a few weeks ago. They had kayaks and I was talking to them and they said, 'You wanna check it out?' And I said, "Yeah.' So they let me try it out and they said, 'Hey, we're gonna go to the river in a few weeks. If you want, we have an extra boat.' So I'm going to do that in a couple of weeks."

Turns out, for a good-looking, healthy, active man like Phillip, remaining single may be one challenge he hadn't really counted on. "There are so many women out here," Phillip says, his eyes like those of a kid in a toy store. "I went on a date with a woman I met at the city library, and another woman I met down at the park along the river."

Driving home from Sacramento, with more than an hour to ponder our conversation, I wonder: Would I date someone if he told me he had been in prison for twenty-plus years for committing a murder? If I answer yes, is that a positive reflection on my character, or should my instincts be more discerning? Maybe if I *knew* the man before he went to prison, from high school or college. If I had a history with him and knew how the murder happened. I hope I would have an open mind.

So, I take it one step further. I know Phillip. What if I had met him in the library, or down on the beach at the river, and we had talked? It's possible. I may have been surprised to hear about his past. Maybe that would have ended any possibility for a date right then and there. Or maybe not.

A month later, nearly nine months into his freedom, Phillip calls. He's practically singing into the phone. "I've met someone."

"You've met someone? I know," I jest. "You've met a lot of someones!"

"No, this is different," he says. "I'm in love. She's amazing. Her name is Desiree."

I don't even try to hide my surprise. "I thought you were going to wait. It isn't a year yet. What about all the other women you were dating?"

"I know. I know." Phillip laughs at himself. "I tried. Nine months is pretty good. About three weeks ago I was facilitating a training for IPP [Insight Prison Project] in Marin. We met and just hit it off. She has been working with IPP inside prison, working with the restorative justice program for a while."

"Is that okay? I mean, is it okay if you date someone who is volunteering inside a prison?" I ask, a bit worried. "I thought there were rules about that."

"I don't know," he says. "It's kind of on the low. We're not broadcasting it. But I thought you would want to know."

"Are you happy? Is this what you want?"

"You know," he says, "I never thought I'd meet someone like Desiree. It's still pretty new but we've been spending all our time together. She comes up here for weekends."

"Where does she live?"

"That's a bit of a problem. She lives south of San Francisco near the ocean. . . . " His voice trails off. "And that means I have to get a pass to go see her. She's been coming to Sacramento. So far, it isn't a problem. We're taking it slow—just see how things develop. Who knows, maybe I'll move to the beach."

Three months later, in the early evening warmth of an August night, I drive with my husband through the valleys of West Marin and up into the thick, forested hills of San Geronimo. Up, up, and around I follow the twists and turns of the single-lane road until I reach the house, just below the top of a ridge at the end of a rutted dirt lane. Parking my car along a high, worn redwood fence, we cross the road and enter a secret, herbed garden of rosemary and lavender. It's quite a place to celebrate a paroled lifer's first year of freedom.

A small pond here, a bench under a cherry tree there, and a choice of stone paths lead to a dark-shingled, meandering cabin, with its windows lit up. So this is where San Quentin's dedicated volunteers recover?

An open door leads to a warm, bustling kitchen filled with people who have just had their first glass of wine and are moving, talking, laughing, cooking. I say my hellos and keep moving. Like my big shepherd dog, I like to get a feeling for the whole layout of the place before I settle down. Beyond the kitchen, past steaming pots of noodles and sensory-overload stir-fry, I make my way out past small groups to a big wooden deck that stretches out beneath a towering redwood tree. The fresh-air escape offers a seductive view of the canyon below and mountains in the distance. Back inside, I continue wandering.

Just around the corner from the comfy, arts and crafts living room, I catch sight of Phillip. He's in the kitchen standing intimately close to a woman about a head shorter than him with long, dark, wavy hair, full lips, and deep, sincere eyes. That must be Desiree. Phillip sees me and waves.

"Nancy! This is Desiree," he says, wrapping his arm around her shoulder.

She smiles and reaches out her hand. "So good to meet you. Phillip's told me a lot about you."

Desiree is not a flippant, superficial person looking for a quick romance. She is a grown woman over forty with a history and a life all her own. I'm fascinated. She puts her arm comfortably around Phillip's waist. Is this it? How can you tell when people meet and are meant for each other? When they have that special tongue-and-groove sort of compatibility? We stand chatting like people do at parties, with no real depth to the conversation but establishing the first, early grounds for later get-togethers. I watch Desiree and Phillip out of the corner of my eye all night—curious.

Just before hostess Rochelle Edwards, a volunteer with the IPP program Phillip worked with inside San Quentin, announces dinner, Phillip takes my arm, leans in, and whispers in my ear, "After dessert, don't leave. I have a little thing I'm doing and I want you to be here."

"Sure. I'll stay," I whisper back. "What is it?"

"I can't tell you, but I want you to be here," he says, looking me in the eyes. "It's just a little something."

Everyone picks up a colorful plate and fills it with curry and spicy dishes hand-flavored by friends. Some sit around picnic tables out on the deck; others scatter around the house, taking seats in comfortable couches and chairs with breathtaking views.

Like a secret society made of the rare American with access to the real lives of people locked up behind bars, they share stories about things happening inside Q without worrying they have to explain their insight. There are updates on programs and the latest news on lifers, those who have gotten a parole date, been denied one, or lost their dates to the governor. It has been a year since the California Supreme Court ruled in *Lawrence*, and now judges throughout the state are more frequently issuing orders to free lifers who have been found suitable for parole and have either been denied parole by the Board of Parole Hearings or had their parole date reversed by the governor. There aren't many gatherings like this, where card-carrying volunteers can comfortably share their stories and anecdotes about the men they all know inside. Over and over, throughout dinner and dessert, names are called out with the refrain, "Did you hear about Stone?" A chorus of voices follows: "No. What?" That's when everyone within earshot stops and waits for the announcement: "He got a date," or "His date was taken," or the most desired of all, "He's getting out."

With nearly 20,000 lifers in state prison serving sentences of life with the possibility of parole, there is always the possibility there will be good news. More familiar is the dull groan, followed by "How long was his denial?"

People turn, pick up their forks, and take a bite of the food waiting in front of them, hoping the taste will take the sting away. But with Phillip bouncing around the party, smiling and laughing, it's hard to stay down for long. He's proof it works. All the programs and classes and letter campaigns to the governor—it all works because here he is, free at last.

With the sun setting and a long drive down the dark mountain road ahead of me, I finish my dessert and begin to make my rounds to say good-bye, starting with Phillip.

"No," he says, a look of panic on his face. "Wait. I have my little surprise. Don't go yet. Help me get everyone in the living room."

"Sure."

Word spreads. By the look on everyone's faces, it appears nobody knows about Phillip's "little surprise." I ask Phillip if I can record whatever is going to happen. "I don't know. I guess it's okay."

Like a slow-moving cloud, everyone moves from their candlelight conversations into the living room, scrunching together on couches, sitting in pairs on chairs, or standing before the west-facing window, the last of the sun's golden rays beaming onto the faces of the widening circle surrounding Phillip.

A sweet ripple of anticipating laughter runs around the circle. These friends and coworkers know one another—well. They are all devoted to the common purpose of helping men inside get the help they need to transform their once-criminal lives into lives committed to healing the gulfs of pain floating in a society troubled by crime. Over time, through persistence and patience, they have maneuvered through the web of prison rules and regulations to get as reliable as possible access to an exclusively inaccessible population. Being with Phillip on the outside tonight is a high point in their often anguished work. Someone in the circle asks everyone to hold hands. Like a conduit, a spark moves hand to hand. A prayer is said. Amen.

"First I want to say to everybody thank you so much for this wonderful night," Phillip says. "This feels beautiful. This will probably take me weeks, maybe months to take this all in, to be a part of this gathering. It's not just something for me, it's for all of us."

Then he turns to face Desiree. "I just want to say a couple nice things to Desiree in front of everybody," Phillip says, his voice rising and falling like a little roller coaster. "One of the things I wanted to say to you, sweetheart, is ever since I saw you at the training—I thought to myself you were beautiful, and you were at a VOEG training, so she has a beautiful heart—and we got to talk a little bit, and I thought, 'She's wise. She's got a beautiful mind. And she's talking to me!'" Everyone laughs. "So that was the start. And I really know that this is right. It's been three months, everyone. Fast but we've talked about a lot of things. And it is something I know in my heart, that I want to spend the rest of my life with you, baby."

Reaching in his pocket, Phillip pulls out a small square box. Gasps of surprise escape from mouths; eyes stretch open. Phillip looks around the circle at the expectant faces and drops to one knee. Taking her left hand in his, he looks up into Desiree's eyes. "Desiree, please marry me."

Desiree's face is equal parts surprise and shock. Watching her, I'm not sure whether Phillip is going to get the answer he is hoping for. Unlike a younger woman who might feel pressured to accept in front of all their friends, even if it isn't the right answer, Desiree is a once-married, now wiser woman. Does she want to marry Phillip? Are they ready for this step? Some people get engaged after three weeks of romance, but Phillip isn't just any man. For a moment, it's painful. He has made a public declaration of his new love. He has exposed himself to the possibility she might deny him. How can she deny him now? That's the beauty of the moment. Phillip loves Desiree for being the steady, mature woman she has become. No one in this room of professionally trained counselors and therapists wants Desiree to compromise, to agree to a marriage before she's ready. But the unspoken pressure swirling around the circle is palpable. Is it possible she loves Phillip enough to say yes? Is she willing on this summer night to commit the rest of her life to Phillip, to share the long-term baggage of his past?

"Phillip," Desiree says, "I'm going to kill you. In front of all these people!"

"That's not an answer," Phillip says, standing up, his heart laid out, exposed for all to see.

"So, let me say a couple of words," Desiree says, her voice present, emotional. "The thing I love about you the most is you take absolutely nothing for granted. So when I'm with you, it's almost like I'm seeing life again with younger eyes. I like that. You make me feel so alive and so happy and you're so sincere and beautiful. I'm still scared. This is very fast."

I look around the circle, then back at Phillip. Like many in the group, I lower my eyes to avoid watching the emotional train wreck. It probably is too early, but saying no now to such an early love with the potential for something greater could be catastrophic. What can she do? A conditional promise. One second. Two. The room is still, waiting while Desiree carries Phillip's hope and promise, and makes a decision.

"Provided that this will be a long engagement"—Desiree laughs a little—"I'm going to say . . . yes."

The room erupts in yelps of released happiness; hope and relief fill the room as Phillip slips the bright, shiny diamond ring onto Desiree's left ring finger. "She said yes!" Phillip yells. "She said yes!"

What a difference a year makes.

Part of a lifer's reintegration into the free, stimulus-rich world he left so long ago involves pacing himself, taking one measured step at a time. Unlike Don Cronk, who has Kathleen to provide plenty of time to adjust and lots of steady, reliable support, Jesse Reed has to hit the ground running, alert. The stakes are high. Taking too long to translate the mixed signals in his neighborhood or inside his addiction-infected family has proved to be, and most likely will continue to be, risky.

It's been months since Jesse got out of prison, and unlike Don, who really has to think only about himself, Jesse has his brothers and sisters, his nieces and nephews, and their children to think about. After twenty-five years inside prison, there are big expectations and big pieces to pick up. Jesse wants his brothers and sisters to change their ways. He knows some of them are using drugs and even suspects his brother might be dealing drugs. "My mother is blind to the risks," he says.

At his mother's house, he has moved into one of a maze of rooms downstairs, and with some money his family has pooled together has bought some new clothes, starting with a smooth black leather jacket and some button-down shirts.

"You like these?" he asks, waiting for me on the sidewalk outside his mom's house, a massive smile spreading across his face.

We've made plans to have lunch but he isn't sure where to go. "It's all changed since before I went in," he says, looking down the block. "I don't know where to go now."

"We'll just take a drive around," I suggest, "and pick a place."

Before heading out, he offers to give me a tour of his room. Pushing through the short white metal gate, we walk back along the side of the house past a broken swing set and a too-pruned apricot tree to the large, unkempt backyard.

Pulling a single key out of his pocket, Jesse steps up to a small, square pad of cement outside a bare door and turns the key. Inside, the room is dark. A heavy set of maroon curtains has been pulled across the single sliding-glass window, blocking out any and all natural light. Jesse reaches up and flicks on a bare bulb high up on the wall. It takes a few seconds for my eyes to adjust. It's a good-size room, maybe twelve by fifteen feet. A queen-size bed set up high on a dark frame in the center of the room doesn't leave much floor space to walk around. On a small computer table just to the left of the door is a coffeemaker and not-too-new computer. "I know it's not much," Jesse says, "but it's been a good place for us to land."

That's when my eyes lock on the bottle of perfume sitting on one of the end tables. "Us?"

"Yeah," Jesse says. "You know, Lisa's living here with me."

"Lisa?" Hm. My mind sifts through images, faces. "Was she at your celebration picnic?"

"Yeah, she was there."

"Right? And she was . . . " I put it together. Jesse is in a behind-the-scenes relationship with Lisa. But why? Lisa is a beautiful woman. Why not just put it out there for all to see? I pepper him with questions: "How long have you known each other? Did you know her before you went in?"

"No," Jesse says, "we only met about five years ago."

"So you met each other inside, before you got out?" I ask, wondering how that was possible. "And now you're living together? Already?" I have to admit, I'm a little disappointed. Jesse gets out of prison after almost twenty-five years in a shared cell and immediately moves into a basement bedroom with a woman he met inside. Is he really giving himself enough time to get adjusted?

"I don't know. We're not staying here for long." He walks back out the door. "We want to get our own place. It's just that we don't have enough money saved yet. And there are complications," he whispers, pointing to the door leading to the rest of the bedrooms on the first floor. "I'll tell you about it while we eat lunch."

It has been so long since Jesse went out to eat, he doesn't know where to go or what to suggest. We drive around scanning the neighborhood, looking for the right combination of good food and lunchtime ambience. One place is mid-lunch empty. Another is too loud. We finally settle on a seafood restaurant at the far end of a mixed-use strip mall, just around the corner from Pottery Barn and IKEA.

Sliding into the dark, padded booth, Jesse struggles to order.

"Does this look good to you?" I ask, wanting it to be his choice.

"Everything looks great," he says. "Why don't you order for me?"

"I don't know what you want." I remember the trouble Don had with ordering when we went out for lunch, and I recognize the signs. There must be a hundred choices on the triple-fold-out glossy menu. He's panicking a bit, turning the menu around in his hands, opening it and closing it, mumbling a little under his breath, "I don't know," over and over. Jesse wants it to be perfect but he doesn't know what "perfect" looks like or tastes like. I order the standard fish and chips. From experience I reason fish and chips in a seafood restaurant is sort of like potatoes and eggs at a diner. There's an unspoken agreement between customer and proprietor not to screw up something so basic. Jesse sees it all very differently. He doesn't want to make a bad choice, and now everything and anything is possible. I'm probably not helping when I say, "Choose anything you want. It's on me."

A few waitress walk-bys later, Jesse settles on sweet potato fries, warm and spicy artichoke dip, and shrimp and chicken jambalaya. I order an Italian soda.

"What's that?" Jesse asks. I explain it's sparkling water with a touch of syrup. "I'll have one of those, too," he says.

"It takes your breath. You're so used to disappointment that when the good news comes, they really said I'm really goin'. Like that!" Jesse snaps his fingers. "You're finally overjoyed it's not bad news. Then when you do get out of the gate it takes time to wrap your arms around it, see it for what it is. Then it's like, what do I do now?"

When Jesse talks about prison, he uses the full name, "San Quentin." I look around, worried people nearby will hear it and be anxious. If they are, they keep it to themselves.

"It's wild. There's so much going on," he says.

And there's so much food left over at the end of the meal, Jesse packs it up to eat later back at his mom's house, where he can savor it alone, without the pressure to finish at the restaurant.

After lunch we drive out to the Marina Park, a spit of land that juts out into the wide waters of the San Francisco Bay. It's a glorious midweek summer day, and no one is around, save for some retired power-walkers. We sit together on a park bench, looking west across the sparkling waters. The warm sun shines across Jesse's upturned face, turning his cheeks and forehead a deep, golden black.

"This is beautiful," Jesse says, "except for that." I follow his eyes across the glint of the water to the far northern tip of the bay. There they are: the telltale sand-colored buildings of San Quentin State Prison.

"There it is," he says. "Man. I spent twenty-five years inside those buildings. Man. You know, it's great being out, being free. But that's the thing: I can't get the guys still there out of my mind. It's survivor's guilt. I was locked up there and now I'm out here. But all the guys I know are still in there. It stays with me."

"And that was a close call with the Emeryville police," I say. "How are things with your family? Are you still giving them rides?"

"No." He blurts the word flat out, like an edict from a higher power. "No. No. No. I was terrified. I told my family they'll have to find their own rides. They don't understand what it means to be on parole. I mean"—he stops himself—"they think they understand but they don't. Some of them have done a night here or there in the county jail, but they don't know what it's like to do twenty-four-plus years inside prison. They have no idea."

"What's it like at home?"

"It's bad. My brother is using. My mother is in denial. He was even storing large boxes of drugs at the house." He says he suspects Jayvonce was dealing drugs from the house. "I told my mom, 'This has got to stop.' He said he wasn't going to do it anymore, but I saw a big bag of it down in his room. I gotta get out of there."

"If your parole agent knew about that, would your parole be at risk?" I ask.

"Absolutely. That's why I'm moving out. I can't take a chance anymore."

"Where are you moving to?"

"That's the question. It's expensive. When I got out, they gave me $200. That's it. That's if they'll even rent to someone like me. I really want to get my own place so I can have some peace and quiet."

"Are you and Lisa going to find a place together?"

"Oh brother. That's a can of worms. I mean, I think Lisa's great. But man, it's hard. She freaks out," he says. "Sometimes I just don't know what to expect. It seems to be going along great, then she blows up. But I can't afford to move out by myself. It takes first and last [months' rent] and security [deposit]. I went to a few places and so far nothing's come through."

I tell Jesse that I heard from another lifer who had just gotten out of San Quentin that after being turned down by one apartment manager after another, he finally got as far as an interview with a company managing some apartment buildings in San Leandro, a middle-class community in the East Bay flatlands, before he was turned down. He said, "When I told her I'd done twenty-three years in prison for homicide, she closed the folder on top of her desk, pushed her chair back as far as she could before hitting the wall, and said, 'You need to go find a felony-friendly apartment building.'"

"That's exactly it!" Jesse says. "They just close the door on us. But we have one place we're going to go look at where they said they would still talk to me, so maybe that'll work out. I just can't stay at my mother's house. It's too dangerous."

"How did you and Lisa meet?" I ask, changing the subject.

"We met inside. She was a nurse inside San Quentin's hospital. Still is. I was working as a janitor. I saw her and thought she looked good. So we hooked up. We really hit it off."

"Love at first sight?"

"Pretty much," Jesse says, laughing. "It started fairly slow, then we got to know each other more."

"But how much time can you really spend together inside? I mean, people are always around. You can't really do anything. . . . "

"You'd be surprised," Jesse says. "There are all kinds of nooks and crannies around the prison where you can be alone. We fooled around quite a bit. It was a relationship."

"So how much can you get away with? I mean, you didn't have sex, right?"

"Sure, we did," Jesse says.

"More than once?" I ask, openly surprised.

"Of course."

"Where?"

"Exam rooms, offices. Everywhere," Jesse says. "The problem is now that we're living together on the outside, it's all different. Things have changed. She always wants to know where I am and when I'm going to be home. It's like checking in at Four Post [the officer's post inside San Quentin where inmates check in on their way to the chapel]. 'Where you going?' 'What time you going to be back?' Sometimes I feel like I've just exchanged one cell for another! Knowing her inside, I never knew this would happen. I wish I could just live by myself, but there's no way."

Listening to Jesse, I see options. "But why don't you stay at your mom's a little longer, until you save enough money to rent an apartment all by yourself?"

"Can't. It's too dangerous," he says. "And I have nowhere else to go. Don't worry. It'll be okay with Lisa. We'll work things out." I wonder if life will ever look like more than a frying pan and a fire to Jesse.

It's raining the day Jesse moves. I stop by, curious to see what $900 a month will get you in Oakland in 2010. Over the Bay Bridge, through a maze of freeway interchanges, I follow Google maps, drive down an off-ramp, make a couple of quick rights and park, the freeway visible through the tall hedges. On one side of the street there are trees and turn-of-the-twentieth-century houses turned into apartment buildings, their wood-framed windows and open porches a reminder of another, gentler time in Oakland. On Jesse's side, a series of four-story, poorly designed, slapped-together apartment buildings line the block, black steel gates and a call box preventing anyone from entering who doesn't know the code or the name of someone who will buzz them in. Stepping up to the security front door, I search the long list of names, the white plastic letters pushed together in a row . . . Reed. There it is. I push "star," then his code. There's a loud dial tone followed by a cackling ring. "Hello?"

"Jesse, it's Nancy."

"Nancy!" his voice brightens, booming through the speaker. "You found it! I'll come down and get you."

While I wait, a beat-up truck stops in the middle of the street in front of Jesse's building. Piled high in the back of the flatbed is a collection of brand-new couches, chairs, and an ottoman, each piece wrapped in sheets of thick, clear plastic, the ends taped closed. Two men, one in his seventies and feeble, the other younger, the brawn of the duo, stand outside the truck, looking up at the building. From inside the thick glass door, Jesse appears. He tries to cover the anxiety of the moment with his reliable smile, but there's just too much going on. He's got furniture coming. And now he's got debt.

"Is that yours?" I ask.

"I think it probably is," he says, looking out at the truck parked in the rain-drenched street. Meeting the older of the two delivery men halfway up the steps, Jesse points to the parking area under the building and indicates his apartment number. "I'll meet you there," he tells the man.

It's a big day. Jesse is moving into the first home of his own after prison. We turn. Jesse walks ahead, up some open tiered steps, around a smudged wall, and down a wide walkway past identical black mesh–covered security doors, each spaced twenty feet apart, to his apartment. While I wait for him to unlock the security gate, I step back and look up. Above us are five stories of tiered walkways leading to rows of apartment doors. It looks so familiar.

Security gate open, Jesse invites me in. Immediately to the left is a shiny, clean bathroom, with a small floral carpet on the floor and an array of towels draped evenly over the bars. Straight ahead is the bedroom Jesse will share with Lisa. It all smells sweetly of Jesse and his signature cologne. To the right of the front door, a white galley kitchen wraps around to a living room, which, in anticipation of the yet-to-arrive furniture, is bare—except, that is, for a big forty-two-inch flat-screen television. Today Jesse is watching an old *Perry Mason*. "I like to figure out what's going to happen before the end. If I'd had Perry Mason, I probably wouldn't have done twenty-five years."

On the far side of the living room, a curtain of plastic vertical blinds covers a large, double-wide sliding glass door. Like a dog checking out entrances and exits before settling down in a new home, I pull back the blinds, unlock the sliding door, and walk out onto the cemented five-by-fifteen-foot walled patio, the apartments high above in the courtyard looking down on Jesse's little bit of escape. Back inside, the two delivery men have already managed to carry the sectional sofa, coffee table, and ottoman inside, and have gone back to their truck for the last piece, a chair.

"This is just great, Jesse," I offer, a bit excited to see the parcels unwrapped. "Do you have scissors? We could take the plastic off!"

"Yeah. Let's do it," Jesse says, sorting through some papers scattered on the top of the computer table and coming up with a big pair of scissors, he hands them to me. "Here."

Cutting and ripping, we expose the sectional couch and place it just the way he wants it, against the far wall, the long end in front of the television. He unwraps two red, gold, and green designer pillows and places them carefully in the opposite corners of the couch, a brown throw blanket over the long end. Picture perfect.

"The last piece is the chair," Jesse says, looking down, "but it's not *the* chair. It's just *a* chair for now. I couldn't afford *the* chair I wanted. But I'll get it. Eventually, I'll get it."

"What was *the* chair like?" I ask.

"Well, it was red and it leaned back so you could relax in it. I've always wanted a chair like that," he says. "But we already spent too much on all this, so I couldn't get the chair."

"How did you buy all this?"

"We bought it on credit. I didn't have any credit cards, so I thought if we buy this, I'll start to build my credit up. It's expensive, though." He winces. "Man. Everything costs so much."

They went to a furniture store, he says, that didn't require a good credit report. The interest rate was high, but they'll pay it off and then he'll have credit. "Now I've got one secured credit card," he says as the movers maneuver the unwanted, not perfect chair into the room behind him.

The movers gone, we sit on Jesse's brand-new furniture and chat about his mom and Lisa, the two women bookending his life. He has just walked away from one and moved in with the other. "It's so bad right now. I've just spent all this money moving in to this apartment and now I'm broke."

Dreaming about being free and actually being free are two very different pictures.

nineteen

MONEY

2008–2011

If free love is one sure vision on a locked-up man's mind, the very next thought likely to occur to him every day of his incarcerated life is about money. And great as it is to get out of prison, living on parole after twenty-plus years behind bars is like being given a get-out-of-jail-free card without any property on the board or cash in the bank. And after spending between $50,000 and $100,000 or more a year to keep a lifer locked up in a California prison, the government doesn't want to spend another penny of the taxpayers' dollars keeping them out.

The expectation is that freed lifers will either take care of themselves or get others to help. Before a lifer can even get out of prison, he has to prove to the parole board that he has his free life already worked out. He must produce signed letters from family, friends, and people he has met on the inside who have promised to help with his transition, and confirm that he has a safe place to live and a full-time job with a living wage. Everything must be arranged before his release.

Then, for the first few days and weeks after he emerges from his Rip Van Winkle years, there are distractions: people to see, places to go, and things to do, all within the fifty-mile parole restriction. In the early days, family and friends pull out their wallets and pick up the tab for drugstore goodies and the little immediate things that need to be covered.

Then slowly, steadily, the money issue reemerges. It takes a lot of cash to be free. A one-way bus ticket across town to see a parole agent costs $2. A tank of gas runs about $40. Just stepping out the front door seems to cost money and that's if he doesn't have to worry about paying for his first few days, weeks, and months of housing.

No grown man is going to live with his mother and/or father forever. And even in a perfect world, first jobs don't usually last. So the question that everyone knows is hanging overhead but doesn't want to ask is: What next? What will he do after his first plans for being free change, morph, and fall through? And how on earth is he going to make enough money?

Phillip Seiler's parole plans were rock solid. He had kept in contact with his family, his friends, and his former employer. He was going to move back in with Mom and Pops, get his old job back as a plumber, build up his savings and credit, and eventually find his own place.

It would take time, but if anyone knows how to pace himself, how to take one step at a time and be patient, it is a man who has served an indeterminate sentence.

At least he wouldn't have to hit the pavement asking strangers to rent him an apartment or give him a job. That probably wouldn't go over very well. They would want to know who he was. They would want him to explain the twenty-year gap in his residential and employment history. Phillip was lucky enough to have a safe landing place and a plan. Unfortunately, neither would last.

By the time the governor finally gave up fighting Phillip's court-ordered parole, it was August 28, 2008, just two weeks before traders working for the global financial firm Lehman Brothers were seen on national television carrying boxes out of the building on a Saturday night. "If I'd been released in 2003, when the parole board first found me suitable," Phillip says, referring to the bull market and growing economic crisis, "it would have been a different story. But I'm not complaining. I'm happy to be free."

Phillip certainly isn't the only lifer facing a post-prison, post-bubble world. By the time Don Cronk was paroled on April 13, 2009, the crisis was old news, and the economy seemed far from recovery. No one was even pretending there could be a quick clean-up of the devastation.

And on June 11, 2009, when Jesse Reed was driven out of San Quentin's east gate and taken to his mother's house, the "R" word had finally, after months of national denial, been brought back into circulation.

A recession is scary for even the best-prepared Americans. No one knows how long it's going to last or what the world will look like when it's over. It's even more unnerving to face a worldwide economic downturn if you've spent the flush years, the good times, in prison, when help-wanted signs faded in shop windows and plentiful jobs were easy to get.

The only upside, if you can call it that, is that lifers have been locked up so long they haven't had an opportunity to accumulate debt. Newly released prisoners don't have credit cards, and that makes them easy prey for businesses offering high-interest loans on things like new furniture and cars. And even if they had wanted to apply for the plethora of easy-to-get, hard-to-pay-for home-equity lines of credit that took so many gullible Americans living on the financial edge down the path to financial ruin, they wouldn't have qualified.

Still, it couldn't have been easy, sitting inside San Quentin, waiting for word whether the governor would let them go, all the time watching the television news programs documenting, for those willing to watch, the early signs of a collapsing economy.

It's not as though Phillip, Don, and Jesse weren't used to working. There are jobs in prison. Most of them pay about 50 cents an hour. Having a full-time job and keeping the home prison running smoothly is all part of doing a life sentence in California. Of the 50 cents an hour most lifers make for their Monday-through-Friday, seven-to-five work, some is applied to the victims' restitution fund; most of the rest is put in their personal prison account so they can buy things like toothpaste and Top Ramen at the canteen and a plate of fried chicken when programs inside hold food sales. And some of it is put in a personal savings account for the day they get out. So with nonexistent credit histories and a résumé they'll be at pains to hand out, lifers enter an unfriendly marketplace.

—

Eddie Ramirez learned how to work with sheet metal inside prison. When he got out of San Quentin in prerecession 2005, it took a little while, but eventually, at the age of forty-five, he landed a union job working for an air-conditioning and heating company making about $12 an hour, or $350 a week, take-home. "I was embarrassed. I couldn't believe it," Eddie says. "I was making just enough to fill the car with gas." At first no one but the bosses knew he had been in prison. Then word spread. In the lunchroom he could feel the sideways glances in his direction. But he knew how to avoid trouble. He'd had plenty of practice.

When the recession hit three years later, in late 2008, Eddie was one of the first to be let go. Lupe still had her job and with her income they managed to meet the monthly mortgage while their savings were used to satisfy the other monthly bills, such as the payment on his truck, gas, food, and utilities, with a little left over for essentials. But work was important to Eddie. He needed to be busy. For weeks and then months, he looked for another position, scouring Craigslist and applying for every job he could find. No one would hire him when they discovered he'd been in prison for twenty-two years for murder. On the verge of depression, and with his and Lupe's small savings draining away, Eddie decided to turn his attention to something with long-term investment value. Instead of moping around the condo he and Lupe bought at the top of the market, he put his hands and skills to work tiling the kitchen backsplash and building out the small attic into an office space, pulling all the boards and materials up through the small access hole in the ceiling. All that mattered was that he was busy. Two years later, in 2010, his union called him back to work. This time, as a journeyman sheet-metal worker, with overtime and time and a half, he would take home more than $1,400 a week. They could start building up their savings again. He and Lupe would survive.

Before he got out of prison in 2006, Richie Rael knew what he would do for work. Inside San Quentin he worked as a carpenter in the prison's wood shop, building shelves and cabinets for the warden's office and furniture for wherever the prison needed it. When the parole board asked for documentation to show he had a guaranteed job on the outside, his older brother Ron wrote the letter. He owned a window business and needed to hire someone to do installations. Richie figured it would make a good transition job. He would get the $200 the prison gave all paroling prisoners on their release, and he had $900 saved up in his prison account. If he lived with his mom and dad for a while and worked for his brother full time, he could save enough money for first and last months' rent to get an apartment. He was grateful for the job offer but knew working for his brother wasn't an ideal situation: "My brother doesn't want to pay me a full salary. He pays everyone else more."

Two years after getting out of prison, Richie was ready to move on. All set with a bright blue flatbed truck and a small nest egg growing in his bank account, he moved out of his parents' house and into a small one-bedroom apartment at the back of a quiet complex about a mile down the road. "I'll never move very far away from Newark and my parents," he said then. "It's my home."

Tired of being underpaid by his brother, Richie quit his job and began an independent contracting business. "I'm pretty excited," he said at the time. "I think this is the right thing to do. Now I can stand or fall on my own two feet."

If the recession of 2008 hadn't hit quite so hard, he might have made it. But in the fall of 2010, Richie called his brother. Would he take him back? No one else would hire a man who had been in prison for murder.

Before Phillip Seiler committed the murder that got him locked up in prison for twenty years, he had worked as a journeyman plumber and carpenter for small companies in Sacramento.

Looking back at his hire two decades earlier, Jerry Greenberg, the owner of ACE Plumbing, says he saw something promising in the face of the young father of two: "Prior to getting in trouble, Phil worked with me. He was a hard worker. I knew when he grew up a bit, he'd be an asset to my business."

Not that hiring Phillip as a young man was all smooth going, even for Greenberg. "Early on when he worked for me, I had a little problem with Phil. He was actually stealing some of our material and doing some side work. I caught him and fired him. I said, 'This is it. You're done.' But he begged me for a second chance. So I asked him, 'How much did you take from me?' He said, 'Probably a couple thousand.' I said, 'Gee, that really bothers me. You got any ideas on how you might pay me back? That might make me change my mind.' Phil had a '76 Harley Sportster and he said, 'How about if I give you my motorcycle to keep my job?' I said, 'We can do something like that.' So early on, Phil realized he had made a mistake. I kept him on, forgave him. He paid his debt to me and I never had another problem with the guy. Never. He was perfect."

But before Phillip could temper his twenty-something immaturity into something harder, more durable, he'd left his job with Greenberg and gotten a job in construction. The day Phillip got laid off from that job was the day he made the deadly mistake that would forever alter his life and the lives of those who knew him.

Still, that murder conviction wouldn't be enough to change Greenberg's early faith in Phillip. A hardworking father and self-starting businessman, Greenberg attended Phillip's trial. For the next two decades, while Greenberg nurtured and grew his small plumbing business, he took time to nurture Phillip's growth and development in prison.

In 1998, with Phillip's first appearance before the board approaching, Greenberg put his money where his mouth was. He wrote a letter to the parole board, and later to the governor, guaranteeing he would give Phillip a full-time $20-an-hour job if the state let him out. Phillip's mom signed another letter guaranteeing Phillip would have a place to live. In 1998 the letters and Phillip's clean prison record wouldn't be enough to convince the board to give him a second chance at freedom.

Then in 2003, the board found Phillip suitable for parole. One hundred and fifty days later, Governor Gray Davis said he wasn't convinced and reversed the board's decision. By the time the court ordered Phillip's release in 2008, his old job as a plumber was still waiting for him, just as Greenberg had promised. "Phil's a good guy. I think he deserved a second chance and I was happy to get him back," Greenberg says while giving me a tour of his new operation, a two-and-a-half-acre plant of spotless warehouses and offices in Sacramento. "He's a good boy. He did something horrible but he paid his price. I always told him, 'If you want your old job back when you get out, come see me.' That's what he did. Now he has his own [company] truck and he does his own sales."

"How does that work?" I ask, not familiar with how plumbing services are sold.

"He'll go out on a job and he'll find perhaps a bad sewer line and he talks to the customer about making a repair. If he's a good salesman and can give a good reason why it should be fixed, it's his job to sell what they need, and yet not sell anyone something they don't need, 'cause I won't allow that. But if they truly need something, I want them to go to town and make it happen. That's how we stay in business."

Not everyone was on board when Greenberg rehired Phillip after he got out of San Quentin. Greenberg recalls, "One of the secretaries made the comment, 'How do you know it's safe for us?' And I said, 'Just trust me. I wouldn't put him here if it wasn't. And once he's here, if at any time anyone feels there's a problem, I want to hear about it and we'll reconsider.' Since he's been here, everyone loves him. There's never been any problem with any of the secretaries. He's never done anything inappropriate, here in the office or in people's homes. I would bet my life that Phil's going to be fine for the rest of his life. Positive."

As he lived with Mom and Pops and worked for Greenberg, Phillip's plans were working out perfectly. But not for long. A few weeks after he got his job back, his parents threw him a curveball, unexpectedly kicking him out of their house. Again, Greenberg came to his rescue, offering a rent-free apartment until he could get things sorted out. "I thought, 'I have a place and he needs a place.'"

Then, again, for a short while, things settled down. Phillip had his own plumbing truck and was moving up in the business, beginning to sell services on commission.

A few weeks after my talk with Greenberg, Phillip met Desiree, and a short time after that he made what he saw as a long-term investment in happiness. He was in love with Desiree, and now that she had accepted his proposal with the condition that it be a long engagement, his future lay with her in the Bay Area.

Leaving Sacramento would mean walking away from the safe, professional relationship he had spent more than twenty years building with Greenberg and applying for jobs a hundred miles away, where no one knew his record, good or bad. "It's okay," Phillip assures me. "I'm sure it'll be okay. Desiree says there's no real rush to get a job. She can carry the mortgage on the house for a while. But I'm determined to get a job as soon as possible."

Yet even with Greenberg as a top-notch reference, it's more difficult than Phillip imagined. One job prospect after another falls through. "They don't even call me back," he says.

Meanwhile, to bring money into the household, Phillip gets some side jobs doing construction.

One day he decides to cold-call a few businesses in the area that look well established. Places he would like to work. He gets sit-down interviews with five construction and plumbing companies. “In four of the interviews, they were all like, ‘You’re hired.’ They didn’t act like *it* was a big deal, but I think *it* was the reason they didn’t hire me.

“One job I interviewed for at a plumbing place, he asked me a bunch of plumbing questions, and about how I get along with people. He seemed pleased with my answers and I gave him my ACE Plumbing card, said he should call my boss in Sacramento about what kind of plumber I am. Before he could ask me about where I’d been for the twenty-year gap in my work history, I told him, like I did with all of my interviews. He looked surprised. He asked me about my crime. I told him everything. He said, ‘Everyone deserves a second chance. But our only catching point is we have to check with corporate to see if they’ll do this, because you just got out of prison.’”

A week later Phillip and Desiree come over for breakfast. The news isn’t good. “I didn’t get the job. The manager said he really went to bat for me, but corporate wasn’t going for it. Apparently, for corporations to get a 20 percent discount on their insurance, they have to be able to say everyone has been background checked, and they didn’t want someone on parole. He even apologized and wished me luck. He said maybe in the future after I’ve worked in the area, if they’re hiring I could apply again. So now I have to start all over. I don’t know what I’m going to do if I can’t find work. It was so easy with Jerry. Now that I have to tell people about my past, it’s hard. They look at me like I’m a monster and my crime is the only deciding factor.”

Meanwhile, Phillip’s work and experience inside San Quentin with Insight Prison Project takes a turn on the outside. Jacques Verduin, the project’s executive director, is beginning a new program working with troubled teens in Bay Area high schools called Inside Out. Verduin wants Phillip to join the program as a part-time staffer. “I really like it, but it’s a lot of travel and I’m not making enough money to pay my part of the household expenses," Phillip says. "They're only giving me six to eight hours of work a week. I need more hours than this. I don't know what I'm going to do."

Months after moving to the Bay Area, Phillip is hitting a wall. It's 2010 and the construction trade is tanking. No one is hiring. Local news reports warn of escalating regional unemployment. There's only one thing, Phillip says, for him to do. Try harder. He makes more cold calls and one day, on his way home, stops off at a construction business he passes on the way home. "The brothers who own the business gave me an interview and he [one of the brothers] said, 'That's quite a few years you did in prison.' And right up front, I told them, 'Here's my history.' I said it was a serious crime. I told him what happened but I didn't go into detail 'cause he wasn't, like, on the edge of his seat. It didn't seem like it mattered a whole lot to him. I said, 'When it comes to carpentry I know my stuff.' After he hired me, I asked, 'What do you think about my history? Is that something that's going to come up?' He said, 'You know what? It's none of their business.' I'm not sure what his reasoning was. From time to time we kick it at the end of the day if I see he isn't busy. At one point he told me my crime wasn't a factor. 'You did your time. That's behind you. I can tell you've changed and as long as you're not going to go off on anybody or anything like that.' I told him I don't do that anymore. They took a chance on me and I won't let them down."

By now Phillip has been out for a little more than two years. One person who's supposed to know just how well Phillip is meeting the conditions of his release is his parole agent. His agent is willing to sit down with me and talk about Phillip's parole as long as I don't identify him by name.

We meet at the agent's office in a nondescript office building. His job, he says, is to help his clients or parolees with their rehabilitation when they get out of prison and to make sure they comply with their parole conditions. Of the sixty parolees he oversees, he says six of them are paroled lifers. "Actually, my lifers are doing pretty good right now." And that's not surprising considering, he says, what a lifer has to do to get out of prison on parole. He was especially impressed when he visited Desiree and Phillip at their shared home in Pacifica. "They maintain a very stable home. It's one of the nicest homes on the block," he says, laughing. "For the most part, I try to give the guys a fair chance. I could have denied his request to move the location of his parole from Sacramento to here, but there were no factors present why I should deny it. The house was stable and he had plans to work. As a lifer he knows if he gets into any trouble and goes back into prison, they'd have to go through the approval process all over again. And what are the chances? The governor before this one wasn't letting any lifers out. So Phillip was one of the lucky ones. And we're going to have a new governor and we don't know what's going to happen then."

For years inside prison, Don Cronk worked as a clerk in San Quentin's chapel. It was one of the better jobs inside prison. He had his own small office with a door that had to be kept open, ajar at all times. He could read, write letters, and get up and walk around when the pain in his neck got to be too much. Except for moving some books every now and then, it was a job that didn't require heavy lifting. This was fortunate—Don says that after years of sleeping on a prison-issued spring bunk bed with a two-inch cotton mattress, he was all but disabled by neck pain. "My fingertips were often numb and I couldn't move my head more than a few inches in any direction without screeching pain."

In 1998 the California Department of Corrections and Rehabilitation paid for a surgeon to fuse vertebrae in his lower back to ease the pain. Initially that helped. But the damage continued, moving up his back to his neck. Two months before he was paroled, the CDCR paid a private doctor some $100,000 to fuse together discs in his upper vertebrae, the same doctor who later accused Don of banging on his doors and windows.

By the time Don got out on parole, he had saved up a little of his wages to add to the $200 cash he expected the prison to give him at his release. But by 2011 Don says he still hasn't received his gate money. "When my parole agent finally came to collect me, he asked if I wanted to wait for the paperwork to be processed for my cash. I told him I just wanted to get out of there. He said he'd get it to me, but I still haven't seen my two hundred bucks. I mean, it's just $200, but it's the principle of the thing. It's all they give us when we get out."

Even without the state's $200, Don's landing at Kathleen's made his transition back into the marketplace unusually smooth. Kathleen had lived alone for so long she knew how to keep the mortgage paid and the refrigerator stocked without any additional funds from Don, at least for a while.

From inside prison, planning for a post-prison life is difficult at best. Internet access is illegal and all phone calls have to be placed collect to the receiver. Potential employers receiving collect calls "from an inmate in San Quentin State Prison" might be hesitant to commit to a hire, especially when the call is interrupted every few minutes with countdown warnings: "You have five minutes remaining."

One way to get a job offer to show to the parole board if a lifer hasn't kept up contact with previous employers is to ask people who volunteer inside to help arrange work on the outside. All the lifer needs for his parole hearing is a letter guaranteeing he'll have a full-time job at a living wage when he gets out. Everyone on both sides of the wall knows with fewer than 1 percent of lifers getting out on parole each year, a promise made to a lifer most likely won't have to be kept.

As a regular visitor to San Quentin, Reverend Melissa Scott ministered to the lifers in the Protestant chapel. In Don's case, Scott promised him a job when he got out. And, true to her word, a few weeks after he was released, Scott offered him $25 an hour to work alongside a half dozen other construction workers refurbishing a massive mausoleum she owned in the Oakland Hills. Some of the gold leaf had flaked off the trim on the moldings and around the tall stained glass windows and it needed patching. So that he could get to the mausoleum, nestled high up in the Oakland hills far from any bus lines, Scott also gave Don a freshly tuned up minivan, the annual insurance premium paid up.

"It's not much of a car," Don says, taking me on an early morning visit to see the mausoleum, "but it works great and it's mine."

"She doesn't want you to pay anything?"

"Nope. She gave me the title," Don says. "I mean, eventually I'd like to get something a little more sporty, but this is fine for now. Reverend Scott said she would give me a hand, and she has. I just don't know how long I can do the work. In order to scrape the plaster and paint, I have to stand on a scaffold and reach up over my head. Even though I had the operation on my neck I still don't have full range of motion. I get headaches and my fingers are starting to go numb again. But it's a job and I'm grateful for it."

For the year that follows, Don has just about the most perfect post–life sentence life imaginable. He is settling in and adjusting to life with Kathleen. He's making a decent wage and he has his own car. Yet sweet as it is, it doesn't last.

Just before Christmas, Don gets word. The recession is taking a toll on Scott's investments. She can't afford to keep such a large staff of workers on the restoration project. The last hired, Don will have to be the first laid off.

"I understand," Don says matter-of-factly. "I mean, she couldn't keep me on the payroll because I just got out of prison. Now I'm sort of scrambling to find some other work. The money I make I give to Kathleen to pay for the utilities and expenses. I can't just sit around."

Problem is, because of his disability, he says, he can't do most of the jobs he might have considered. "I can't do any heavy lifting and even sitting for extended periods of time gives me severe headaches. When I was at the mausoleum, I almost blacked out a few times and had to lie down over lunch and rest. I'd like to do something with my associate alcohol and drug addiction counseling credential, but I'd have to do hundreds of hours of internship before I could really get a job that would pay. I need something now to keep us going."

Kathleen isn't panicking even though there isn't a whole lot of padding to keep them afloat. "When Don was inside, I spent $15,000 on an attorney who said he could get Don out. I didn't have to pay it all at once. He said, 'Give me $3,000 for this writ and $5,000 for that.' Before I knew it I'd spent nearly all my savings and the lawyer didn't get anywhere near getting Don out. In the end, it was writs that Don and his friend Rusty wrote on the inside that got him out. The lawyer didn't do anything. I'm still angry about that. He all but promised if we gave him the money, he'd get Don out. That was before Don was even found suitable. I still have my job [as a travel agent]," Kathleen says, "but people are calling and canceling their cruises. The industry is hurting."

To keep a little money coming in, Don takes on small jobs fixing decks in Kathleen's neighborhood and repairing electrical fixtures. "It's hit-and-misses. I'm keeping busy. Here," he says, pushing the sliding screen door to the side and stepping out onto the deck off the kitchen. "Let me show you the latest thing I've been working on here at home. See that little shed?" He points to a small playhouse-like building in the corner of the backyard. "I pulled off the old lattice around the bottom and see how the white lattice is all fresh? I just put that up this morning. I've still got to tack it permanently to the bottom of the little shed but it looks so much better."

"So what is that little house?"

"Some friends came over and said it's the most organized workshop they have ever seen. I keep all my audio and electrical tools in there. I still do some odd jobs when I have time."

"Oh, so it's your space? Kathleen said you can have it?"

"It's Kathleen's," Don corrects, a big smile stretching across his face, "but she said I can use it. And see that bed of dirt that's all turned over just to the right of the shed? It used to have a big rosebush that went up the fence and over the shed, but I pulled it out. Now that's where my vegetable garden is going. It gets sun all afternoon."

By mid-2010, Don is at his wits' end. "I don't know what I'm going to do. I've applied for every job I can think of that I can actually do, and no one's hiring me. I can't apply for jobs I'm not capable of doing and I can't not work."

With nothing to lose, Don applies to the US government for Social Security Disability benefits. The long application process is rigorous. There are doctor evaluations and interviews. In the end, it all pays off when the federal government declares that Don is physically disabled. "It's a combination of things," Don says. "It is partly genetic, but the catalyst that set the whole thing off was the spring cots we were forced to sleep on and not ever being able to sit up straight in the cell. That's what contributed to the three surgeries I've had on my neck, and now I'm disabled." The US government grants Don full disability benefits, including a three-digit monthly stipend, and the education and training he needs to create a new career. "It's really something. For the rest of my life, with regular checkups, the federal government will give me about $1,000 a month and they'll pay for me to go to college to learn a new skill."

The very next semester Don enrolls in computer technology program at the local community college. In two years, he says, when he finishes his program, he'll be certified as an IT guy. "I'll be one of those Geek Squad guys driving around in those funny cars taking care of people's computers. Isn't it amazing?"

If a bird were to fly directly from Don and Kathleen's rose-colored bungalow in San Anselmo to Jesse Reed's low-rent one-bedroom apartment in Oakland, it wouldn't take more than twenty minutes as the crow flies. But no bird in its right mind would want to make the trip. Given the choice, it surely would want to stay in San Anselmo, where the air is quiet and clean rather than head into the congested foothills of the east bay. Not to press too hard on the contrasts of their lives, it's hard to imagine things more black and white.

"You'll never guess where I am right now," Jesse says, his voice sounding a little hushed over the phone.

"I give up. Where are you?"

"I'm in Sacramento inside the CDCR's administration building," Jesse says, lowering his voice. "They're treating me so nice. It's so strange."

Immediately I am alarmed. "What are you doing inside the CDCR? Is there a problem with your parole? Are you in trouble?"

"No," Jesse says with a laugh, trying not to draw too much attention to himself. "I'm getting a green card!" This is an official photo ID that allows a visitor to enter a Department of Corrections facility—for example, a prison or a juvenile facility—without an escort. "It's wild. At first I was really scared to come in here. I mean, these are the officers who controlled my life for twenty-four years. Now the same people who treated me like an animal are treating me like an equal. They said, 'Please, sir,' and 'Thank you, sir.' It's amazing."

There it is. Over and over again, these formerly incarcerated men find it amazing to be treated like regular people.

"So, why are you getting the green card?"

"Reverend Earl Smith, the former chaplain inside San Quentin, finally called me back. He's starting an IMPACT [Incarcerated Men Putting Away Childish Things] program for juveniles who are locked up in the Department of Juvenile Justice facilities. I already went inside a couple of times with Earl and it was great."

"So, let me get this straight," I say. "You just got out of prison after serving twenty-four years for murder. The governor even reversed your parole date, and now the CDCR is paying you to go inside juvenile prisons to teach kids how to turn their lives around?"

"That's it. But I gotta tell you, being here in the CDCR headquarters is freaky."

The next time I see him, it's his one-year free anniversary. "That sure went fast," I say, approaching Jesse, who's standing outside his apartment, holding open the thick black security gate. "How would you like to spend the day?"

"Any way you want!" he chirps, giving me a big hug. "I'll leave it up to you."

Pulling onto the freeway at just after nine in the morning, we head northwest. "Have you ever been to Point Reyes National Seashore?" I ask.

"Nope," Jesse says, "but if that's where you want to go, I'm game. I just have to be back by one thirty for my car pool with the guys to Stockton for IMPACT. We share the driving duties and the price of gas so no one gets too burned out."

"We can have lunch in Point Reyes," I suggest, happy to share one of my favorite places on earth with Jesse on his anniversary. "There's a nice little café there with great milk shakes. Do you like milk shakes?"

"You bet," Jesse says, settling in for the journey. "I like everything."

It has been a long year since Jesse returned home to his mother and all the problems hidden behind her tears of joy. I'm glad he and I will have a chance to talk, driving along, with no distractions. So much has happened with his brothers and Lisa. I wonder how his perceptions have changed from that day to today. Is freedom still as sweet?

Fifteen minutes into our celebratory drive, we reach the top of the Richmond–San Rafael Bridge heading west. I hardly ever take this bridge. There, like a bull's-eye in front of us, with no way to turn left or right, loom the walls, cell blocks, and towers of San Quentin. "Whoa," Jesse murmurs, shifting in the front passenger seat.

"I've crossed this bridge a dozen times over the past year," he says, staring straight ahead, "and every time it feels the same. My chest tightens up and I feel it. I spent half my life inside those walls. My friends are still in there."

The way the floating road drops down from the apex, it feels like we're going to drive straight into the San Quentin yard.

"Let's see," Jesse says, pulling his sleeve back to look at the face on his watch. "Right now it's about nine forty-five. Everyone's pretty much at work. It's painful knowing how beautiful it is to be outside and so many brothers are locked up for nothing. They've already done the work to get out. But they can't leave. Just locked up."

That's the thing about bridges: you gotta keep moving. Suddenly the melancholy memory of the years he spent wishing for freedom, and his private worry for those left behind, is out of sight.

"Have you been out to the hills of Marin, since you got out?" I ask.

"Nope. I keep meaning to, but just one thing after another. Gas is expensive and I'm broke. Absolutely broke."

"But what about the job with IMPACT and Reverend Smith?" I ask. "Hey, let me see your new CDCR green card."

He reaches back and pulls the driver's license–size card, encased in hard, clear plastic, out of his wallet. As I turn it around in the sun, it looks just like the CDCR photo ID card with the holographic image Lieutenant Sam Robinson flashes when he passes through the sally port.

"Is it enough work?" I ask, handing the card back. "Can you survive on what you're going to be making with IMPACT?"

"No. Not at all," Jesse says with a moan. "I go inside the facilities three days of the week. But the DJJ facilities are between an hour and a half and three hours away. There are six of us, all former lifers who were involved in IMPACT on the inside and now we're teaching it to these kids who are locked up. So we try and carpool. We leave Oakland at about one, one thirty in the afternoon and drive an hour and a half to Stockton to the O.H. Close Youth Correctional Facility. It's one of two juvenile facilities just outside Stockton. One day of the week, we drive to Preston, which is 125 miles, or a three-hour drive each way. We go inside at around three and stay inside working with two different groups of juveniles and leave at around seven thirty or eight at night. We don't get home until around ten or ten thirty at night. It's a long day."

"How much do you make?"

"Reverend Smith doesn't like us to talk about how much pay we get, but I make about $25 an hour for the three to three and a half hours, sometimes four hours a night, three times a week. That doesn't include the time it takes for us to get there and get home. It really takes us about nine hours from the time we leave to the time we get home. So that's about $300 a week for about thirty hours' work. It really isn't much. I need to get more work. And the worst part is I haven't been paid in three months. The state hasn't passed the budget for the year and we aren't going to be paid until the budget is passed. Right now the state owes me about $4,000. We don't have enough money to pay our utilities and rent and eat, it's so bad. I don't know what's going to happen. The other day, my auntie showed up at our apartment with bags of food. It was huge. Our cupboards were literally bare. I don't know what I'm going to do. We've already borrowed money from Lisa's mom and a little from my family."

"What about Lisa? Is she still working as a nurse inside San Quentin?"

"Yeah. Thank God. We couldn't survive without her pay. But that's the other problem. I don't want to be dependent on Lisa. Things aren't great between us. We just see things differently. I think I should have gotten my own place, just to have some time to myself after being locked up for so long. But I couldn't afford it then and I can't afford it now. To tell you the truth, she's even threatened to call the police and report her car stolen if I go out at night."

"What about moving back home into the room downstairs alone, without Lisa? So you have that time alone?"

"No way. That is not an option. I was over there the other day and Jay is still up to his old business. I can't go back there. I'm really stuck, and right now there's no way out. I just wish Lisa would back off, give me a little room to breathe. Man," he says, as if invisible walls are restricting him, "if she just gave me a little room, we'd be okay. But she loses her mind and I can't take it." He stops as if to remind himself he isn't at home with Lisa, arguing. Right now, at this moment, he's in a car moving under leafy green trees. Sparkling in the sun, a creek is rushing by over boulders and pebbly stones. "This is beautiful, man. I had no idea. If the guys could see this, they wouldn't believe it."

We continue west on Sir Francis Drake Boulevard, up and around, following the curves of the road past the turnoff to Don Cronk's house, through one small, mostly white town after another. Jesse looks out the open window and takes a few deep breaths. Forty-five minutes after leaving Jesse's apartment in Oakland, we reach the top of a rise that separates suburbia from rural wild. Dropping down into a long stretch of valley, we pass through rolling green pastures spotted with thick, old-as-the-hills oak trees. A little farther along, we enter a redwood grove as we push on to the Pacific.

At just before ten thirty in the morning, we pull into Point Reyes Station, a small everyone-knows-everyone Main Street town in western Marin County with a bar, bookstore, and farmers' market. At the far end is the Pine Cone Diner. Aching for a good breakfast, we sit down outside the screen door at one of the long worn-wood picnic tables. Jesse's face is beaming. I stare, trying not to take any of his private joy, but desperate to understand it, to know what it feels like to live inside prison for so long, then sit at a picnic table on one of the most beautiful days in June, breathing the freshest air in the world.

It's cheeseburgers and milk shakes, the Pine Cone's specialties. With two hours until he has to be home, I make a proposition. If we hurry, we can still get to Limantour Beach with just enough time to make it back for his car pool to Stockton. "If you think we have time, I'm all yours," Jesse says. "Is it worth it?"

"If there's one place in the world you want to spend your first free anniversary, it's Limantour Beach."

"Let's go."

Driving around the southern tip of Tomales Bay, the spit of land stretching north that separates the American Plate from the Pacific Plate, a key fact to geologists, we zoom up the eastern face of a mountain thick with pines of all sorts to the very top, then back down the grassy, barren, wind-swept hills of Limantour Beach and an endless stretch of wild dunes and beach.

Sitting on the sand, looking out at the enormity of water, horizon, and space, his back against the grass-covered dunes, Jesse rolls up his pant legs, pulls off his brown leather shoes, strips off his socks, and wiggles his toes in the sand. It's a perfect moment in a life scattered with bad.

I walk farther on down the beach, to give Jesse time alone. There isn't enough time but it's better than none. Sitting down, I close my eyes. As I stretch my hands to either side, the hot sand reaches up through my palms to my forearms and shoulders. My face turned to the sun, I can feel the heat washing over me. Good idea, but it's time to go.

Lifting myself off the sand, I walk back. By now Jesse is walking in the shallow, rolling waves, curls lapping at his rolled-up pant legs. Then, like a young boy with just a few minutes left at the beach, he raises his arms into the air and runs around in a wide circle, laughing.

We spent longer than we should have on the beach and now have to rush to get back to Oakland in time for Jesse's car pool.

"Do you like your job working with the kids in the juvenile prisons?"

"I really think we're making a difference with these kids. We stand there in front of them and tell them who we are, what we did, and how we changed our lives. They see the nice clothes we're wearing, and listen to us. They know we all did twenty to thirty years in prison for murder, but at the end of the night, they watch us walk out, free because we changed. We tell them change is real, so start now, before they do something stupid and end up spending decades of their adult lives behind bars."

I want to see this for myself. "Do you think the CDCR will let me go inside the juvenile facilities to watch one of your IMPACT sessions?"

"It won't be easy. I don't even know if they allow the press inside," Jesse says. "You'll have to get permission from lots of people. First call Reverend Earl Smith. He's in charge of IMPACT. Then he'll tell you who to call inside the CDCR to get permission."

We make it just in time for Jesse to get in another car for the two-hour drive to Stockton.

It takes more than three months and an endless string of phone calls and e-mails, but eventually, with the help of Bill Sessa, the press secretary for the CDCR's Department of Juvenile Justice in Sacramento, it's all arranged. I may go inside the N. A. Chaderjian Youth Correctional Facility, one of two maximum-security juvenile lockups in the state.

Early in the fall we head east on the freeway, away from the cool Bay Area and into the heat of California's central valley. Again, while we drive Jesse has time to tell me things he might not otherwise. "Ask anything you want, Nancy. I've told you. If by my telling my story it will make it possible for my brothers who are still locked up to get out, I'll answer any question you've got."

The state still hasn't passed a budget, he and Lisa are beyond desperate, and he can't seem to find a second job.

"I must have made more than two hundred calls looking for work, any kind of work, but no one calls me back. When I go for jobs, they just say no, flat out, when I check the box."

"What do you mean, 'the box'?"

"There's a box on job applications. It asks if you've ever been convicted of a felony. Well, I figure they're going to find out sooner or later, so I check it. No point in trying to hide it. And they ask me what I was in for, and when I say homicide, well, that's the end of the discussion. Over and over again.

"I need to make money. So far the only work outside IMPACT that I've found is cleaning the Oakland Coliseum after the games. I go in at midnight, right after I get home from IMPACT, and work all night until eight in the morning picking up trash and cleaning the place up. It's disgusting what people leave behind. When I leave at eight, eight thirty, I'm completely exhausted. Then I go to sleep for a couple of hours, until it's time to get up to go to Stockton or Preston. Preston is a long day. When I get home that night, I'm so tired. And when Lisa gets crazy when I get home, I can't take it. I don't know, Nancy. It's not what I expected."

"Do you think about how you could do this freedom thing differently?"

"Sure. But it's going to take time. I want to start my own janitorial business, but I can't do that until I have enough money saved up to buy the equipment I need: you know, a professional vacuum cleaner, floor buffer, and all the [cleaning] solutions."

Meanwhile, Jesse says, Reverend Smith is trying to get the CDCR to expand the IMPACT program in other juvenile facilities. But that's going to take time. "What really makes it hard right now is since we aren't getting paid until the budget is passed, we aren't making enough to pay for the gas to get to Stockton and Preston. So me and the other ex-lifers pool our money, carpool, and spend time together."

It's nearly three in the afternoon when we finally reach Stockton and stop for a quick lunch. "If we don't eat now," Jesse says, "we won't have another chance to eat until eight tonight when we leave the facility. We usually just stop here at this gas station and get the stuff they sell: you know, hot dogs and chips."

"I don't think I would survive on that. I'm really hungry. There must be some good Mexican food. Let's look around a little before we settle for gas station food."

Treasure-hunt driving, I pull into a large grocery store with *menudo* written in large letters on the side of the building, "I think we might get lucky."

Inside, women with aprons stand ready to build a Mexican-style feast. Jesse orders a giant burrito with carne asada. I order some tacos. Sitting in a booth with long plastic bench seats, Jesse and I devour our lunches. "That was delicious!" Jesse says. "Much better than the gas station. I'll have to tell the guys about this. And it only cost $2.50."

Like most CDCR prisons, the N. A. Chaderjian Youth Correctional Facility is located miles from the freeway. Following Jesse's directions, we head down a two-way road past random farmhouses and businesses, turn right at a stop sign in the middle of nowhere, and keep going. Just when it looks as though there's nothing left but dry farmland and bare, empty dirt, I begin to see the telltale razor wire and high fences stretching along the road for what seems like miles. At the first break in the fence, we turn left into a black-topped parking lot planted with scattered trees that lean in the persistent wind.

As I open the car door, everything seems to fly around: my hair, my jacket.

"It's always windy here," Jesse says.

We stop at the sally port of a twelve-foot-high fence. Inside a window I see an officer turn and look at us. Simultaneously, he picks up a phone and reaches with his free hand to push a lever. A deep bank teller–style drawer opens on our side. Jesse pulls out his CDCR card and puts it in the open drawer. I retrieve my driver's License and place it next to Jesse's ID.

The officer on the other side looks at me. "Put your equipment in there. I'll need to check it." I place my tape deck and microphone in the box next to our photo IDs. The officer pulls the drawer closed. Lifting our IDs out, he holds them up to our faces, then picks up my deck and microphone and places them on a table behind him. Unable to record, document, I feel bare, anxious.

"You can go in," he says to Jesse, "but she'll have to wait for someone to come get her and take her inside."

"I was cleared by Bill Sessa in Sacramento," I offer, dropping the biggest name I have in my reporter arsenal.

"I don't care who cleared you," the officer says. "You'll have to wait for someone to come get you and take you inside. I think they're in a conference right now, so you'll have to wait."

"I have a couple of names of people here who may be responsible for me," I suggest. "Do you want them?"

"Sure. What do you have?"

I pull out my notes and read off a couple of names of counselors and authorities I've been in contact with at this institution. One of the names rings true to the officer. "Just a minute. I'll give 'em a call."

"Maybe you should go in without me," I tell Jesse. "I don't want you to be late for your session."

"I'm not going in without you," Jesse says. "We'll just wait. The others can get the session started without me. You know, it's an awesome feeling every time I come in here. Going in behind the gates, the alarms. It's like, wow."

We take a seat on a narrow bench below the window. The wind is whipping around; pieces of dirt and dust blow into our eyes and hair. It's unnerving somehow. Ten minutes later I don't know which I want more, to get out of the wind or to get inside for the IMPACT program.

"Hi. Nancy Mullane?" A man dressed in casual pants and a button-down shirt approaches from the other side of the high, chain-link fence. He's this institution's public information officer. "Glad you could make it," he says. He looks up, makes eye contact with the officer, and nods his head. I'm in. The officer behind the glass pushes a button. Slowly the fence rolls away.

"Wait," I say before passing through the gate. "I need my deck and microphone. The officer said he wanted to clear it, but I've been given permission from the press office in Sacramento to interview staff."

"No problem." Another nod and the officer behind the window places my equipment in the sliding drawer. Lifting the equipment, I step over the gate rail.

"Hey, Jesse," says the officer who came to fetch me, holding out his hand. In this prison, Jesse is an insider among the powerful. I watch the exchange. It all makes perfect sense—Jesse is here offering his experience and knowledge to kids playing serious games with crime—but still, it's odd to see him on the inside, dressed in street clothes, confident.

"Before we go over to the program, we need to stop in here in the admin building," says the casually dressed information officer, turning to me. "There are some people waiting to talk to you."

"I'll just head over to the library," Jesse says. "See you when you're done."

Before climbing the stairs, I catch a look at Jesse's back. He's stretching his legs in broad strides to get across the wide grounds of short grass and skinny trees to the compound of buildings off in the distance. There isn't another soul in sight.

I'm planted in a dark, cluttered office to wait. "We've got a couple of parole agents who work as counselors with the juveniles in the IMPACT program. I thought you'd want to talk to them."

First one thirty-something man, a parole agent's badge hanging from his belt buckle, walks in and takes a seat, then another. One is dark and calm, the other blond and fidgety.

"IMPACT is probably one of the best programs we've ever had here at the institution," says the darker agent, Harvey Casillas. And he should know a good program when he sees it. For the past eighteen years, he has worked at a number of juvenile facilities in the state and now is a parole agent II supervisor, working primarily with intervention services and programs for the CDCR's Department of Juvenile Justice. "The one thing our staff struggles with is developing a strong bond, rapport, trust with the young men in the facility. The men in the IMPACT program come in and they have instant credibility because they've spent a number of years behind bars—been there, done that. It's hard to explain but when these guys come in, not only don't they make excuses but they don't allow the young men to make excuses. They try to get our young men to think with a different mind-set about concepts they've experienced and dealt with in the prison environment, things like snitching and gang affiliation. I've never seen the young men win an argument with the IMPACT facilitators. Some young guys won't listen, but you can see their heads are spinning. They know what these guys are talking about. These kids aren't easy to impress and they see through top-down institutional programs—aren't interested. But this is different. The men in IMPACT talk their language. They know what it is to do time, and how to change.

"A couple of the kids have completed all eight of the eleven-week modules and have signed up to take the whole course all over again.

There's 'Man's Essential Make-Up,' 'Violence Prevention,' 'Relationships,' and 'Financial Literacy.' One ward has taken it more than three times and it's made a huge difference. I don't know how long they're going to keep it. You never know. But if we had our way, it would stay."

I wonder what he thinks, as an experienced parole agent, about the men leading the IMPACT program, and their criminal pasts.

"When I see an Eddie Ramirez and a Jesse Reed, I have to take them at face value. You know, I believe Eddie did time at Preston and he would tell the guys, 'These are the same units and halls I was on, and still I spent another twenty-two years in prison.' My interactions with these men are pleasant. I don't see them away from the job setting, but when I see them inside, they are very positive, very professional. They come across as ethical. The language they use is articulate. I've never heard any foul language coming from the men. Everything is just positive. That's what these guys out here need to see. They need to see offenders that are not coming in and being negative about the system or looking for excuses as to what things happened. When I interact with the men, I see them as good, law-abiding citizens. I would never say I didn't want these guys as my neighbors."

Approaching the facility's pitched-ceiling library at the edge of the education complex, through a wall of windows I see some two dozen young men and teenage boys sitting, mostly slouching, in rows of chairs facing Jesse and three other former lifers who are standing in front of them, leading the class. As we step through the door at the back of the room, the boys-to-men casually turn and look, then face the front again. This is a group not easily surprised, or shocked. Dressed in low-hanging dark blue sweatpants and cotton khakis, gray T-shirts hanging from their youthful shoulders, they have the body language of the outwardly bored, inwardly trapped.

Today's first group is just finishing up an eleven-week module on addiction, and it's time for the final review before the next day's test. On the table in front of IMPACT's three facilitators is a pile of candy bars and chips.

"First question," announces Sterling Scott, one of the facilitators. "According to IMPACT's definition, what is addiction?"

A few scattered hands shoot up. Others raise their half-bent fingers slowly, so they don't appear too excited. Scott, a tall, impressive man with years of behind-bars experience, eagerly points to one student, more man than boy, sitting at the end of the second row.

Opening his mouth just wide enough to be heard, the young man says, "Still using with adverse consequences?"

"That's the right answer," Scott says, to the sounds of whoops and hollers. "Using with adverse consequences. You used the key words. Come on up and get your prize."

As the young man pops up off his chair, the boy-men around him slap him on the back and shoot high fives. He struggles to accept the half-joking accolades and hold on to the rim of his pants that, as he stands, slip below his hips. It wasn't much of an answer, but he tried and he got something back for his efforts.

"All right," Jesse calls out, "who can tell me what the cycle of addiction is? Give me three components to the cycle of addiction."

One young man tries but doesn't quite get it right. The facilitators help him along and he manages to spit it out. He gets a prize.

"Give me three symptoms of addiction," Scott booms.

"Denial, stress, and peer pressure," calls out a teen with as much confidence as attitude, clearly enunciating each word.

"Denial, stress, and peer pressure," Scott repeats, not giving full credit where it isn't due. "Denial would be one symptom, but the other two are causes. What are the other symptoms?"

Another student in the program tries: "Denial . . . denial, addiction, and . . . relapse." The group howls with laughter.

Another tries: "Denial, abusive behavior . . . and continuous . . . use?"

"Come get your chips," Scott says.

The pre-exam review continues for another half hour as the grown-up men standing in front, dressed in snappy street clothes, model what a man who has done time and learned how to make it back out to the good life on the outside looks like and sounds like to this gaggle of lost boy-men. It's satisfying to see it happening. Boys to men and now men giving back to boys, trying to cut into their juvenile bullshit with their hard-earned experience.

When Bill Sessa, the press secretary for the Department of Juvenile Justice in Sacramento, had set up my visit a few weeks before, he made one thing clear: "If the counselors think it's appropriate, you may have a chance to interview one of the juveniles in the group. They have to be over eighteen, so we don't violate their juvenile right to privacy, and you can't record it. You'll have to take notes."

Now that the session is ending, I ask one of the counselors standing near the back door if this might be a good time for me to interview one of the program participants.

"Sure. Which one do you want to talk to?" he asks.

"Doesn't really matter. How about the one that answered that question?"

"Who else?" he asks, looking past me at the group of boy-men getting ready to walk away.

"Um, how about the tall, sort of skinny guy in the second-to-last row?"

"Sure. And you really should talk to James. This is the third time he's been through the program, and he has really made huge strides."

"Is it okay if I record the interviews?"

"Sure. That's fine," the counselor says.

He summons the three young men and leads the first of them down a wide hall to a locked office. Unlocking the door, he turns back to me and says, "Here. You won't be disturbed. I'll keep everyone away from the area."

This is too good to be true. I'm in a quiet office alone with a boy-man incarcerated for I don't know what.

Twenty-year-old James Piggee falls into the chair and moves a little until he's comfortable. He tells me he's from Southern California and that he's been locked up ever since his mom passed away when he was fourteen and he began breaking the law. His dad died while

James was locked up. He has now been in "Chad" for six months. Before that it was the youth facility in Chino for a year; before that, the Ventura fire camp, the Southern Reception Center, juvenile hall, and before that, home. "These people [referring to the men like Jesse who are leading the IMPACT program] have been through what I don't want to go through and they show me not to give up. There was a time I didn't care about maxing out [serving a maximum sentence of life in prison] or ever going home because I had a lifestyle addiction. I was an active gang member for a lot of years. I dedicated my life to it. I don't remember who it was, which facilitator, but he asked me if I was willing to give my life away forever. I really couldn't answer that question. He said, 'Well, you planning on being a gang member forever?' I said, 'Yeah.' He said, 'Well, then, you planning on giving your life away forever.' At that point I recognized I'm not willing to let anybody or anything dictate what I'm going to do. I'm going to dictate it for myself. So I left the gang-banging and it opened my eyes and I looked at the bigger picture: my values and priorities, which is my family, the people who have been here for my incarceration, not my gang members. It made me see another side of life I hadn't recognized."

"Do you know what the men standing in front of you were convicted of?"

"Murder. And I'm in for a similar crime. But it shows to me that if they can change, I know I can. 'Cause they've been to a bigger place, a worse place. And for them not to get dragged in [to gang lifestyle in prison], they got to be strong-minded men. It would have been easy for them to say, 'Oh, I got life so it doesn't matter.' I don't want to be that type of person. I can learn from other people's mistakes. On the streets I was willing to give away my life for something I never owned, that I didn't control, something I let control me. If I go out there and control my life and live a good life, good will come. I want to be a school counselor. I plan to go to college when I get out. It's a whole new experience. I mean, they're here showing me they made it, and that we can make it—that it's not over."

It's after six by the time I finish the third interview and make my way back to the library. Already the second IMPACT session of the night is under way and there's another group of boy-men slouched down in chairs facing the men at the front of the room. Taking a seat among them, I'm exhausted. It has been seven hours since I left my office in San Francisco, picked Jesse up in Oakland, and drove to Stockton, and there are two hours to go before this session is over.

Later that evening, before getting on the freeway to head home, Jesse and I stop to get gas at the hot-dog station. Reaching into the frozen case by the cash register, I pull out two double-chocolate ice cream bars. Back in the car, I pull them out of the brown paper bag and hand one to Jesse. "Have you ever had one of these?"

"Nope," he says, laughing, "but I'm game if you are."

Pulling off the cold wrappers, we head down the freeway, the sweet taste and rush of the chocolate taking the sting out of the long ride home.

twenty

DISNEYLAND

2010-2011

Eddie Ramirez has been counting the days. For five years, he has lived a free life tethered to parole. It's a world far better than being incarcerated in prison, but it's not an unfettered, kick-up-your-heels, and spontaneously take a drive across the country kind of free. If he wants to drive to Sacramento with Lupe to visit his stepson and step-grandsons, he first must request and wait for the slow-moving gears of the parole system to give him permission. Sacramento is one hundred miles away, fifty miles outside his parole radius. He can't have a beer or drink a glass of wine without risking a technical violation. Getting off parole isn't something these men talk about, but it's always on their minds.

On February 24, 2010, Eddie Ramirez calls his parole agent. After twenty-two years in prison and five on parole, his debt to society has been paid in full.

But, as there always must be, an unexpected problem arises. His agent forgot to submit the paperwork to finalize Eddie's release from parole. It's going to take at least another month to get it all done.

Reflecting on how far he has come in the five years since he was released from San Quentin, Eddie writes a letter to Governor Arnold

Schwarzenegger. "I want the man who signed my parole papers," he tells me, "the last man to decide whether or not to let me go free, to know who I have become on the outside. I want the man who took a chance on me to know I've gotten married and bought a home. I want the governor to know his decision to parole Eddie Ramirez was a good one."

When he finishes the letter, Eddie signs it, seals it, and drops it in a nearby mailbox.

A few weeks later, he gets word. Thirty years after being convicted of second-degree murder, he is free. He is an equal in a society without walls. He can drive to Sacramento or take a trip to Europe. But that's not what he has in mind. He knows exactly where he wants to take Lupe to celebrate.

They pack their bags, fill the tank with gas, and head south on the freeway. Pushing through the turnstiles at Disneyland, just like he remembers from when he was a boy, holding his father's hand, Eddie walks into the Magic Kingdom with his wife and the children they share as a family. It's a dream come true.

Holding Lupe's hand, giddy with childlike anticipation, Eddie joins the throng of humanity parading down Main Street USA, up through Cinderella's castle, and into Fantasyland. As he sits in a wide-bottom boat, floating through "It's a Small World," past the hundreds of little mechanical dolls singing in a dozen different languages all around him, Eddie's cell phone buzzes. He looks down at the screen and sees it's his old cellie, a man still locked up inside San Quentin's North Block. Eddie flips open the phone.

"Where are you, man?" his cellie asks from inside North Block.

Eddie laughs out loud. "I'm in Disneyland, man. I'm free."

A few weeks later, I'm sitting in Eddie's new truck driving to a strip-mall Mexican restaurant a couple of blocks from his home for lunch. Sliding into a red vinyl booth in the mostly empty room, he promises that the place "doesn't look like much, but it's good food." Now that

Eddie is off parole, he can have a beer at lunch without worrying he might have to take a surprise urine test. We order his favorite, lemonade. "When I got out of Q, I thought nothing would compare to that feeling. I thought, 'Now I'm free.' But that doesn't even compare to getting off parole. It's like I can finally breathe. I don't worry that I might make some little misstep that could send me back. Lupe and I are going to Hawaii and I don't even have to think about calling my PO to ask for permission."

Watching him talk about his life and his plans, I try to think back to the first time I ever saw Eddie, four years earlier, back in 2007. He was standing in a small half circle with a half dozen paroled lifers at a party celebrating Bryan Smith's parole. From across the room, he looked massive and dark, a brooding man with tattoos on his thick neck and chunky forearms. I didn't want to go to the Saturday afternoon party; I had weekend errands to finish up. But that annoying little voice in my head, the one that wakes me at night or interrupts conversation, wouldn't let go: "You have got to go. Who knows who you'll meet or what you'll see." I'm glad I listened.

For the two years since he had been released from Q, Eddie lived anonymously in Sunnyvale. He had a job and a wife. No one had to know about his past unless he decided to tell them, one by one by one. Then I had handed him one of my business cards and asked if he would tell me the story of his crime and his parole. It would be on microphone, on the record. He didn't have to. It wasn't a condition of his parole. Like the tens of thousands of people before him who had committed murder and been paroled throughout the country whose pasts remained sealed, he could have simply said no. He didn't even have to give a reason. Instead, he took a chance. I took a chance. Now four years later, sitting in this booth with me, he's as free as I am.

"You know," Eddie says, staring across the table at me while I nibble on deep-fried chips and hot salsa, "you're more likely to commit murder than I am. I mean, I know what it means to make that kind of horrible decision. I know what it costs. I know how to take the steps to avoid getting into a situation like that ever again. But people who have never been there, who think they can get away with one bad decision after another are more dangerous. They think they can get away with things that lead people, in a split second, to commit murder."

Lunch *is* good, but I can hardly taste it. Listening to Eddie talk about his new fully ripe liberty is mesmerizing. It's a freedom that, since the night he drove his car into a block of cement, was never guaranteed. First he had to do an unknown number of good-time decades in prison. Then he had to convince commissioners on the governor-appointed parole board he had truly, deeply changed and that if they let him out of prison, he wouldn't be a threat to anyone's public safety. Then he had to wait for word whether the governor was going to sign off on his freedom. Out on parole, he had to do five years without a single glitch or violation.

Getting off parole is the final frontier tying a person convicted of murder to the state and to his crime. Cutting the thick cord connecting a lifer to his parole agent isn't automatic. It requires five years of clean urine tests, regularly scheduled and kept check-ins with the parole agent, and no flagged contact with law enforcement. "I got stopped for a traffic violation once," Eddie says. "I was leaving the Preston Youth Facility in Ione one night after doing the IMPACT program, and my truck trailer hitch was obstructing my license plate. The Ione police officer pulled me over and asked me why I was in Ione. I told him I worked at the youth facility and pulled out my CDCR green card to show him. The minute he saw my green CDCR card, his attitude completely changed, like 'you're one of us.' The officer said, 'Have a good day, Mr. Ramirez, and take care of that trailer hitch as soon as you can.' Other than that, I don't even cross the street outside the crosswalk."

twenty-one

DIGGING DEEP

2011

Just before midnight January 1, 2011, Jesse Reed calls my home phone. I'm out with friends, celebrating, and don't see there's a message until midday, January 1. He sounds happy, like his life is settling into a little bit of the dream he had inside: "This is going to be a great year! I just know it."

Jesse is right . . . for about a week.

The next time I hear Jesse's voice, his hopeful, patched-together world has turned upside down. "I'm going through a lot. My mom is in the hospital," Jesse says, his voice raw. "She's really sick. I don't know what's going to happen. She's my mom."

I'm stunned, both to hear Jesse's voice sound so low and to hear his mom has been hospitalized. I flash back quickly to the last time I saw her, only three months before. She looked pretty good for a woman in her late sixties. "What happened?"

"It's been hell. I'm working all the time and trying to juggle everything. The doctor says she has stage-four liver cancer," Jesse says, repeating, "She's my mom." He says it as though he can't believe it, as though he's trying to remind himself that it's his mom this is happening to.

Early the following morning, a Sunday, I drive over the Bay Bridge to Alta Bates Summit Medical Center in Berkeley. Jesse meets me at the elevator doors just down the hall from Lois Parks's hospital room. "It's bad," he says, pulling back from a hug. "It all started three weeks ago. My mom was nauseous. At first she thought she'd had a heart attack. That's when my sister noticed her blood sugar level had spiked to over five hundred. The doctor said to take her to the emergency room."

Slowly I walk with Jesse down the hospital corridor. Standing in front of a large picture window, looking out on a hospital garden, Jesse is overwrought. "One thing led to another. They did some tests and found a number of blood clots and a mass on her liver. They gave her an MRI and decided to do a biopsy of her liver. In the process, they nicked an artery and that caused internal bleeding. They didn't catch it right away, and she got increasingly sicker in her bed. She couldn't breathe. They had to rush her back into surgery to close the artery, stop the bleeding. It looked like she was going to die right then and there!" Jesse says, his big shoulders slumped. "I mean, this is my mom. I don't know what will happen to the family if anything happens to her."

With the cancer diagnosis, the doctors needed someone to make decisions. No one in the family knew if she had a will or had signed a medical power of attorney. Maybe no one saw it coming, but now it was happening. Someone needed to step in, take charge, make life-and-death decisions.

Jesse recalls the first critical decision: whether to insert a breathing tube. "'If you give her a breathing tube,' the doctors said, 'you won't ever be able to take it out.' I said, 'No. Give her oxygen.'"

Lois's breathing resumed. They were out of the dark woods.

Then word came: things were worse than anyone had thought. "Three days ago the doctors said my mom has stage-four cancer in her liver. They aren't talking days or weeks," Jesse says, "but months. The doctor told us he would be surprised if she was still around in a year. I was there with my sister Angie when they told my mom and she just yelled, 'No! No! I'm going home!' The doctors wanted to operate on the tumors but Mom is sure they're wrong. She says she doesn't have cancer. She doesn't want anyone to do anything more. She believes God will take care of her. The doctors say without surgery or drugs, she won't live more than three months."

As I walk into the shared hospital room that for now Lois has all to herself, Jesse's mom looks over and reaches her hands out to give me a hug. I'm not family, but to Lois Parks, family casts a wide net. There's an intravenous line in the back of her hand to give her fluids and slow drips of morphine; a pale blue hospital gown is pulled across her broad black chest. Careful not to disrupt the lines and needles, I take a seat on the edge of her bed. She is wearing a nearly real-looking wig of shoulder-length straight black hair, the long bangs combed to the side. Her full, rose-colored lips are dry and chapped; her eyes are warm, drugged. Jesse stands at the foot of the high bed, staring at his mom. Jayvonce, his younger brother, is at his mother's side, feeding her small bits of cold, overly peppered scrambled eggs. She tries to eat them but can't swallow. A nurse comes in to sort things out, take Lois's blood pressure, and adjust her pillows. Moving any part of her body causes her to wince in pain. To break the tension, Jesse and Jayvonce banter about the football game on the TV and the upcoming Super Bowl between the AFC Pittsburgh Steelers and the NFC Green Bay Packers.

"In high school, Jesse was a star player," Jayvonce says. "He was a power on the field, a champion."

"I was good," Jesse says confidently. "I first played for Emery High School."

"What position did you play?" I ask.

"Linebacker," Jesse says. "I always tried to take two to three players out every game."

A cousin and his wife pass the nurse on their way in and jump right into the conversation about football: "Jesse was powerful on the field," his cousin says. "Every time he took another player out, he got another sticker on his helmet. They called him 'the Assassin.'"

"I went on to play at Laney College," Jesse says. "I didn't have the grades to go to a four-year college."

"Did you go to see Jesse play football?" I ask Lois.

"Every game," she says, her eyes fully open. "Home and away." Looking at the television and coughing a little, Lois says she wants the Steelers to win the Super Bowl. Her two sons challenge her, calling for the Packers to win. It's a safe topic in a room of fragile souls.

Lois is tired. Jesse walks me back out to my car. "You know, when I was inside and my dad died I knew I wouldn't be able to take it if anything happened to my mom," he says. "So here we are. I've had a year and a half to prepare for this moment. Now I'm ready to be the oldest son, the leader. I'm going to keep my family together. They're a mess with alcohol and drugs, but I'm not going to let that destroy my family."

But between work and family, Jesse is stretched to breaking. "Now I'm working five days of the week for IMPACT and that means every day driving to Stockton and Preston and five nights I have my cleaning jobs and I gotta come here for my mom. So it's difficult. It's very difficult, but I'm ready for what I need to do. If I weren't here, if I were still inside, it would be chaos."

True to her word, Lois refuses all treatment and goes home. It's not that she wants to die. She loves life and all the power and trouble it has brought her along the way. It's that she believes from the bottom of her God-loving soul that he will protect her and if the doctors are right, he will save her. After all, God answered her prayers and brought her eldest son, Jesse, home from prison. In time, she is sure, God will free her second son, Gregory. Yes. At home, where she is safe in God's care, she will live free of cancer. It's faith, pure faith.

A week later, things aren't as Lois had hoped. "We brought her home three days ago," Jesse says. "She wouldn't sleep downstairs. She wanted to be in her own bedroom. It wasn't easy. But it's what she wanted."

From inside Lois's bedroom, immediately to the right of the second-floor front door, I hear soft, soothing gospel music. Jesse gently pushes opens the half-closed hollow white door and stealthily peeks inside. It's cool, dark. Only the most determined of winter morning rays reach through the worn, heavy dust-covered drapes that have been yanked closed, blocking out both the sun and any gasps of fresh air. On the wide, king-size hospital bed that fills the core of the room, the twenty-three-year-old granddaughter Lois adopted as her own daughter is curled up next to her full, dark body, fitting into Lois's curves like a fetus outside the womb. Lois's eyes are closed. It's so still, so private that I want to turn and leave.

"Momma?" Jesse calls out softly. "Momma, it's Jesse."

His mother shifts slightly, slowly opens her enormous eyes, and smiles, then winces. There is pain with every movement. The daughter/granddaughter lying next to her rises, looks into Lois's face, and strokes her arm.

Out of nowhere, Jayvonce struts through the door carrying a plate of cold scrambled egg and broken bits of bacon. Moving in between Jesse and the edge of the bed, he pushes the food onto the teeth of a fork and holds it in front of Lois's mouth. She shakes her head, then opens her mouth just enough for Jayvonce to force the fork between her thick, dry lips. She chews, coughs.

"She needs water," Jesse says.

His niece moves to the opposite side of the bed and offers Lois a straw jutting out of a glass of water.

"She needs more morphine," Jayvonce cries out. "She's in pain. I don't want her in pain. I've upped the dosage." Jesse shakes his head.

Jayvonce leaves the room and returns with a minute-by-minute chart of the drugs he has administered. There are notations detailing when his mother vomited and how frequently she had a bowel movement.

"I don't want her drugged up so she's out of it," Jesse shoots back as if for the hundredth time in the days since his mother collapsed. "I don't want you giving her more drugs."

It's all new, this power struggle. Jesse is the eldest son, but he was gone, locked up for more than twenty-four years. Since he has gotten out of prison on parole, he hasn't had quite enough time to regain his position in this fractured family. As long as Lois stood tall, no one dared challenge her authority. But now that she's injured, lying weak before them, the future of the family is blurry. No one knows whom to listen to, who is second in command. Even as they stand on either side of the bed, their mother struggling for her life, small skirmishes break out.

Standing outside the house a little later, Jesse says, "Things are rough with Lisa but I can't come back here with Jayvonce living here. It's too dangerous. He's here every day. I'm just coming over in the morning before I go to Stockton to work, and then back at night. I can't just drop everything to take care of this situation. I'm the only person in my family who owns a car. I get calls every day: 'Jesse, can you come pick me up and take me to the store?' 'Jesse, I need to come see Momma. Can you come get me and the kids?' It's all day and night. I'm the only one. We don't really know how long we have with my mom. I have to keep my jobs. Every day I go to Stockton and when I get back at ten, I still have to do my janitorial work until two or three in the morning. I'm so tired, but I just gotta keep going."

Every afternoon I try to take my dog, Gigi, for an afternoon walk on the beach. One afternoon Phillip calls and asks to join me. It's beautiful and breezy out as we traipse along the low tide of the bay, toward the Golden Gate Bridge. "I wanted to tell you," Phillip says, "Desiree and I aren't going to be living together anymore, and the engagement is off. But everything is fine. We are great friends, and we still see each other all the time. In fact, I was over last night for dinner. It's just the way we live is real different."

We walk and talk, stopping every once in a while to throw my dog a hard stick. Phillip says they gave themselves a few months to really be sure this is what they wanted and in the end, it was. "I'm renting an apartment near my work. I like it. It's not exactly what I want. It doesn't have a garage, but I'll get that eventually. For now this is fine."

"Phillip is an absolutely incredible human being," Desiree tells me awhile later, "in terms of his level of integrity and respect. One of the most respectful and kindhearted people I have ever met, and I've met a lot of people. It wasn't for a lack of character substance or self-control or any kind of lingering sort of problematic behavior that we broke up. It was more a question of pacing. After so many years of being taken out of the work, out of society, out of life, living in an isolated subculture, he has a sense of 'I don't want to miss another moment of living.' So Phillip lives with a lot of intensity. He doesn't want to waste any time. And frankly, the pace with which he was moving exceeded my capacity to keep up."

I wonder if there's something she isn't telling me about Phillip. I've known him for three years, have spent hours and hours with him in all sorts of environments, but is it possible there's something I haven't detected? Maybe I shouldn't, but I have to ask her. "I have to examine every doubt," I tell Desiree. "You chose to be in a relationship with someone who committed murder twenty years ago. Are you ever afraid that part of him might put your life in danger?"

"Never," Desiree says. "Never, and I can say that with unequivocal certainty. He is one of the people I trust most in my life. We've had disagreements, and we've had, like every other couple, fights and never, never did I think, 'Oh my God, he could hurt me right now.' Never did I feel any aggressive energy towards me. This man has truly done his work. He would never hurt me and I know this. And you know something, because he did the classes, and did the psychological and emotional work around it and really looked at everything that happened, and because of his high level of awareness around it, he's a very safe guy to be around."

There is a sadness that follows these men. It isn't mysterious, just inevitable, that after being incarcerated for so many years, they want to live every minute and that desire can make having and keeping a relationship with someone who hasn't had that experience difficult.

A few days later, my cell phone buzzes. It's Johanna Hoffman, one of the attorneys who represents lifers inside San Quentin. "Nancy, did you hear about Bobby Brown?"

Bobby Brown. Tall with a short crop of wiry black hair that eventually was shaved to bald. He was one of the first lifers I met inside

San Quentin, in that little room across the hall from the chapel. He was also Jesse Reed's former cell mate.

"He went in for neck surgery," Hoffman says, her voice cracking, "and something went wrong and he died at the hospital."

Like people do when they hear some tragedy, I search my mind for a memory of Bobby. It settles on the day the board found him suitable for parole. It seemed the whole prison celebrated his pending freedom. But before his file even got to the governor's desk for a likely reversal, the state authorities determined Bobby didn't have a safe enough place to live on the outside and they reversed his parole. His south central Los Angeles family, long plagued by drug and alcohol addiction, had been either unable or unwilling to offer him a safe place to live on the outside, a key condition of parole. Bobby was devastated by the reversal. The next time he went before the Board of Parole Hearings, Johanna Hoffman was by his side. But even her legal representation wasn't enough to get another parole date. "This time," Hoffman says, "I couldn't even get his sister to return my calls." He was denied parole and told he would have to wait three years before he would be eligible for another parole hearing.

I remember. The last time I was inside, a month earlier, Bobby looked drawn, depressed. There is so much sadness inside San Quentin, it's easy to overlook one more lifer having a really bad day.

When I get through, Lieutenant Sam Robinson tells me he doesn't know how or why Bobby Brown died. "There's going to be a coroner's inquest. I'll let you know when I get the report. We're planning a memorial service. Do you want to come in for it?"

I call Jesse and give him the news. "Man. Bobby Brown," he says. "He never got to be free."

Driving across the Golden Gate Bridge on my way to San Quentin for Bobby's memorial service, I call Jesse to see how his mom is doing and to let him know I'll be seeing some of his old friends inside.

The minute I hear his voice, I know.

"Oh my God," he says. "My mom just died. What am I going to do? It's my mom."

"I'm so sorry, Jesse. When did it happen?"

"Just now," Jesse cries into the phone. "She just passed. We're waiting for the coroner to come and take her body away."

"I have to go inside Q for Bobby's service," I tell him, "but I'll come straight over after I get out. At least your mom got to see you on the outside, free. Can you imagine how you would feel if you were still locked up and you lost your mom? You had time together."

"I know. But what are we going to do now?"

Yes—that is the question. What is Lois Parks's family going to do without her?

The San Quentin Protestant chapel is packed to overflowing. Men in blue are sitting in chairs and wandering in the lobby outside, unable to sit still. It's hard to say good-bye. One of the ushers hands me a program. The memorial isn't just for Bobby Brown. It seems two other lifers have died in custody in the past couple of weeks and instead of holding three separate memorial services, the prison has lumped them all together, family members from the outside filling the first five rows of chairs in the front of the church.

Volunteers from the outside and inmates line up together along the far wall each patiently waiting their turn to offer condolences and tell stories about the three men who have died. To people on the outside, they might have been convicted murderers, but on the inside, these were men with friends and family who loved them. When I tell some of the lifers standing at the back of the sanctuary that Jesse's mom passed away, there are gasps and sighs. "Tell him we're with him." But of course, they can't be with him.

By the time I leave San Quentin for the twenty-five-minute drive to Jesse's house, it's a drizzly, gray kind of gloom. It's a day of death and memory, lives lost and hope extinguished. I park my car on a side street and walk the half a block, slowly.

At the Parks house, things are chaotic. If there was a thread tying together this troubled family of brothers and sisters, aunts and uncles, grandbabies and nieces, Lois's death has set it unraveling. Women and soaked, bewildered children sit disheveled at the curb in cars patched together with duct tape, their doors half open. Men and boys wander inside the yard in the rain, separate. Jayvonce stands on the bottom of the stairs calling out his bottomless anguish in slurred, too-quick words, unopened bills in his mother's name clutched in his fists, symbols of his power in a world that is disappearing around him. Standing at the top of the steps, Jesse is watching the scene below. Catching my eye, he waves me up.

"They just took her away," he says, opening the screen door. Inside family elders dressed in their Sunday best sit on the edge of the couch, holding the hands and rubbing the shoulders of a family looking for someone to soothe the dull emptiness filling the room. One of the women lifts her outstretched hands in the air and sings, calling for God to heal the family that has lost its mother. It's this family's first hours of the first day without their mother, and forever is just beginning.

Inside the kitchen, where dirty dishes are piled high and packaged goods are stuffed in the corners, someone has placed a large aluminum pan of cooked chicken, a grocery store sweet potato pie, and a big plastic bowl of ambrosia fruit salad on the sticky counter.

There are things to be done, decisions to be made, but not today. Today is reserved for surviving grief. Like a spiraling vortex, loss swirls around the edges of the living room threatening to suck down everyone standing too close to the center, too far, too fast. Jesse stands to the side, holding back, watching the world he dreamed about and longed for inside prison collapsing.

Placing his large hands on the waist-high railing that leads to the basement and the maze of rooms below, Jesse drops his head. Without his mother to lift his troubles, to soothe the pain, he is alone.

Days later, with his mother's body waiting to be buried, someone has to take charge. "There isn't a will," Jesse says over the phone. "We don't know what she wanted to do with the house. Mom told me awhile back she wanted me to have the house, but no one can find a will. The house is such a mess, even if there was one it could be covered up, or hidden under a mattress. But there's no money. There are bills that haven't been paid. I don't think she paid some for the past few months. We have to keep paying the mortgage to keep the house. I went to the mortuary and luckily, my father bought his plot and a plot for her, so we don't have to pay for that. But the funeral with the casket and flowers and limousines is going to cost about $8,000. The church is donating $500, but we have to raise the rest and I don't know how we're going to do it."

Jesse and I meet at Mama's in Oakland for breakfast. He looks spent, drained. "Jayvonce is out of control. He's high all the time. I have to be careful. He's threatened by me. He told everyone he wanted me to come home, to help share the burden of the family, but now that I'm out, he doesn't want me around. He hasn't really worked in years and has been living at my mom's. Now that world is over. A neighbor gave him $200 for the funeral and he took some of it and bought beer."

"What are you going to do?" I ask, looking across the table at his barely hidden frustration, pain, and anger.

Staring back at me, his face steadying, his eyes turning steely, he says, "You know, inside I learned how to think. And that's what I'm going to do. When things get to be too much, I know how to step back, take a breath. Sometimes that's all you need to do is create a little space, take time to get a little perspective so you don't make a stupid move. I know what that is. I take breaths all the time. That's the difference. I used to just react. Now I take the time to take breaths. This is hard. Getting my family through the funeral and dealing with the house is going to take time. Right now that's all I've got."

I was a little worried about going to Lois Parks's funeral. So much of what I'd observed already had me wondering how this troubled family would handle saying good-bye to the one person who for years had held them together.

Walking toward the address Jesse gave me for the Miraculous Word Christian Center, the site of his mother's funeral service, I wonder if I got the address wrong. Boarded-up, graffiti-scarred buildings and industrial storage facilities, surrounded by razor wire–topped chain-link fence, bookend the block. Not much of a church environment. But halfway down the long block, a hearse is parked outside a white, double-wide commercial-looking building. Could that be the "church"? Approaching, I step inside a small crowd of men and women dressed in purple: purple shirts, hats, dresses, shoes. Opening the back of the hearse, pallbearers dressed in dark purple rented tuxes and light purple shirts pull the white coffin out onto a dolly and push it through the church's double doors.

Joining the procession as it makes its way through the narthex, I catch sight of a man who looks like a taller, older identical twin to San Quentin's Lieutenant Sam Robinson.

"I'm Sam Robinson," he says, "the pastor of this church."

"Sam Robinson?" I ask. "You look just like a Sam Robinson I know who works at San Quentin."

"I'm Sam Robinson Sr. That's my son, Sam Robinson Jr. My father adopted Lois Parks when she was around fourteen years old. So Jesse's mom was my sister. My father was her father. We're family."

I stare up at the elder Robinson, putting two and two together. Sam and Jesse grew up in the same troubled neighborhood, within the same extended family. Sam went one way, Jesse the other.

Walking into the sanctuary, the only white person, I look for somewhere to sit where I won't be noticed. Every single chair on the family side and friend side of the aisle is taken. Sam Robinson Sr. is standing at the back of the church, watching. He reaches into the sound booth, grabs a plastic chair, plops it midway down the aisle on the friend side, and points to me. It's a small world.

Midway through the wrenching, wailing service, Jesse rises from his chair in the front row. Taking the microphone, he sings "Heaven on My Mind" to his mother: "I'll admit there have been times where I've faltered along the way, but I'll keep trying 'cause somehow I've gotta make it. You see, I've got a charge on my life and I've got a job to do and I can't stop until it's through."

Shortly afterward, things begin to fall apart. The fire department is called. One of Jesse's sisters has fainted and needs to go to the hospital. Outside the church, Jesse's brother Jayvonce refuses to get in the family limousine. A kind uncle takes control of the sideshow, escorting Jayvonce down the sidewalk away from the cars lining up for the funeral procession. I watch to see how's Jesse's doing—not well.

Later, up at the hilltop grave site, next to the pile of dirt that will cover Lois's casket deep in the earth, Sam Robinson Sr. stands beside Jesse in the rain. "Let us pray," Robinson calls out to the few family members who have left their cars to say a final farewell. "The Lord is my shepherd. I shall not want. . . . "

When it's all over, after his mother has been lowered into her grave and the last of the day's prayers have been said, Jesse turns away from the gaping hole in the ground. There, standing behind him, are Demetrius Daniels and Jerry Elster, two lifers he knew on the inside who have come to support him in his hour of need on the outside. His mother is gone. The men who know what he has done, where he has been, and how hard this all is, are there. Jesse is not alone.

Lifer reunions happen all the time. There are large backyard picnics with wives and girlfriends, children and their children all invited to join the brotherhood of men who survived prison. And there are small get-togethers, the daily car pool to Stockton for the IMPACT program, meet-ups at speaking engagements, and phone calls. "It was kind of taboo inside," Eddie Ramirez says, "to talk in the line, on the tiers. You were setting yourself up for people overhearing. If you wanted to talk to someone you trusted, not really to get answers, often just to vent, to find a commonality you would say, 'Hey, wanna take a lap?' And we would take a lap on the yard, walk around the track. Talk things through. I got a call from a good friend I knew on the inside who got out, and he was having a tough time. He said, 'Got time to take a lap?' We took a lap and we cried, bounced stuff off. I told him, 'We've been through a journey and you're here. Tomorrow will be better.' Sometimes we go camping or out for a day of fishing; it's taking a lap and having people you know and trust to talk things through with."

One of these reunions ends up coalescing around the second memorial planned for Bobby Brown. Unlike the memorial inside, this one is on the outside for the lifers and volunteers who weren't allowed to go inside San Quentin to pay their respects.

Up at the Russian River, writing, it has been storming. The winds and rain have left behind strewn wreckage. Driving around the wild litter, down rural roads slippery with mud slides and through one-store towns, I finally reach the freeway, emerging as if from a cave. Retreats can be like that.

To get to the church, an hour and a half south, a Google map leads me past San Quentin State Prison. It has been four years since the day I met Bobby Brown, Don Cronk, Bryan Smith, and a half dozen other lifers inside that little room across from the prison sanctuary. It has been four years since I began my quest to find out what really happens to people who commit murder, decades after their crime. Moments, inside and out, flash before my eyes like film images clicking across the shutter of a projector.

First Don, then Eddie and Richie, Phillip and Jesse. There are others, but these five men took me into their lives, inside San Quentin and out. I discovered a healthy mix of trouble and fun, love and heartbreak, hope realized and dreams broken. They are men who committed horrible crimes. They did their time, reformed their thinking, fundamentally changed their behavior, and were found suitable for parole but remained locked up, living in nine-by-six-foot cells. Eventually they were given a second chance. Now they are out, their wisdom and insight lost on all but a very few in a society too afraid to witness it, see it, learn from it.

Passing by the last exit to San Quentin and heading up over the Richmond–San Rafael Bridge, I gasp a private breath. I am driving past what remains a secret, isolated, walled-off community of more than 5,000 people in the middle of one of the most liberally minded, eco-friendly, justice-oriented counties in the United States. Looking down from their million-dollar houses on the hills or glancing at the prison from the freeways that skirt three sides of the massive institution, what questions pass through the minds of the free?

Do they wonder who is in there? What is it like? Is prison effective? Is locking 'em up and throwing away the key making free people safe? Is this an effective answer to crime and punishment? Or is it a punishment born of social ignorance?

How many people on the freeway with me this Sunday morning look at San Quentin and wonder what's going on behind the thick sand-colored walls? Or is it a big yellow "black site" in the middle of our democratic world? A place and a people to be haphazardly legislated, paid for out of taxpayers' increasingly shallow pockets, and ignored?

Reaching the far side of the bridge, I follow the map and park my car across the street from the redbrick, white-steepled church high on a hill in Point Richmond. Walking up the uneven sidewalk, I see Jesse standing up the street, beyond the church. He has the biggest smile I've ever seen on his face—which comes as a surprise after the hard time he has been going through.

"Nancy," he says with a laugh, "I went on a retreat of my own to Stinson Beach. I rented a small hotel room for two nights. It was raining. I walked on the beach in the rain and I sat on the sand in the rain. I cried for my mother. I walked and walked. I was soaked. I just kept walking. It felt so good. I've never done that before. But it's what I needed."

"I'm so glad, Jesse," I say, taking a good look at his smile. "That's what retreats are all about: finding some kind of peace."

Inside the sunlit chapel, a woman is sitting at a dark wood grand piano just to the right of a podium. The classical music she's playing fills the intimate sanctuary. Like half of the people scattered throughout the pews, she met Bobby Brown volunteering inside San Quentin. The other half are men who, like Bobby, committed a murder. Now, decades of guilt, sorrow, self-forgiveness, and acceptance later, they have changed. Unlike Bobby and the 775 prisoners serving life sentences with the possibility of parole who from 2000 to 2009 died waiting for the state to let them out, the men in the chapel this morning are the lucky ones. They got out of prison by governor orders or by order of a court judge. Now out in the free world, their debt to society paid, they are doing what it takes to survive and thrive.

They find someone willing to give them a job and do everything they can to keep it. They fall in love and do their best to keep that love alive while they negotiate the ups and downs of a long-term commitment without the references most middle-aged men have to years of short-term dating. Some break up. A few have children. Others share the lessons they've learned with other people's children, the ones who need to hear what they've learned.

Today, here in this chapel, they have come together to remember one of their own who never got a second chance.

When former lifers get together, no longer wearing prison blues, they stand out, distinct from one another. They talk North Block shop, about their still-incarcerated friends on the inside, always the first topic of conversation: who has a date and who has been denied; who is waiting for the governor to decide, or worse, who has had their parole date "taken."

They have cars and the latest edition 4G cell phones; their skin is flush with color; their bodies are filled out and relaxed.

Standing on the sidewalk outside the chapel, one of the men lifts his cell phone and shoots a few photos. Later someone will print them to send to the lifers inside, so they can post them on the chapel window, the faces of the lifers outside.

epilogue

THANKSGIVING

2011

It takes shoving four long tables end to end to make enough room for forty-four people to sit down to Thanksgiving dinner. Old friends and family mix with the new.

Looking down over the linen and flowers, I see Eddie and Lupe leaning in over the candles, talking to Lupe's son, Daniel, who has traveled all the way from Los Angeles with his girlfriend for dinner.

Early that morning, Richie's mom made her homemade flour tortillas. After placing them on the counter, Richie turns to me, beaming: "Nancy, I'm in love." A few weeks ago at his high school reunion, he says, he fell in love with April, a girl he knew from elementary school. "She said, 'I've waited all my life to meet a guy like you.' Can you believe it? Now that I'm off parole, I flew to Chicago to spend the weekend with her. Now she's moving back to Newark."

Jesse and Phillip said they couldn't make it. Jesse is cooking Thanksgiving dinner for his brothers and sisters in his apartment, "right down," he says, "to the sweet potato pies." Phillip and Desiree are having a quiet Thanksgiving at their house with her parents.

One table down, Don and Kathleen are laughing with the mother of a friend in the neighborhood. It's a normal holiday dinner scene, but with a twist: today the men I met so long ago inside San Quentin are joining in the celebration with my family and neighborhood friends.

Who would have thought more than four years ago that this could or would happen? That fear of people unknown to me, people locked up in cells in the nearby prison, would fade and in its place I would feel acceptance and appreciation for how far these men had come and how much they have to give. It's hard to pinpoint the moment it happened, but somewhere along the way, on this reporter's journey to find out who people who murder become years, decades after their crimes, I changed. Somewhere along the way, the men and their families became friends. It didn't happen all at once, but over the years my self-imposed armor of fear cracked and fell away.

Like the 57,000 men and women convicted of murder who were released from state and federal prisons from 2000 to 2009, Don, Eddie, Richie, Phillip, and Jesse could have chosen to live the rest of their lives anonymously, their criminal histories a secret.

With this book, their anonymity and privacy will be compromised. And still, when I call and ask for more, they give it—whatever it takes, they say, so people know the truth.

How could they have known back in 2007 and 2008, when I first asked them to give their consent to be interviewed, it would come to this? Yes, they said, then yes. But neither they nor I knew where my questions and their answers would lead. Over the years, from inside prison to out, not one of the men I met inside San Quentin has withdrawn his consent. In fact, each has quietly encouraged me to keep going, to tell their stories, their whole stories.

As they have each said to me at one point or another, "If it helps the guys still inside who have done their time, who have done everything they can to change get out, it's worth it."

EDWARD "EDDIE" RAMIREZ

Conviction: second-degree murder, 1982
Sentence: fifteen years to life with the possibility of parole

Incarcerated: twenty-three years
Parole reversed by Governor Gray Davis
Parole approved by Governor Arnold Schwarzenegger
Paroled: February 24, 2005
Released from Parole: March 2010

Eddie and Lupe live in Sunnyvale with their dog, Spunky. Eddie finished five years of training to become a journeyman sheet-metal worker. But the recession has meant fewer full-time opportunities. Over the summer of 2011, Eddie joined the IMPACT program, going into the same juvenile facilities he was locked up in more than a quarter of a century ago, only now, counseling the young men who committed crimes. "This is what the twenty-three years was for: for this! These kids need to hear this as they begin their journey. A lot of time I drive home crying because of the conversations I've had with them. I see me in them." After years as a local public school administrator, Lupe is taking a less stressful position as a teacher. Now that Eddie has been released from parole, they take frequent trips to spend time with his two sisters and relatives, to Sacramento to be with Lupe's son and grandsons, and to Los Angeles to care for Lupe's aging mother and father and see her other son. One day they'll go to Hawaii for their honeymoon.

DONALD CRONK

Conviction: first-degree murder, 1984
Sentence: twenty-five years to life with possibility of parole
Incarcerated: twenty-eight years
Parole reversed by Governor Arnold Schwarzenegger
Paroled: April 11, 2008, by order of the Sacramento County Superior Court

Donald and Kathleen are living together in San Anselmo. Donald is enrolled in his second semester at the College of Marin in a computer technology program. When done, he'll have a Microsoft A+ certification.

Kathleen is officially retired but works a few hours each week as a travel agent. When her boss offers them his season tickets, they attend the San Francisco Symphony and Giants baseball games. On the weekend, Don and Kathleen have family and friends over for dinner, and on Sunday mornings attend the local church. After nearly twenty years in love, Don and Kathleen are happy together.

PHILLIP "PJ" JAY SEILER

Conviction: second-degree murder, 1988
Sentence: seventeen years to life with possibility of parole
Incarcerated: twenty years
Parole reversed by Governor Gray Davis and Governor Arnold Schwarzenegger
Paroled: August 27, 2008, by order of the California Court of Appeal

Phillip is working full-time with a construction company in south San Francisco and volunteering with Insight-Out, a nonprofit program working with at-risk youth in Bay Area high schools. After being released from prison, Phillip's older son, Phillip Jr., is in a drug rehab program. Phillip's younger son, Anthony, is still in prison. Over pancakes one Sunday in December, I noticed Desiree was again wearing her sparkling engagement ring. "We're back together," they announced, "and we're getting married. We realize we belong together." On Friday evenings, when the wind is up and the workweek is over, Phillip joins my husband and neighborhood friends for a sail on the San Francisco Bay.

JESSE REED

Conviction: first-degree murder, 1985
Sentence: twenty-seven years to life with possibility of parole
Incarcerated: nearly twenty-five years

Parole reversed by Governor Arnold Schwarzenegger
Paroled: June 11, 2009, by order of Alameda County Superior Court

Jesse lives in his own apartment in Oakland, about a mile from his family. He works for the California Department of Corrections and Rehabilitation with the IMPACT program, traveling more than a hundred miles, five days a week to counsel incarcerated young men in the state's youth facility in Stockton. On the weekend, he sings second tenor with a Christian gospel group, the Redemption Band. The band members originally met inside San Quentin, where they sang "God's praises" every Sunday morning. On May 21, 2010, Jesse became the first former inmate to graduate with a diploma in Christian ministries from the Golden Gate Baptist Theological Seminary's contextualized leadership development program, after beginning his studies inside San Quentin in 2006. To use some of the janitorial and maintenance experience he learned inside, Jesse opened his own company, Jess-Clean Maintenance: "For a smart clean, call Jess-Clean." Jesse says his parole agent has told him he will be released from parole on June 23, 2012. Jesse plans to celebrate by taking a trip, somewhere beautiful, maybe with Lisa.

RICHARD "RICHIE" RAEL

Conviction: second-degree murder and assault with a deadly weapon, 1982
Sentence: twenty-two years to life with the possibility of parole
Incarcerated: twenty-four years
Parole reversed by Governor Gray Davis in 2005
Paroled: September 16, 2006

Richard Rael lives in an apartment in Newark, less than a mile from his parents' house. He is working for his brother's company installing windows in businesses and residences. In the evening he likes to work in the vegetable garden in his small backyard and play his guitar. On the weekend he spends time with his family and attends the early Sunday services at the Catholic church across the street from his apartment. At a recent high school reunion, Richie met and fell in love with April, a classmate from the fourth grade. They had their first kiss the very next day, sitting together in the stands of the Oakland sports arena watching the Raiders make their first touchdown. Chatting at the Fairmont Hotel under blinking Christmas lights, the nurse and mother of two says, "He's a good man. He isn't his past. I had to wait twenty-seven years to find a man like him." Richie smiles and holds her hand.

Bryan Smith now lives with his wife in Tucson, Arizona. He is a senior at the University of Arizona earning a degree in psychology. Bryan regularly speaks at universities, colleges, high schools, and faith-based communities, where he shares his story of change and personal transformation. He also speaks on panels related to restorative justice and reentry. In February 2012, Bryan and his wife became the proud parents of their first child, a baby girl.

On January 2, 2011, Jerry Brown became governor of California for the second time. Within weeks of his inauguration, it was clear there would be a new policy coming out of Sacramento regarding executive review of lifers found suitable for parole.

Steve Acquisto is Governor Brown's chief deputy legal affairs secretary. In my earliest conversations with Mr. Acquisto, as I have done at times throughout this book, I referred to the "decisions" of the parole board as "recommendations." Mr. Acquisto asked me why. My answer was that over the years, while reporting on lifer issues, the staff of the Department of Corrections and Rehabilitation had repeatedly instructed me to describe the parole board's actions as recommendations to the governor. According to staff, the governor was in charge of making any final decision. Mr. Acquisto said they were wrong.

"It is inaccurate to refer to the board's decisions as recommendations," Mr. Acquisto said, "and I think doing so tends to diminish the board's authority. The board is an independent decision-making body that is charged with the authority to grant or deny parole to inmates serving indeterminate prison terms. Its decisions do not require governor approval to be effective. And the commissioners who serve on the board have many years of experience in law enforcement and corrections, so they are well qualified to make parole determinations that do not jeopardize public safety. Rather than characterize the process as the board making a recommendation that the governor must adopt or reject, it is more accurate to say that the board is making a decision that it has the expertise and legal authority to make. When the governor conducts a parole review, he is assessing whether there is reason to take the step of interfering with the board's decision."

True to Acquisto's word, since Governor Brown was sworn into office on January 3, 2011, the parole board has found 430 people convicted of murder and serving life terms with the possibility of parole, suitable for parole. Of those grants, Governor Brown has reversed (or interfered with) seventy-four and sent two back for reconsideration by the full board, effectively taking no action (accepting the parole board's grant of parole) for 356, or 83 percent of the parole decisions.

If Governor Brown continues this trend throughout the four years of his first term, he could oversee the parole of some 1,200 of the approximately 17,000 inmates in the state's prisons who are serving life sentences with the possibility of parole for murder. Taken one step further, if Brown were reelected and he continued with a policy of allowing 83 percent of parole board decisions to stand, some 2,400 lifers could potentially be paroled by the year 2020, saving the state tens of millions of dollars each year. That would leave 15,000 to 16,000 people incarcerated in the state's prisons serving life terms with the possibility of parole.

The question that remains is: What next? California's three previous governors reversed between 75 percent and 99.9 percent of all parole recommendations sent to them for review. After Brown, will the political door to parole shut? Will state legislators pass laws that will make it even more difficult for rehabilitated lifers to get out of prison on parole? Will future governors see the parole board's decisions as mere recommendations?

In August 2011 Senate Bill 391 was introduced in the state legislature. If enacted, it would reverse the California Supreme Court's ruling *In re Lawrence,* creating law that would permit the Board of Parole Hearings and the governor to use the original crime as the sole reason for denying parole.

California Assistant Attorney General Julie Garland argued in opposition to *Lawrence* before the state supreme court. She says no one from the legislature contacted her before SB 391 was introduced. If they had, she says, she would have told them SB 391 would violate the due process liberty interest of the law that states, "One year prior to the inmate's minimum eligible parole release date, a panel of two or more commissioners or deputy commissioners shall again meet with the inmate and shall normally set a parole release date."

Today, if the Board of Parole Hearings denies parole or the governor reverses a grant of parole, life inmates in California have limited options. In January 2011, the US Supreme Court ruled in *Swarthout v. Cooke* that in the context of California's parole statute, there is no federal habeas relief for errors of state law. In other words, the court ruled there is no federal constitutional right to conditional release. Any review of a state's decision to deny parole is limited to whether the inmate was provided an opportunity to be heard and a statement of reasons that parole was denied. The federal court has no authority to scrutinize the merits of denial. Period.

In other states, the same issues remain.

In Maryland and Oklahoma, governors also have the power to review and reverse parole board recommendations for prisoners serving life sentences with the possibility of parole. In both states very few, if any, lifers convicted of a murder offense are being paroled.

In Maryland, it's been difficult to tell how many of the state's 2,600 lifers have been recommended for parole by the state's parole board because all recommendations are, according to the state's Office of Pardons and Executive, "confidential" until the governor has acted on the recommendations. And for a parole recommendation to become final, the governor had to actively confirm that recommendation. Unlike in California where the governor has 150 days to act on a parole board's decision, until this year in Maryland there has been no time restriction on the governor approving or denying a recommendation so information on how many or who have been recommended has been a mystery.

What is less mysterious is the actual number of lifers in Maryland who have been paroled. From 1970 to 1994, 193 lifers were paroled from Maryland prisons. From 1995 to 2007, thirteen lifers were paroled. Since 2007, not one lifer has been paroled.

But the secretive nature of parole board recommendations in Maryland may change. In March 2011 the Maryland legislature passed House Bill 302. Under the terms of the new law, which went into effect on October 1, 2011, the governor has 180 days to reverse *in writing* a recommendation for parole. If he does not submit his reversal in writing by the 180th day, the parole board's decision stands. In March 2012 the people of Maryland will find out whether the governor will actively reverse the parole board's decisions or "take no action" and allow the board's decisions to stand, granting parole to lifers found suitable for freedom. Under this governor however, the outlook for change is bleak. Since March 2011 when the new law was passed, Governor Martin O'Malley began addressing the backlog of standing recommendations for parole or sentence commutations for lifers by acting on 48 cases—reversing them all.

Acknowledgments

There is only one way to begin thanking the many people who made this work possible, and that is to acknowledge the contribution of Don Cronk, Ed Ramirez, Rich Rael, Phillip Seiler, and Jesse Reed. If they had turned away and refused to answer my very first questions, this book would not exist. But they didn't turn away. With a willingness that to this day continues to surprise and amaze me, they bared their private guilt, remorse, and shame, and their hard-won redemption for all to see. Some readers may ask whether I chose them or they asked to be chosen. It didn't happen that way. It just happened that they became the "five." There were many others I met inside and outside who could have been the sixth or seventh or more lifers to tell their stories. But one fewer than five and the work didn't feel complete. One more and I would not have been able to tell the stories completely.

Don, Ed, Rich, Phillip, and Jesse never had to speak to me on the record. But one by one, they looked me in the eye and said, "What do you want to know?" With honesty and openness, they took me into their lives and faced my early fear and probing questions with acceptance and transparency.

Now, years later, I thank each of them for their honesty, for always returning my phone calls, for making time to talk, and for the constant encouragement they gave me to keep going, keep asking, keep telling.

I can't go another word further without thanking the women in the lives of Don, Rich, Ed, Phillip, and Jesse for accepting me and my journalistic inquisitiveness. Lupe, Kathleen, Desiree, Lisa, and April could have put up their hand and said no. That may have put an end to it. But they didn't. Graciously opening their private worlds, they took me into their professional, college-educated, confident, self-reliant lives, and shattered the misinformed stereotype of women who love men who have committed murder. To them, I say thank you.

Inside and out, I am grateful to Demetrius Daniel, Nathaniel Ray Rouse, Troy Williams, Hector Oropeza, Rusty Trunzo, Michael Harris, Leonard Rubio, Jerry Elster, Juan Haines, Arnulfo Garcia, Julian Glen Padgett, and Stephen Liebb for their kind smiles and thoughtful interviews.

Flozelle Woodmore at the New Way of Life Reentry Project in Los Angeles opened my eyes and ears to the families on the outside trying to help loved ones on the inside negotiate their way through the parole board process. I must also thank Sister Mary Sean Hodges and all of the men at the Leighton House, especially Emmit Ward, for inviting me to their celebratory barbecue and sharing their beautiful home with me.

There are three men to whom I owe a debt that can never be repaid. When San Quentin State Prison Warden Robert Ayres and Public Information Officers Lieutenant Sam Robinson and Lieutenant Eric Messick realized the depth of my reporter's interest in inmates serving life sentences inside the prison, they gave me unheard-of and often exclusive access to the prison and its administrators, officers, programs, and prisoners, encouraging me to tell the story. I can never thank them enough for their confidence in my work and for giving up so many evenings and weekends to usher me through the institution for one more program and "just one more interview."

Before the book was a thought, there were radio stories. One after another, they gave me the opportunity to report on life in prison. My story pitches were met by some of the best radio editors in the country. I'd like to thank Alisa Joyce Barba at National Public Radio; Krissy Clark at Weekend America; Mincho Jacob and Alex Avila at Latino USA; Holly Kernan, Ben Trefny, Martina Castro, and Rina

Palta at KALW News' *Crosscurrents*; and last but clearly not least, Ira Glass and Robyn Semien at *This American Life*. Thank you all for giving my stories a home.

A very special thank you to Niki Papadopoulos for listening.

In 2009 the Open Society Institute honored the early direction of my work examining the impact of a 1988 law granting the governor of California the authority to reverse parole board decisions and take away a lifer's parole date, with a Soros Justice Media Fellowship. I'd like to thank Adam Culbreath for calling with such good news and for his support and encouragement. Thank you, Christina Voight, for all your behind-the-scenes nurturing over the years. And to all the Soros Justice Fellows, who have taken time to speak with me about the book in its first steps, thank you.

Over pizza in Chicago, Soros Fellow and author Amy Bach told me I had to do more than produce a two-hour radio documentary. She said I had to write a book. She said it would be the hardest thing I would ever do, but that she would be there every step of the way. I didn't believe her at the time but both have come true.

Diane Fraser helped me craft the book from the earliest stages to the final edits. Bridget Kinsella showed me the way, more than once. Early on in the book's development, Stephen Hubbell of the Open Society Institute, Laura Lent of the San Francisco Public Library, Edmund O'Reilly of the National Library Service for the Blind and Physically Handicapped, and Ellen Towell of Weldon Owen Publishing made important structural suggestions, all of which helped more than they will ever know.

Along the way, Justice James Lambden took time out of his pressing schedule to make tea and explain how the courts participate in the process of determining justice for life inmates. Paul Comiskey, Michael Satris, and Donald Miller were a tremendous help explaining the history and impact of Proposition 89. Keith Wattley and Thomas Master described the changing landscape of liberty law in California. John Dannenberg kept the court records straight. I would like to thank Steve Acquisto in the governor's office for all the frustrating off-the-record conversations and for eventually giving me a paragraph that was worth waiting for. Julie Garland from the state attorney general's office couldn't have been more helpful or candid. Shadd Maruna and Jonathan Simon opened many doors ahead of me with their critical work examining the punitive natures of societies. Walter Lomax of the Maryland Restorative Justice Initiative and Tracy Velazquez of the Justice Policy Institute have been very helpful in providing updates on lifer parole in Maryland. Lunches with Claire-Elizabeth DeSophia helped me sort through the emotions woven into the fabric of long-term reporting on prisons and parole. Jody Lewen inspired me with her wealth of perspective gained from years of running the Prison University Project inside San Quentin. No matter how late in the day, Terry Thornton and Bill Sessa of the California Department of Corrections (and after 2009, Rehabilitation) willingly took my calls and patiently led me through the state's incarceration policies and parole process. And thank you, Terry and Jay Atkinson, for processing my Public Records Act requests. James Austin of the JFA Institute offered the one critical link to the one person at the Bureau of Justice Statistics in Washington, D.C., who could help me crunch the numbers that had never been crunched before.

The day my agent, Gail Ross, said she would represent this book, I knew I would hold it in my hands. Anna Sproul performed not one but two miracles.

It was in my earliest conversations with Clive Priddle at PublicAffairs that the real weight of what I was going to be writing about hit home. Furiously taking notes and hearing my vision in his words, I realized I had found the perfect editor for *Life After Murder*. And when Brandon Proia sent me his thoughtful edits, I was awed by his perceptive grasp of the book. Special thanks to Managing Editor Melissa Raymond and Project Editor Melissa Veronesi, for moving the book along with attention and care, Antoinette Smith for her comprehensive, catch-every-single-thing copyedit of the manuscript, and Pete Garceau for the perfect cover. I am ever grateful.

From the very beginning of this work to the end, I have had the support of friends and family who have shared in the rigorous journey: Margit Wennmachers for opening her heart and home; Mary Beth Sanders for years of faithful friendship; Leigh Johnston, David Samra and Erica Pearson for always checking in and celebrating the good moments with champagne; Howard Devore for his wisdom; David Tateosian for his enthusiastic support, and his uncle Charles Tateosian for his inquisitiveness; Nicola Tateosian, Dionne Woods, Jay Seiden, Andrew Germond, and Nancy Bella Lopes for helping me find the perfect place to write; my sister Kate Robertson for cheering me on; my daughter Nayeli Mullane Maxson for her grace, intellect, and love; and my husband Dennis "Max" Maxson for everything.

A Note on Sources

My professional work as a journalist has been as a radio reporter. And the interesting thing about radio reporting is that, like photo journalists who have to be *there* to get the photograph, radio reporters have to be *there* as well to capture the voices and sounds of the story on "tape" (now on a digital flash drive). Over the years, I have grown accustomed to being there and capturing the voices of the people I am reporting on by standing or sitting in front of them, microphone in hand, asking questions.

From the very outset in 2007, before I even had the slightest idea my work covering prisons would result in this book, I approached this "story" as one interview after another with people who I thought might have the answers to the compounding questions. From inside prison to outside, I held my microphone, looked people in the eye, and asked questions.

As a result, this book is nearly entirely based on recorded interviews with authors, researchers, lawyers, academics, justices, legislators, wardens, correctional officers, prisoners, and their family members; and on unpublished data based on information that was provided by, and compiled with the help of, the California Department of Corrections and Rehabilitation through Public Records Act requests and unpublished data compiled from the Bureau of Justice Statistics in Washington.

In addition, published case law, probation officers' reports, original documentation, and the California Department of Corrections and

Rehabilitation's own research dating back to 1945 were very helpful in uncovering sentencing and parole trends. It was in poring over the CDCR's reports, tables, and charts that I realized what was missing and that led to my filing the first of many Public Records Act requests.

So, although more than four years of investigation and research went into writing this book, the core of the information presented is based on first-person interviews.

Nancy Mullane
February 2012

Index

ELISABETH FALL

Nancy Mullane develops, reports, and produces feature stories for Public Radio International's *This American Life*, National Public Radio, and the NPR affiliate KALW in San Francisco. For her work examining the impact of governor review of parole, Mullane was awarded a Soros Justice Media Fellowship. She is a member of the Society for Professional Journalists, the Association of Independents in Radio, and the International Women's Media Foundation. In 2011 she was the recipient of a National Edward R. Murrow Award.

PublicAffairs is a publishing house founded in 1997. It is a tribute to the standards, values, and flair of three persons who have served as mentors to countless reporters, writers, editors, and book people of all kinds, including me.

I. F. STONE, proprietor of *I. F. Stone's Weekly*, combined a commitment to the First Amendment with entrepreneurial zeal and reporting skill and became one of the great independent journalists in American history. At the age of eighty, Izzy published *The Trial of Socrates*, which was a national bestseller. He wrote the book after he taught himself ancient Greek.

BENJAMIN C. BRADLEE was for nearly thirty years the charismatic editorial leader of *The Washington Post*. It was Ben who gave the *Post* the range and courage to pursue such historic issues as Watergate. He supported his reporters with a tenacity that made them fearless and it is no accident that so many became authors of influential, best-selling books.

ROBERT L. BERNSTEIN, the chief executive of Random House for more than a quarter century, guided one of the nation's premier publishing houses. Bob was personally responsible for many books of political dissent and argument that challenged tyranny around the globe. He is also the founder and longtime chair of Human Rights Watch, one of the most respected human rights organizations in the world.

• • •

For fifty years, the banner of Public Affairs Press was carried by its owner Morris B. Schnapper, who published Gandhi, Nasser, Toynbee, Truman, and about 1,500 other authors. In 1983, Schnapper was described by *The Washington Post* as "a redoubtable gadfly." His legacy will endure in the books to come.

Peter Osnos, *Founder and Editor-at-Large*